SENIOR RESIDENCES

SENIOR RESIDENCES

Designing Retirement Communities for the Future

John E. Harrigan, Ph.D.

Jennifer M. Raiser, M.B.A.

Phillip H. Raiser, M.S. Arch.

JOHN WILEY & SONS, INC.

New York   Chichester   Weinheim   Brisbane   Singspore   Toronto

This publication is designed to provide accurate and authoritative information in regard to the subject matter covered. It is sold with the understanding that the publisher is not engaged in rendering professional services. If professional advice or other expert assistance is required, the services of a competent professional person should be sought.

Library of Congress Cataloging-in-Publication Data
Harrigan, John E.
   Senior residences : designing retirement communities for the
future / John E. Harrigan, Jennifer M. Raiser, Phillip H. Raiser.
       p.   cm. — (Wiley series in healthcare and senior living
design)
   Includes bibliographical references and index.
   ISBN 0-471-19061-6 (cloth : alk. paper)
   1. Life care communities—United States—Planning.   2. Retirement
communities—United States—Planning.   I. Raiser, Jennifer M.
II. Raiser, Phillip H.   III. Title.   IV. Series.
HV1454.2.U6H36   1998
362.1′6′068—dc21   97-41757

Printed in the United States of America
10 9 8 7 6 5 4 3 2 1

To Helen and John Raiser,
the ultimate enterprise team.

Who have always defined
the importance of integrity,
the endurance of quality,
and the value of family.

CONTENTS

PART I

CRITICAL SUCCESS FACTORS

PART III

STRATEGIC RESEARCH

ACKNOWLEDGMENTS

Many individuals and organizations contributed to the form and substance of this book. Gratefully, the authors wish to acknowledge those who made this enterprise possible.

Very special thanks are due to James and Mary Coleman and the dedicated and enthusiastic executives at *The Cypress at Hilton Head*, for sharing with us their knowledge, their experiences, and their most cordial hospitality. Robin Larzelere, architect and artist, made a most significant contribution when she translated the CCRC executive strategy into defining logos and artwork.

The managers who brought their dedication and talent to the building of *The Stratford* and The Raiser Organization, Nancy Rancatore, Larry Tarter, John Shivers, and Cliff Scott, deserve our commendation and thanks. The hard-working and creative leaders of Raiser Senior Services, Wendi Giordano, Susan Kellerman, Marianne Nannestad, and Kathleen Nelson, deserve great credit for their collaboration and innovations. Ann Murray has persevered with grace. Fred Furland provided extensive support and encouragement. Pamela Johnson interpreted our transcriptions and text with aplomb. To the present and past members of The Raiser Organization and Raiser Senior Services, our respectful appreciation for your ongoing efforts—you make brilliant practice out of evolving theory, and exemplify the best of family business.

Many others contributed to *The Stratford* in their vision of what a forward-thinking retirement community could be. Our hard hats off to the many subcontractors, laborers, and artisans who made a personal commitment to excellence in their trades. The dedicated colleagues who gave large amounts of time and talent to serve on the Senior Community Services Board provided wisdom and counsel in myriad ways. The professionals at Backen, Arrigoni and Ross; Seccombe Design Associates; Watry Design Group; Hansen, Bridgett, Marcus, Vlahos and Rudy; and Sumitomo Bank of California contributed significant effort and knowledge. Also deserving of our thanks are the analysts, inspectors, and supervisors of the local and state agencies who provided our guidelines and regulations, who protect our citizens and ensure the continuity of the senior care industry.

Our colleagues have provided crucial peer learning and encouragement. In particular, we wish to thank members of the Associated General Contractors, the Senior Managers Group of Retirement Communities, and the Social Venture Network for their perspectives and insights.

This book was originally conceived under the auspices of the College of Architecture and Environmental Design's Executive Graduate Program at Cal Poly, San Luis Obispo. Dean Paul R. Neel, F.A.I.A., and Professor Allan Cooper, A.I.A., deserve our grateful acknowledgment. Senior Editor Amanda Miller of John Wiley & Sons deserves thanks for her advocacy on behalf of senior living issues.

Most significantly, Cynthia Raiser Jeavons and John Jeavons deserve commendation for their positive attitudes and their own sense of dedication. Erin Raiser made a daily contribution with her business insights and critiques that so challenged the authors. Donald Bacon, Eliot, and Adelaide provided their own objective correlative, and emphasized the ultimate standard of performance. Jessica Harrigan, RN, showed us that "care" is a daily obligation and the joy of the profession.

When the challenge is to understand what is important to people and bring their knowledge to life, to match thought with word, Janet Harrigan is our scholar-in-residence.

SENIOR RESIDENCES

THE EXECUTIVE STRATEGY

As the American population ages, the retirement community industry grows. The promise of this expanding customer base has attracted a host of developers, architects, contractors, and health care and service providers looking eagerly toward a great market opportunity. But size of market does not necessarily assure success. To become the customer's choice, retirement communities must be forward-thinking, functional, solvent, and adaptable.

Looking to the future of the retirement community industry, this book does not purport to be a manual on how to develop, build, and manage a successful retirement community. The examples are too numerous, and the individual situations too complex, to even attempt to specify what works across geographies, management philosophies, competitive situations, and corporate constraints. Rather, this book provides case studies to test the reader's own assumptions, interviews to illuminate perspectives and best practices, and a study of the critical success factors that underlie every executive deliberation. Rather than a manual, this book at best may serve as a consultant, reminding and encouraging avenues of thought that will lead to a more cohesive, responsive, and successful retirement community product.

For professionals new to the retirement community industry, the executive strategy is a guide to success in this highly competitive and demanding business. It specifies all the critical aspects of a retirement community enterprise and provides the means to gain an understanding of organizational success. Students undertaking graduate, certificate, and continuing education studies will find that the executive strategy helps them think realistically about their professional responsibilities within the retirement community industry. This book may help university faculty and research center associates take into account the full complexity of the retirement community challenge. The executive strategy pertains directly to regulatory and legislative deliberations that so dramatically affect the lives and resources of the elderly.

We are particularly concerned with the profit-oriented approach that characterizes many new entrants to the industry. As a result of demand, we see aggressive moves by organizations seeking to explore or expand their positions on the basis of short-term returns, often at the cost of longer-term value to residents and the greater community. It is possible for a retirement community corporation to promote increased share value or profitability and still maintain the quality of life for every resident. But will shareholders understand expenditures that go beyond the resident contract or will they force financial parsimony at the expense of residents' quality of life? To be truly successful, executives in this industry must emulate those organizations that generate reasonable profits without compromising their responsibility to present and future residents, staff, and the community they serve. Service and profit are not incompatible if retirement community professionals share a performance and ethical standard that incorporates competing needs into the overall executive strategy. But organizations that sacrifice care for the sake of short-term dollars are risking the credibility of the industry and their own corporate continuity at the same time.

■ The Elderly

We use the word "elderly" with the awareness that this label may evoke an unfortunate stereotypical image. We cannot allow the term elderly to obscure what must be learned—how individuals and groups of individuals view themselves and the places and events around them, and that unique needs and wants always exist. With our increasingly well-founded understanding of the expectations and requirements of the elderly (for our purposes, those 75 and older), we must discard stereotypes and perceive the elderly to be in personal, social, political, and economic evolution, a process that we should know more about. We must be alert to the fact that the daily life of the elderly is becoming more complex and their needs for perfected physical settings and services more pressing. We must invest in the research needed to identify and understand every challenge facing the elderly, lead communities in the development of new concepts for achieving quality of life for the elderly, and, most particularly, create the means to husband every dollar invested in the development of housing and services for the elderly. Industry professionals who achieve this expertise will provide extraordinary value to the elderly and their families, create residences and services that anticipate expectations and requirements, and prevail over their competition.

The elderly are becoming an increasingly powerful force for their own best interests. By studying and promoting the executive strategy, the elderly guarantee that what they know will be applied. To safeguard their interests, they must participate directly in executive strategy applications. We want the elderly to learn to speak for themselves, to confound those who still think of them as passively living in a home setting when they should perceive and value the elderly as interested in opportunity as much as younger people.

The Benchmarks

The retirement community industry characterizes itself through a simple spectrum of living arrangements—independent-living facility, congregate seniors' housing, assisted-living facility, and continuing care retirement community (CCRC).[1] Each has its own potential and may be suitable for specific situations. However, these words are nothing more than labels. They convey little of the fact that the development and operation of a retirement community is one of the most complex undertakings in which an individual can be involved. Since this book is intended to address the full complexity of the retirement community challenge, as well as to speak to the future, we have selected the *equity CCRC* as our focus. The CCRC is our finest retirement community industry product. It is responsive to every need. It is certainly a model for the future. The associated "equity" concept—where CCRC residents purchase their own condominiums and retain all property rights—is the best possible strategy for assuring the financial success of the enterprise, while providing long-term stability and security for residents. As we seek to demonstrate the best practices for the retirement community industry, the equity CCRC is useful as an umbrella concept that covers our entire product line, from independent-living facilities to assisted-living, skilled nursing, and special-need settings.

After reviewing many exemplary retirement communities, two of America's foremost CCRCs were selected as our case studies—*The Cypress of Hilton Head*, a 100-acre condominium campus located on Hilton Head Island in South Carolina, and *The Stratford*, an eleven-story, high-rise equity CCRC located in the center of the San Francisco Peninsula. The first case study is a benchmark for enterprises striving to achieve a resortlike residential experience and the second is a benchmark for enterprises challenged to provide residences and services within a densely developed city environment. The scores of residents at *The Cypress* and *The Stratford* with whom we strolled, dined, and

The Cypress: **Aerial view of the campus**

The Cypress: **The Clubhouse**

The Stratford

chatted would support the view that a great deal can be learned about the best by studying these two CCRCs. Committed to advancing the retirement community industry, the executives of these enterprises made available all their documents for review and spoke most insightfully about their challenges and strategies for the future.

In keeping with our focus on executive leadership and action, we interviewed developers, architects, attorneys, and executive managers of marketing, health care, and residential service programs associated with the development and operation of *The Cypress* and *The Stratford*. At the end of our research, we had accumulated hundreds of pages of transcribed interviews, resident association manuals, eligibility screening documents, market studies, pro formas, and a complete portfolio of drawings, specifications, photographs, and master plans.

The selection of these benchmarks in no way overlooks the elderly with limited resources who may never qualify for an equity CCRC. On the contrary, these models of best practices provide a basis to evaluate and critique proposals designed for those with limited resources.

The CCRC Executive Strategy

From the beginning, the authors recognized the need for a tightly argued executive strategy with the primary objective of exceptional business results. The central theme of the executive strategy is the search for development possibilities, characterizing what is needed to meet the quality-of-life demands of the elderly, respond to government regulations, apply social service guidelines, develop action plans, and assign enterprise responsibilities. The executive strategy is a response to the need to husband resources and increase returns. The strategy is responsive to the matter of risk. Even when capably leading retirement community enterprises, we work in situations with the possibilities for failure facing every development—overbuilding, changing market demands, neighborhood and community resistance, prolonged review processes, premature obsolescence, and ineptly conceived and arbitrarily applied codes and regulations. Work pace is also a factor of the executive strategy. Investments begin to perform only when we are far enough along on a project to start selling property or leasing units. The executive strategy is also responsive to business development. It structures our attempts to establish a market reputation for exceptional achievement and develop our potential for future growth.

Cooperation, Collaboration, and Shared Responsibility

The CCRC executive strategy is about the people in the CCRC industry, their challenges, and how they work through their problems. Certainly, the greatest challenge is how to get the most out of people. The executive strategy promotes the view that a successful retirement community enterprise is dependent on the contributions of all participants working with a sense of cooperation, collaboration, and shared responsibility for project success. The importance of this view is directly related to these questions:

- How do we learn and apply what investors and lenders know about opportunity and profit?
- How can we learn from legal and financial professionals to safeguard investments, manage financial activities, and comply with regulatory and licensing requirements?
- How can we benefit from and apply the accumulated knowledge and experience of developers and architects in regards to the attainment of facility value, performance, and image?
- How can we apply what health care and service providers know about attaining quality of life for every resident?
- How can we learn from communities of interest such as families and neighborhood groups, regulatory entities, social service consultants, and gerontologists, who have special interests and knowledge?
- How can we learn from the elderly themselves, who have the most insightful understanding about the best way to meet their residential, health care, and service expectations and requirements?

Executive Strategy Structure

The executive strategy has three parts (Figure 1).

Part I: Critical Success Factors

The thread that binds the parts of this book into a systematic executive strategy is the concept of critical success factors. The premise is that eight factors set the conditions for a successful equity CCRC enterprise:

1.0 Enterprise Concept
2.0 Executive Organization
3.0 Finance and Law

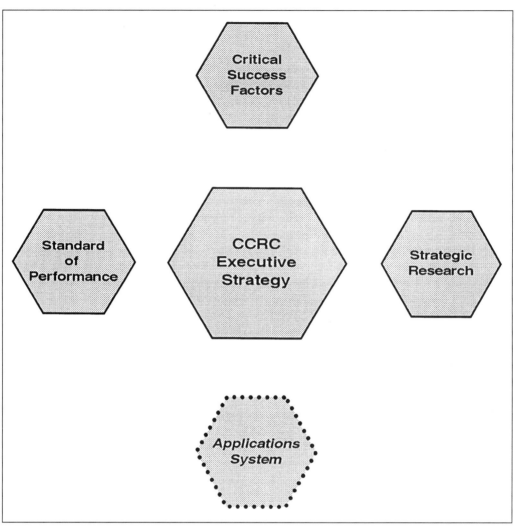

Figure 1. CCRC executive strategy

4.0 Marketing and Sales
5.0 Residents
6.0 Health Care
7.0 Residents' Services
8.0 Design and Build

Part II: Standard of Performance

The standard of performance decomposes the critical success factors into mutually exclusive data and information entities. This detailed, 200-question item expansion of the critical success factors—shown in its entirety in the Appendix—particularly distinguishes the CCRC executive strategy.

Part III: Strategic Research

Whereas the standard of performance decomposes the critical success factors into mutually exclusive data and information entities, strategic research brings all the components together. The primary objectives of strategic research are to support and guide decision makers in the most practical manner possible. This problem focus is why we use the term "strategic research."

About Part I: Critical Success Factors

The concept of critical success factors is the foundation of the executive strategy. These are the essential beginning points for a CCRC enterprise, the points at which investors, lenders, developers, architects, health care and service providers, communities of interest, and the elderly must achieve a notable degree of organization and be given an opportunity to defend their views and specific recommendations. Whether at an executive organization meeting or development work session, reviewing proposed master plans and facility design concepts, appearing before a state regulatory agency or community planning board, leading a public hearing or investor presentation, critical success factors frame presentations, arguments, and deliberations.

■ 1.0 Enterprise Concept

Consideration of this critical success factor results in a conceptual overview that encompasses every objective, issue, and concern. This does not happen at one particular point in the CCRC executive strategy. The enterprise concept evolves as we study each critical success factor and as more and more people become involved in the enterprise. The challenge during this process of discovery is verification. No unfounded speculations, no unverified assumptions, and the most cautious reliance on prior experience—these are the safeguards that must be maintained while working to identify and assess the potential in a CCRC enterprise concept.

■ 2.0 Executive Organization

The executive organization we build within a CCRC enterprise must include people who can provide a service of outstanding value and who are gifted at sensing and pursuing opportunities and creating a highly competitive organization. The equity CCRC needs people with an exceptional performance standard that encompasses every advance in knowledge and technology. Once this requirement is met, the CCRC executive must invest professional, service, technical, and operations personnel with the responsibility for creating the organization's road to success. The challenge is to let all work as they wish, freely apply their experience and expertise, and still maintain common goals and objectives.

3.0 Finance and Law

This critical success factor is a major part of every CCRC enterprise. The legal aspect is two-sided; that is, the statutory requirements for CCRC developments and operations, and the property and service safeguards for residents. We also consider topics related to investment expectations and achieving sustainable profit, such as financing, investors' perceptions, capital availability, cost of capital, construction financing, profitability, minimizing investment risks, and legal oversight to safeguard and clarify the financial commitments and property acquisition process for residents. Latent in these considerations is the possibility of conflict between legal and financial opinion and the risks the developer is willing to take to compete in the demanding CCRC marketplace. Any discussion between an attorney or financial advisor and a CCRC executive reveals that these advisors have a tendency to give business advice beyond their competency, often losing competitive opportunities.

4.0 Marketing and Sales

This critical success factor addresses the challenges associated with an expanding and heterogeneous population continually evolving in terms of expectations and requirements, a constantly changing regulatory environment, and advances in health care. We note the opportunities that arise for those who can predict the needs of the marketplace and anticipate community concerns. On the other hand, we consider the need to protect ourselves from data and information that distort the reality of the situation. A major consideration is how to make financial options and facilities and services so attractive that buyers are willing to leave their homes and old neighborhoods and accept the challenge of moving to a new living and social setting.

The dimensions of this critical success factor are extensive. We have to be aware of the need to anticipate changes in the market and define the direction these might take. We must deal with such basic considerations as presell strategies, creating a wait list of committed individuals and families, standards for admission, and ethnic and disability discrimination in admissions and services. Exposure in the media, published announcements, direct mail, telemarketing, Internet marketing, and professional and business publications are important topics.

■ 5.0 Residents

This critical success factor challenges us to anticipate life within the CCRC. The goals are verified data and clarified insights descriptive of preferred ways of living at home, in the neighborhood and community, daily and seasonal activities, and lifestyles and traditions. While working to identify the expectations and requirements of residents and weighing the relative significance of findings, we must identify likely areas of change. Our deliberations demand insight into individual perceptions, behavior, and judgment, our most valuable resources for discovering what is important and what should be achieved.

The work undertaken here identifies exactly what is needed in a well-designed residence: places designed to provide comfort and in which to rest, relax, and get well; attractive places to entertain friends and families; and places for residents to share quiet moments and stimulating experiences. It makes the desire to meet the needs of staff also very tangible by fostering well-designed workplaces, which help staff make each day pleasant for every resident and deal with the stresses and frustration associated with this responsibility.

■ 6.0 Health Care

The health care contract and services provided to residents is an essential part of the CCRC enterprise. The challenge is to assure that the health care offering is financially sound, makes advances in medical practice and technology accessible to residents, and complies with the recommendation of agencies that approve, monitor, and regulate health care providers, protecting the interests and rights of residents. Work within this critical success factor begins with an evaluation of proposed health care programs and their financial sustainability and continues through the establishment of an approved continuing care contract to the continual assessment of the common and daily experience of residents. An immediate safeguard is the thoughtful care and considerate attention provided by CCRC staff. The limitations and capabilities of residents must influence staff selection and training and the handling of special events and emergencies. In terms of additional sources of revenue, attention may also be given to the provision of short-stay services to nonresidents and community outreach services such as home care, outpatient physical therapy, and adult day care.

■ 7.0 Residents' Services

This critical success factor recognizes that the ability to provide services that meet quality-of-life and cost criteria is an essential aspect of the CCRC enterprise. To prevail over the competition, we must promote in the minds of prospective residents the extraordinary quality of the CCRC. Prospective residents must be assured that when they contract for services, these will meet every expectation and requirement. To provide value, we have to develop and deliver exceptional service to residents, which includes everything from financing consultations to concierge services.

■ 8.0 Design and Build

This critical success factor deals with the translation of the expectations and requirements of residents and staff into design concepts, schemes, forms, and features. To be a champion of quality, time, and money management, those providing architectural services must be more than designers. Architects must be prepared to meet the expectations and requirements of investors, lenders, and operators as business associates. More than any other selection criteria, contracts are awarded to architectural firms and contractors who are willing to work in their client's interest and invest time and effort to fully understand their client's risks and resource limitations.

Within this critical success factor, we promote the design/build method of construction, arguing that this method holds the greatest promise for all stakeholders. In this method, we need more than skilled designers and construction managers. We need men and women ready for executive responsibility. The design/build process requires exceptional performance leaders, totally committed to the concept of cooperation, collaboration, and shared responsibility. To make design/build developments an opportunity, architects and construction managers must look beyond what they are doing today and create new forms of shared responsibility for enterprise success. This suggests that professionals in the architecture, engineering, and construction industry will increase their value to their corporation and advance their careers to the extent to which they understand the challenges and responsibilities associated with the CCRC executive strategy.

About Part II: Standard of Performance

The standard of performance was specifically conceived as a computer-based applications system. To provide a means to precisely order data and information, the 200 question items in the standard of performance were written as mutually exclusive information categories. Each question item is uniquely identified by index number, title, and topic. The goal is to maintain a real-time view of the enterprise. With this overview, we can track progress, alert ourselves to what is needed, identify where we can contribute, and conduct "what if" deliberations, sharing new possibilities with enterprise associates.

Application of the 200 question items in the standard of performance develops a verified image of a successful project outcome and expands and improves that image throughout the CCRC enterprise. Applications set the agenda for deliberations and provide the means to determine how successfully each critical success factor was addressed. The standard of performance provides a means for accumulating ideas, sharpening perceptions, and rigorous analysis. Answering the question items in the CCRC standard of performance provides the very special benefit of learning how to work with others in a less judgmental and more collaborative manner, in which enterprise achievement is more important than position.

■ Computer-Based Applications System

When the standard of performance is transformed into an applications system, essential capabilities are established. During the course of every enterprise, conditions will change and we will have to adjust to these. The applications system makes immediately available all that has been accomplished, as a reference point when reformulating enterprise direction. Throughout the retirement community enterprise, executives will make dozens of presentations. An applications system that is rigorously maintained means little or no time spent on preparation, because every piece of information is in your laptop and can be projected instantly. The applications system helps people who are there from the beginning of the enterprise and those who join later to maintain mutual understanding of enterprise direction and achievements. It also assures that information developed for one project can be efficiently employed on future business development activities.

The applications system is the principal management tool for achieving the benefits associated with the design/build process.

Monitoring events within the system is a means to assess the performance of enterprise participants, comparing what must be accomplished and what is actually being accomplished. This is one part of the effort to establish the cooperation and shared responsibility needed to make the design/build process work. When work is open to review by the entire spectrum of design/build participants and all interested parties, you have the best of collaborative situations.

About Part III: Strategic Research

The premise of strategic research is that, as we face the future, we cannot succeed financially unless we achieve an encompassing and accurate overview of every retirement community enterprise expectation and requirement. For instance, consider an overlooked regulatory requirement that results in project delay, an unforeseen expenditure because facility design did not accommodate a critical aspect of assisted living, the disruption and cost of requalifying staff because a change in licensing requirements was not foreseen, and a residents' association in an adversarial position regarding points of dissatisfaction that should have been anticipated. Consider the financial downside when presale forecasts are too optimistic or when the property value depreciates because no one identified what is needed to maintain a reputation in the eyes of the community. Think about a company whose last project is in financial distress because the preferences of the elderly were not accurately anticipated. What went wrong? In every one of these situations, enterprise participants failed to anticipate a particularly important aspect of one or more features of the retirement community enterprise.

Within strategic research we approach an enterprise from four directions. We employ Market Research as a means to judge the potential of a proposed CCRC enterprise and establish a market strategy responsive to current, near-term, and future possibilities. In Human Factors Research, we validate facility design and service features in terms of the expectations and requirements of residents. The benefits associated with Design Research are directly related to making design and research one process. The Legal Research presentation works as a safeguard to assure that we anticipate what will be demanded of us by government entities, investors and lenders, and by those who reside in an equity CCRC.

Executive Leadership and Action

How effectively employable is the executive strategy? This is the overriding question. The answer will be increasingly more positive as readers recognize that the executive strategy addresses a CCRC enterprise at its most critical and risky time, the first stages of deliberation and action. This is what is emphasized in the executive strategy and all that is presented in Parts I, II, and III. The strategy tells us that the steps we take in the beginning of a CCRC enterprise determine whether the outcome will be an exceptional achievement or something that will soon become a distressed property with diminished market value.

That executive leadership and action is the single most important aspect of every retirement community enterprise is confirmed when you propose an undertaking to potential investors and lenders. Even as they see promise in your concept, market analysis, master plan, facility design, services, and pro formas, their first question indicates what is really important. "How will you manage the enterprise?" They want to know just how likely you are to fulfill the promise of your proposal. They have learned that notable achievements and the ability to service debt are always the result of leadership and the ability of people to work together, and that enterprises with problems or characterized by lost opportunities are the result of management failure. Examination of failed retirement community developments has revealed that often one or more key figures were not included in deliberations, or were not listened to, or listened to too late, and that there were no means in place to assess the effect of one decision on others. In other words, unsuccessful retirement community developments are characterized by a lack of effective executive strategy, in which the prime requirements are managerial concepts, knowledge, and methods capable of producing what the elderly expect today and will demand in coming decades.

■ Setting the Conditions for Success

Consider the future of the CCRC industry. How can we provide the best possible service to the elderly? What are our standards? Where do CCRC developers, architects, marketing executives, and health care and service providers need new expertise and skills? Where are federal and state regulatory agencies taking the industry? What evolving political, economic, and social situations provide new opportunities? How are advances in technology and medical science redefining the needs and wants of the elderly? Considering all the risks involved, how demanding will

CCRC financing become in terms of presale requirements? How do we compete in this industry and where can firms cooperate to enhance the reputation of the industry? As we ask these questions, it becomes clear that we need to systematically address a very basic question: What is the best possible way to lead a CCRC enterprise?

Applications

Applications of the executive strategy are basically deliberative and research activities that result in a complete and detailed prescription for CCRC enterprise success. The areas of concern include forming the enterprise concept, creating an executive organization, financial and legal due diligence, marketing and sales preparation, the expectations and requirements of residents, health care and residential services features, and the design and build process. Within this framework, the authors anticipate that the executive strategy and associated standard of performance and strategic research methods will be employed when

- Corporate and institutional executive boards formulate strategies for CCRC developments.
- Commercial banks, real estate investment trusts, pension funds, and lending organizations assess the merit of a proposed CCRC development project.
- Financial advisors and attorneys seek to determine the compliance of a CCRC enterprise with all existing and forthcoming statutes and regulations.
- CCRC developers craft strategies to deal with marketability and community acceptance of a project.
- Building industry professionals manage CCRC facility design and construction undertakings.
- Providers create and justify CCRC services, establish costs, and guide staff development.
- CCRC sales and marketing staff help individuals and families create the best possible future for themselves.
- Public officials and government regulators responsible for protecting the interests of the elderly oversee CCRC housing and service activities.
- Individuals, families, and communities of interest work to make their expectations, requirements, recommendations, and concerns known to CCRC developers and community officials.

The executive strategy recognizes that developers, architects, marketing executives, and health care and service providers share many common concerns. Their responsibilities require that they work together to confront the need to identify, understand, and meet diverse and often conflicting expectations and requirements. We emphasize that collaboration and shared responsibility are fundamental aspects of enterprise success. Although we have complete faith in the experience and expertise of retirement community industry professionals, collaboration is the only way to realize our potential. Our response is to standardize all the work we undertake within the framework of the executive strategy. Although the executive strategy may seem more complex than necessary, it isn't. It simplifies our work and provides a guarantee that our work will, at the same time, be more precise, comprehensive, and thorough.

With the sense of direction provided by the CCRC executive strategy, the associated critical success factor framework, the CCRC standard of performance, and CCRC strategic research, every aspect of the enterprise seems to improve, work speed increases, fewer errors appear, and rework efforts occur less frequently. Consider that the work of project participants is often delayed by stalled attempts to determine what will make an enterprise successful. If uncertainty and unwarranted speculation are eliminated and replaced with a clear image of what should be done and how it might be done, people will start to employ their skills and insights efficiently and with confidence.

■ Benefits

In every retirement community deliberation, whether associated with a major enterprise or a small-scale local effort, evolving over a long period of time or fast-tracked, managed by a senior housing corporation or a local developer, the means for setting the conditions for success are found in the CCRC executive strategy. This strategy provides for discovery, clarification, and verification by means of an inclusive process of debate and research. It is a process that assures that people discuss the appropriate things, that what might be misunderstood or ignored is clarified and appreciated, and that the time spent on management deliberations and research produces exceptional performance and results.

Investors and Lenders

Investors and lending organizations benefit when the CCRC executive strategy is accepted and adhered to by all parties. There are no easy dollars to be uncovered in the CCRC business. However, a thorough understanding of market potential and hazards should earn fair profits for those who maintain the standard of performance developed in this work. It is important to note that while lenders safeguard their resources with loan and mortgage minimum performance requirements and technical default restrictions, we are suggesting more. The direct and continuing participation of investors and lenders in applications of the CCRC executive strategy provides a means to safeguard profitability and minimize investment risk.

Retirement Community Professionals

There is a benefit for developers when they share and promote the CCRC executive strategy with others. The more knowledgeable people are about the developer's challenges, the more likely it is that you will learn what people know to be important, and hear promising speculations that will help everyone consider new possibilities. Regarding the value of the executive strategy for architects, consider the significant change in the professional practice of architecture, in which the world outside the office is seen as being more important than the world inside the office.[2] Architectural practice is becoming increasingly client-centered, with a widening number of people involved in the creation of design concepts, schemes, forms, and features. This results in a greater need for managerial methodologies. The marketing challenging is central to enterprise success. The executive strategy advances current practices by revealing more of what it means to attract the interest and trust of the elderly. Applications of the executive strategy will help health care and service providers work with others to anticipate what service and facility design options and alternatives will mean for the daily life of senior residents and staff. The primary goal here is not only to help assure that facilities and services are perfected prior to occupancy, but also to gain the efficiencies that result when people have confidence that what they are doing makes sense.

Financial Advisors and Attorneys

When these professionals recommend and participate in executive strategy applications, they create a means to fulfill fiduciary responsibilities to investors, lenders, developers, and residents. The result is a legal and financial review that is unassailable in terms of detailed oversight of every aspect of the CCRC enterprise.

Communities of Interest

In a CCRC enterprise, decisions are made at all levels—from government regulators, to professional groups providing accreditation, to a son and daughter helping their parents relocate to a more supportive and pleasant situation. These communities of interest will have many types of commitments. Some will be committed to ideals, some will be motivated to protect or increase personal, neighborhood, or public assets, and some will be fulfilling familial or regulatory responsibilities. Each participant brings a variety of expectations and requirements to every CCRC enterprise and the ability to contribute to every deliberation.

Community and Neighborhood Groups.   When competing for the acceptance of their point of view and what they consider the appropriate allocation of resources, community and neighborhood groups demand adherence to an open process of deliberation. Public forums always reveal the presence of conflicts of interest and intent. Resolution begins with the acceptance of the concept of cooperation, collaboration, and shared responsibility that is the foundation of the CCRC executive strategy.

Government and Regulatory Entities.   These are the men and women in local, county, state, and federal offices who oversee the development of CCRCs and associated facilities and services. These elected and appointed public officials and government regulators have a voice in every CCRC development. They must consider the benefits of sharing a common standard of performance with investors, lenders, developers, architects, marketing executives, health care and service providers, communities of interest, and the elderly. Government regulations, standards, and guidelines prescribe only what is known; they do not identify what might or must be discovered. The executive strategy provides the means to respond to situations with appropriate innovations, achieving advances in governmental regulations and guidance.

Gerontologists.   It is essential for this group of professionals to recognize that a CCRC enterprise is a bounded problem, not an open-ended research endeavor. Decisions have to be made within a specified time frame and are literally cast in concrete. The CCRC executive strategy provides direction for gerontological research so that this knowledge can have a direct impact on enterprise deliberations.

The Retirement Community Industry

Within the retirement community industry, we see a steady development of strategic, facility, and service innovations. Markets are now being won with new concepts. Changing requirements and problems are being addressed with a new certainty. The best of executive leadership and action is future-oriented—probing, risk taking, insightful.

Although many retirement communities are worthy of recognition for their service to the elderly and as worthwhile investments, there are also too many communities where promises are not being kept and debt is not being serviced. The remedy for this is the executive strategy, which assures that we think critically during the first stages of a retirement community enterprise. When studying the role of critical thinking in the retirement community industry, what did we find? We saw executives committing themselves to a renewal in intellectual discipline and intellectual openness. We saw executives employing critical thinking to define opportunity, identify promising innovations, and form the performance standards needed to direct and market professional services. It was found that executives in the retirement community industry use critical thinking to avoid the narrow view as they focus on the goal of realizing their potential and mapping the challenges ahead.

Addressing the members of the American Association of Homes and Services for the Aging, James E. Dewhirst,[3] Chairman, noted the challenges the industry is facing and proposed some strategic considerations. Anticipating massive changes in health care, housing, and services for the elderly, Dewhirst called for leadership that ensures that any new system of care, housing, and services preserves the "social components of care" and the "continuum" concept. Of particular significance is that the consumer movement of the last 20 years has created a sophisticated public. Health care is increasingly driven by consumers' demands and needs. They demand to know costs. They want to know about the quality of care. They want to know what your organization will do to satisfy their needs. They expect accountability, efficiency, and value. In his extended remarks, Dewhirst asked the retirement community industry to concentrate on the future, emphasize flexibility, minimize hierarchy, develop a learning culture, and look for partners with special expertise in health care, housing, and service. He concluded that nonprofit innovation led the way in developing homes for the aging, assisted living, continuing care, hospice care, home health care, and many other services. Now, the retirement community industry must provide the leadership for the next century.

The increasing sophistication of the customer, combined with the plethora of housing and service choices available, place increasing competitive pressure on retirement communities. Our research and experience consistently demonstrate that the "future" will always be a matter of executive leadership and action, the ability to mobilize and wisely direct resources and expertise. To meet this challenge, the strategy outlined in this book helps retirement community executives forge links between key associates, and clarify, persuade, and achieve the economies associated with effective management.

Responding to objectives such as these, the CCRC executive strategy fosters the view that those in the retirement community industry must discard old habits, assess their values and priorities, and learn new ways of doing business.[4] The executive challenge for retirement community professionals is related to the premise that a CCRC enterprise must be led, not merely managed. In the most dynamic fashion possible, retirement community executives must maintain a vision of unlimited opportunities. Open to all possibilities, they must experiment with ideas and methods and work to develop new capabilities within their organization. The CCRC executive strategy is fundamentally a business plan; you have every reason to read this book critically and try to incorporate the presented concepts, insights, and methods in your future undertakings.

Risks and Rewards: A Case Study

This case study presents an early trial application of the concept of critical success factors. It supported the refinement of what is presented in this book.

William Sahlman of the Harvard Business School speaks to the challenge of developing a great business plan. "One of the greatest myths about entrepreneurs is that they are risk seekers. All sane people want to avoid risk."[5] Challenged in this fashion, William Leslie, president of a highly recognized development, construction, and property management corporation, evaluates two business opportunities in the following case study by applying the concept of critical success factors.

■ *The Hampshire* and *The Fairford* Opportunities

William Leslie looked at the piles of documents on his desk. On the right side were site plans, economic analyses, and a Sanwa Bank construction loan rejection letter for *The Hampshire*, a CCRC development he had been working on for the past 18 months. On the left side of his desk were residence and care agreements, acquisition documents, economic analyses, and a letter of confidentiality to acquire *The Fairford*, an existing highrise continuing care retirement community. This project was fraught with problems, from inadequate financial and operational structures to a challenging and argumentative resident association, but it was already developed and licensed and half-sold, and now control of the property was available as a package with 100 remaining original units.

Despite the construction loan rejection, Leslie thought he could raise enough cash to go ahead with one or the other project, but his resources would be taxed to proceed with both. A long period of market analysis had convinced him that the CCRC market was ripe for opportunity—and rife with failures. Should he risk *The Hampshire* development with the known potential for excellence or compromise with known problems associated with *The Fairford*? If he decided to go with *The Fairford*, could he convince his investors to back him?

■ The Leslie Organization

The Leslie Organization was a privately held organization founded by Nicholas Leslie in 1962. Originally conceived as a design/build construction company, over the years it had developed a reputation as a high-quality developer, contractor, and property manager of commercial and multifamily residential properties. Its current portfolio of properties managed was valued at $100 million, the majority of which were owned wholly or in partnership by the company.

The company was divided into four divisions: Development, Construction, Commercial Property Management, and Residential Property Management, which included a senior services organization. As part of its strategy to expand the senior services organization, the company had recently appointed a new president, a highly qualified MBA with experience with a national senior care management firm.

A multifunctional support team offered human resources, accounting/finance, and office management services to each division on a flexible, as-needed basis. The organization was accustomed to being flexible, focusing resources on each division as needed to keep overhead low and weather the inevitable business cycles. Core office staff numbered 26, with an additional field staff on each property managed and a construction staff that was added as the work required. The staff was managed by a general manager, who reported to Nick Leslie, Chairman and CEO. William Leslie, his son, had headed the development arm of the business for the past 3 years; prior to that, William's experience had been in commercial real estate brokerage and consulting services.

William Leslie knew that he would need to tap the resources of the entire company to make either *The Hampshire* or *The Fairford* project fly. *The Hampshire* project would provide an opportunity to develop a CCRC with an integrated approach from initial design all the way through to operations. *The Fairford* project would need the expertise of the Development and Construction divisions only in the minor retrofitting required, and the immediate acquisition would pose a serious set of challenges to the Residential Property Management Division, taxing staff resources. Although the organization was positioned for growth, it was unlikely that it could simultaneously invest the resources in both projects to do either justice.

Leslie mulled over the advantages of each project. *The Hampshire* project was certainly more appealing, with its clean slate offering opportunities to take an integrated, streamlined approach to the complex development task. And the pro forma promised impressive returns over a 10-year period and beyond, after serious up-front investment of money and energy. On the other hand, *The Fairford* project would offer hands-on experience with known risk.

At *The Fairford*, for a smaller up-front investment, he could put his team to work right away learning the ins and outs of the business, bringing quicker, although lesser, returns. He predicted the market would be heating up quickly and could be saturated with competitors over the next few years. Could he afford the learning curve and lengthy timeline of *The Hampshire* project? Could he afford the compromises and the aggravation of cleaning up another developer's mistakes on *The Fairford* project? He decided to list the critical success factors in CCRC development, factors he had studied and believed to be the determinants of success in this business. Putting his emotional attachment to the glamour of *The Hampshire* aside, he decided to evaluate each project against eight success factors. By the end of the exercise, the facts would lead him to a decision.

■ Critical Success Factors

Leslie had spent the past 18 months learning about the continuing care retirement industry. He had attended industry conferences, visited fifteen CCRC facilities in the San Francisco Bay Area and others across the country, and met with countless developers, attorneys, financiers, and operators. Although his research had demonstrated the considerable variation in communities in everything from state licensing requirements to financial structure, the successful communities appeared to have certain things in common that the unsuccessful ones did not have. After months of thinking and revising, Leslie had devised a checklist of the factors that seemed to differentiate the good communities from the foundering or ill-conceived ones. These "critical success factors," as he called them, formed the basis for his evaluation of every project, and would be essential in helping him determine the better course to take with *The Hampshire* and *The Fairford*.

According to Leslie, the critical success factors for a successful continuing care retirement community are as follows:

Enterprise Concept

Leslie knew that good facilities are conceived from a vision or concept that dictates the look, tone, and central character of a retirement community. The concept provides a snapshot description of the community, such as "a gated community that serves as a magnet and microcosm of the New England fishing village in which it is situated," or "a spacious university-style campus located a few miles from a premier research and teaching institution." The enterprise concept also extends beyond the characteristics of the retirement community to a financial structure that correlates to the needs of the customer base: fee-for-service, equity-based, or entrance-fee-based. Without a distinctive marketing image and without a guiding vision to lead a myriad of subsequent decisions about design, construction, community outreach, and operations, a retirement community will founder.

Executive Organization

The members of the executive team are the essential messengers of the enterprise concept. Successful communities have a multi-disciplinary group of managers leading the community through development, construction, marketing, and operations. Ideally, the team develops or shares the key decisions that create and reinforce the concept, so that a structure is designed by an architect working with the individuals responsible for selling and operating a community, creating a seamless whole. Leslie found that communities developed by a succession of professionals handing off responsibility for the next function, from developer to architect to engineer to builder to marketer to manager, ended up with significant problems, as each subsequent recipient of responsibility struggled with the independent role of fulfilling his narrow function without input from the previous or to the subsequent manager. In those facilities where a team had contributed to every stage, more consistent marketing, more efficient operations, and, ultimately, more financially successful enterprises were evident.

Finance and Law

A carefully considered financial and legal structure forms the essential skeleton and cartilage of the body of an effective CCRC community. Communities where the developer does not do his legal homework end up with years of conflict with the residents, the staff, and licensing agencies. Likewise, retirement community enterprises that do not plan financially for contingencies or interest rate changes find themselves in foreclosure or worse.

Marketing and Sales

This is the bane of the industry, the most unpredictable and challenging part of creating a CCRC. During his research phase, Leslie heard more horror stories about the problems of selling a community than about any other aspect of the enterprise. The customer was skeptical, could not be rushed, was reluctant to part with his money and home, and perpetually "not ready yet." Moreover, only a small portion of any age and income-qualified population would even consider moving to a retirement community, no matter how elegant or convenient. Although a huge cottage industry of senior marketing firms had emerged to "solve" this problem for the industry, Leslie found that there was no magic answer or formula beyond patience, hard work, honesty, a strong image, and a steady cash stream to keep the marketing effort afloat.

Residents

Once operational, successful communities anticipate and address the concerns of residents in a reasonable manner. Understanding the psychology of the elderly is essential here, as people's perspectives naturally evolve through the challenges associated with aging. A community that does not understand seniors' psychological needs for peer support, individual recognition, power, authority, and control risks a regular series of minor and major disruptions to the operation and the sense of well-being the community is attempting to provide. Issues of grieving, pharmaceutical or alcoholic debilitation, anger, and loss are all powerful processes that must be addressed or they will be subverted into other disruptions. Successful communities make sure that staff understands these issues and have effective programs to channel this energy as constructively as possible.

Health Care

An effective health care program is the primary reason seniors consider a move to a CCRC. To provide continuing care, a community must create and support a means to accommodate the inevitably increasing health care needs of an aging population. This must be done in a manner that is both cost-effective and compassionate, so that the senior can imagine himself or herself, spouse or friend in a situation that is financially and medically preferable to living alone outside a CCRC.

Residents' Services

Without question, a community has to provide quality services to its residents. Services must be consistently and fairly delivered to all residents, with a reasonable balance of efficiency and perceived quality, and the services offered must be considered valuable enough to the population to be appreciated. Although delivery styles varied widely, those communities that offered the right mix of services to seniors had a serious advantage over those that were inconsistent, overpriced, or unreliable.

Design and Build

For a community to run well, it has to be designed well. In his research, Leslie saw a plethora of poorly designed and shabbily constructed facilities that, as a consequence, suffered from marketing problems, operational inefficiency, and resident displeasure. Alternatively, the facilities where the design and construction were well thought out and of a reasonable quality enjoyed positive operations and resident satisfaction. There was a surprisingly low correlation between the cost to buy or join a community and the quality and cost of the design and construction. Some of the most effective communities spent far less money on construction, but spent it after careful consideration of the functions of spaces and facilities.

A Comparison

Having reviewed his success factors, Leslie decided to develop a risk-and-reward profile for the two projects. He decided to review each independently, measuring each against his eight standards, as a means of equating two very different projects with two very different sets of needs, concerns, and opportunities. Which had the greatest potential for his organization? Which, if any, would make his reputation as a leader in the continuing care field? Although Leslie knew which project he instinctively preferred, he wondered which project was really the better choice.

■ Evaluation of *The Hampshire*

The Hampshire project was to be located on a 2-acre lot in the middle of a thriving downtown suburb of a major metropolitan area. Design plans called for a 15-story building consisting of 90 two- and three-bedroom condominiums ranging in size from 1,000 to 2,500 square feet. Units would be located on floors 2 to 15, and have full kitchens, gas fireplaces, balconies, wet bars, and walk-in closets with built-in wall safes. The ground-floor, common-area plan called for a secure entry foyer, living room, library, dining room with outdoor patio, covered pool, exercise room, seminar/activity room, and an assisted-living wing. The inclusive cost to build would be $450 per square foot and the sales price would be $500 per square foot.

Enterprise Concept

The concept of *The Hampshire* would be "retirement in a small European hotel." Residents would purchase and own a unit, and then pay an inclusive monthly fee for a host of hotel-style services including room service, chauffeur service, and unlimited use of the assisted-living facility on-site or skilled nursing services off-site. The high staff-to-resident ratio, small number of units, and above-average sales prices would be designed to create a sense of exclusivity and desirability for the target market.

Executive Organization

Fortunately, The Leslie Organization was well equipped to staff the enterprise team from within the organization. The current heads of development, architecture, construction, sales/leasing, and senior management could be easily brought together to work on *The Hampshire* project. Having all of these individuals on staff would make integration easy, and, as they would all be benefiting from a successful enterprise through the senior employee bonus plan, they would be highly motivated to work together. On the other hand, none of the team members had actually worked on a project in this way before. Although The Leslie Organization had used a team approach for other developments, they had never attempted a senior residential project, let alone a project of this complexity or magnitude. Leslie wondered if he had the right players to form a winning enterprise team.

Finance and Law

Leslie had engaged a legal firm that specialized in writing CCRC contracts to provide his legal documents. He knew this area was loaded with explosive issues and was determined to invest in the legal expertise required to protect his development from future problems. He also knew that he would need expert assistance in passing the regulatory hurdles required by his state to obtain a CCRC license. He had heard war stories from other facilities that had been substantially compromised by loopholes in the resident contracts that enabled estates to stop paying monthly fees when the resident had died and the unit was up for resale. A problem like that could compromise the financial integrity of the operation and cause frustration and possibly hatred between neighbors. Despite his planning and investment, Leslie still worried that his lack of experience might lead him to overlook a crucial component of the legal process.

His financial footing was equally unnerving. The refusal from Sanwa Bank meant he would have to reapply for financing to another lender; although he knew money was starting to be available for real estate loans, he knew his firm's impressive track record on other projects would have to compensate for his lack of CCRC experience. The pro formas of the project showed a positive net return to the developer in year 4; until then, he would be paying hefty interest just to keep the construction and development loans afloat. If marketing went awry, or the real estate market went sour, or the project was delayed in obtaining a license, he could be faced with months or years of carrying costs and additional interest.

On this project, Leslie would make money in two ways, but both of them would take time. He was forgoing his traditional contractor's and developer's profit from initial sellout, and using that money as seed money to provide a free-and-clear site that any lender would require. He would receive a monthly management fee, but this would cover operations, overhead, and little else. He would actually reap profit only on resale of the units, through a 10% brokerage and marketing fee, which would cover ongoing sales expenses and marketing of resales, and collection of 50% of the equity appreciation between the original and resale price. If inflation increased, this could be a sizable amount. If the facility was poorly run or suffered from deflation, the resale prices would not rise and he would be left with only the 10% brokerage fee for all of his troubles.

Marketing and Sales

Leslie had done extensive demographic and absorption research on his market before structuring *The Hampshire* enterprise concept. His market area showed a significant concentration of residents 75 and older who had owned their homes for 30 or more years. This meant most traditional mortgages were paid off, and therefore the investment income of potential residents could support a luxurious life-style. A high-quality community located across town had enjoyed tremendous demand and was now entertaining a waiting list.

Leslie also knew he would have some serious hurdles to overcome in the marketing process. Most importantly, while he was well-known for his other projects, his company had not achieved a reputation in the senior care market. His senior care team leader had been with the organization only 3 months, but was known in the building industry, although not by the potential customer base. The site enjoyed good visibility, which would establish his recognition in the neighborhood, but was deliberately not on a major thoroughfare due to the disruption of noise and traffic. Thus, advertising was going to be an extremely important vehicle for improving name recognition and reputation. Leslie wondered about engaging a marketing firm, but he suspected that marketing efforts directed by the enterprise team would have much more impact.

The marketing program Leslie envisioned would have four components: direct mail, public relations, special events, and print advertising. His reading told him that these four components were the most accessible and credible to seniors, who would read an exhaustive amount before even considering a marketing visit or tour. He would also have to establish a sales office to provide a venue for marketing calls before the project was built. This would need to be staffed by salespeople who understood the special dynamics of selling to this population. Leslie knew that this was not a job for a traditional real estate salesperson and that he would have to do some serious searching to assemble an appropriate sales team.

Residents

Leslie had a profile of his potential resident: married or widowed, in their early eighties, with a net worth of $1,000,000 and an annual income of $100,000. This resident would have traveled extensively and would appreciate the "finer things"; he or she would be willing to pay a premium for ambiance and flair. The competition for this resident was not that great; the greatest threat was posed by his or her means and the desire to remain in his or her existing home, bringing in the assistance and health care needed as he or she aged.

This resident would be quite discriminating and, in many cases, demanding about the service he or she would expect in an upscale CCRC. By setting a higher standard, Leslie was also setting his operation up for higher expectations that would be more challenging to fulfill as the population aged. These residents, or their spouses, had been senior managers and professionals, attorneys, physicians, and bankers, and they were used to having things done their way. If "their" way adhered to a culturally common standard, such as how a table should be set, Leslie felt his staff could be trained to deliver. But could he train his staff to deliver service to the difficult individual, who might assume that staff should know about the finer things in life? Leslie could be setting his staff up for certain failure.

Health Care

The health care question presented a "moving target," as issues of Medicare reform, managed care, and medical advances all threatened to change the face of health care at an alarming rate. Leslie knew he would have to design a program that would take care of the residents, accommodate change, and ultimately be financially viable over the long run. He knew that his legal counsel would be crucial in crafting a health care package that was appealing and deliverable, but would not bankrupt the facility if health care costs skyrocketed.

Leslie was committed to an on-site, assisted-living wing to provide the cornerstone of his health care program. Staffed with licensed nurses around the clock, an on-site care center could offer triage services in an emergency, determine when to transfer a patient to a hospital, and care for residents who had been discharged from the hospital but who weren't yet able to return home unassisted. A care center could also provide an important stopgap between independent living and skilled nursing; many patients remain in a skilled nursing facility because they do not have access to less expensive and more appealing intermediate care. Leslie had made arrangements with a local nursing facility to provide for skilled care as necessary. He had actually rejected the idea of a skilled facility on-site as being too expensive, too complex in terms of regulatory considerations, and a marketing detriment to the "small European hotel" concept he was trying to achieve. A row of wheelchairs in the front hallway would effectively deter independent seniors from wanting to move in; while they might need a wheelchair one day, they certainly did not want to be reminded of it until it was absolutely necessary.

Residents' Services

Leslie knew that operations would determine the community's success once the facility was built. Although prospective residents worry about health care and financial security before they move in, once they become residents, their focus changes to scrutiny of things that affect the quality of their daily life, such as the variety of activities or the thoroughness of housecleaning. The number one question for any resident, of course, is "How's the food?" a source of endless interest and discussion. Leslie had learned that operations cannot make a significant amount of money for a developer, if any, but a poor operation could certainly depress sales and appreciation, ultimately ruining a developer's investment. No one would pay for real estate with services unless the services were worth the price premium a CCRC developer needed to ask. Operations were the "loss leader" of the equity CCRC business. You could not afford for them to be poorly run.

The Leslie Organization's president of senior services was hired for her expertise and high reputation for excellent CCRC operations. She had devised a number of methods for continuous improvement in what could easily become a repetitive and deteriorating part of the business. Most importantly, she invested a great deal of energy in up-front hiring and training, so that the right people were hired to perform the work. She insisted on manager and peer performance reviews tied to a cash incentive twice a year, and a system of checklists for resident satisfaction. She believed in ongoing education on everything, from security, to human resource issues, to medical issues, as a way to keep the inherently cyclical work in a retirement community fresh and interesting, as a matter of both safety and job satisfaction.

The other big advantage William Leslie saw in his concept for *The Hampshire* was his willingness to focus the monthly operational fees on areas of importance to residents. Even though it was out of line for a restaurant, Leslie was determined to spend a large portion of the residents' monthly fees on dinner and was planning to staff the dining room as if it were a fine French restaurant. If people had a bad experience at dinner, he reasoned, they would resent the entire monthly fee, most of which was spent on a host of "invisible" items like building maintenance or long-term care insurance. In this business, Leslie was learning, perception was reality.

Design and Build

The design and construction of the proposed project had been the source of endless vision and revision by the whole Leslie Organization. The original enterprise concept and the building site had dictated a high-rise building with large condominiums and ample common areas, with a mix of hotel-style features such as a covered *porte cochère*, marble entrance lobby, and grand reception rooms.

The atmosphere of a European hotel would extend into the dining room, complete with a mural on one wall, overlooking a formal garden and patio area. The design goal was to be grand without being stuffy, and to convey a sense of taste and warmth through furniture, fine art, and abundant fresh flowers. In short, the idea was to offer a space that surprised and delighted the senses with warmth and luxury, the antithesis of what many would expect from a "senior institution." Although the entire building would be designed to accommodate the needs of the least independent resident, it would need to appeal to the most independent. One of the design challenges was to disguise the many essential elements the building would need. The CCRC license required an abundance of grab bars, pull cords, and other necessities that render the usual senior facility institutional and off-putting. Chairs, for example, would need to be comfortable, sturdy, with armrests to hold onto, tuck in smoothly across carpet, and stand up to heavy use with the occasional but inevitable incontinence problem—all this and appear attractively "European" as well. It was a tall order, just one of literally thousands of design decisions that would have to be made in designing and furnishing the community.

As a design/build company with its own architecture and construction divisions, The Leslie Organization had the distinct advantage of integrating the design and construction functions from the start. The design would need to reflect the enterprise concept and operational functions as well as the realities of the construction code and process. The efficient placement of the elevators or the fireplaces would have a profound affect on structural engineering, piping, and plumbing, which would then affect the architecture of the units, which would in turn have an ultimate effect on sales.

Leslie knew that this kind of integrated thinking would also affect the cost of operations; for example, the placement and speed of the service elevator could add or subtract minutes to the housekeepers' daily routine, which when multiplied by the number of housekeepers and the number of days per year, could have a material effect on the operations budget and the monthly fees. This, in turn, could affect marketing. Leslie wondered how "traditional" developers were able to work with an architect before hiring the contractor or operations team and get the maximum efficiency out of a project; design/build integration was essential to every aspect of a project's success.

■ Evaluation of *The Fairford*

In many respects, *The Fairford* property was Leslie's "ace in the hole." The confidential offer for *The Fairford* had arrived on his desk 8 months after *The Hampshire* project began predevelopment. Now that he knew more about the industry, Leslie knew he should consider *The Fairford* as a serious contender for his development aspirations. *The Fairford* was only 3 years old. However, it had already had an original developer and another interim owner, both of whom had failed to make the project a success. These developers had hired and fired three management companies between them; in 3 years, a succession of individuals had managed to leave their dubious marks and then leave *The Fairford*.

The obvious advantage of *The Fairford*, of course, was that it was already built and partly occupied. The mountain of zoning, construction financing, and other challenges yet to be undertaken in *The Hampshire* was behind *The Fairford*, which meant that net positive cash flow was a matter of months, not years, away. The property enjoyed a decent, although not stellar, reputation in the marketplace, and was in a good metropolitan location. For a first development project, it might be a less risky choice for the Leslie Organization.

Still, William Leslie had serious reservations about *The Fairford*. The common areas were adequate in size, although poorly planned, and would require renovation and refurbishment to meet his standards of quality. But the individual units were a disaster—small, poorly planned, with efficiency apartment features that did not lend themselves to the premium pricing of the continuing care market. The succession of management companies had seriously eroded the residents' confidence in any manager, which in turn was affecting sales of the remaining units. Leslie wasn't sure this was the project that would persuade investors of his potential leadership in the CCRC market.

Leslie knew he could only make a reasonable comparison between the two projects if they were presented in comparable terms. He perused the selling broker's offer pro forma and began to reconfigure the information into his eight categories for success.

Enterprise Concept

The Fairford concept was a middle-priced, middle-class CCRC for residents who were committed to residing within the city center. Whereas the brochures touted "luxury living," the property was more comparable to a midlevel Sheraton or Marriott hotel than a Ritz-Carlton, with prices to match. Units ranged from $99,000 for a 500-square-foot studio with a Murphy bed to $400,000 for a two-bedroom apartment with a pleasing view. Services included a three-meal-a-day dining room, housekeeping, security, 24-hour reception attendant, scheduled van transportation, activities throughout the city, and several optional assisted-living packages.

Executive Organization

Although Leslie had the option of replacing all of the key staff people, the project was fully staffed with a licensed executive director and department heads and a full-time staff. The departing management company was leaving the area and had not offered any of its staff the opportunity for transfer. That meant Leslie would come in as an operator and have to make do with existing staff, which had not been hired to his standards (the Leslie Organization had a very forward-thinking set of human resources policies that emphasized prescreening and rigorous training) or he could fire a number of staff and risk eroding the confidence of those who remained. From his initial visit, he could see that the executive director was not going to work out, and he had serious reservations about two of the five managers and more than a few staff. Leslie's president of senior services would be an essential team leader to help sort out the "keepers." Because the property was already built, the team would not be working with the extensive personnel required to get *The Hampshire* up and running.

Finance and Law

Unlike *The Hampshire*, the finance structure of *The Fairford* was straightforward, but the legal issues were complex. The property was assessed at $40 million, with 100 units currently sold and occupied. Leslie felt he could find a lender to supplement his $6 million pool of capital to meet the $20 million asking price for the 100 remaining units. He would need an additional $14 million of financing to purchase free and clear, although the seller might carry financing. It would take 3 years to sell out and cost a significant amount to keep the project afloat until cash flow became positive. Marketing and negative operational cash flow were difficult to recoup in the future—he would have to consider them sunk costs. But did the cash flow justify the investment and loan?

Leslie was concerned that the current resident contract was insupportable. Those who had already purchased had done so under an agreement that the unit would be resold upon their demise, with the estate receiving 100% of the original purchase price paid or the market price, whichever was higher, less a 10% transfer fee to be paid to the developer and 6% for brokerage commissions. The estates were expected to pay a "nonoccupied monthly fee" for the empty unit's share of the fixed costs of operating the property. Until the property was sold out, Leslie would be expected to pay a reduced portion of the fixed costs for every unoccupied unit, which provided an additional incentive to get the facility sold out. The legal issues were confusing in a number of areas. With effort, Leslie felt he could surmount the licensing challenge; his president of senior services had worked through the licensing of three facilities in her career, although it would be Leslie's first. Leslie reviewed the licensing checklist. It was a daunting amount of information, but at least it kept many competitors out of the CCRC market.

The more challenging issue was the existing contractual obligations that Leslie would have to assume from the previous operator as part of his licensing requirement. Residents didn't understand them, and for good reason. They were written with a combination of legalese and state disclosure requirements that frustrated most attorneys. Separate "side letters" and agreements abounded, with different fees listed for similar services as a matter of course. Leslie knew he could phase in a new, clearer set of documents with each resale, but he would have to abide by previous agreements until the building turned a complete generation. He knew he needed to have his attorney read the legal document binder of every resident to understand his liability. The cost of that job alone would be tremendous.

Marketing and Sales

Marketing and sales were a perennial problem for this property. Multiple approaches and marketing messages had served to confuse or alienate a large part of the potential customer base, leaving a pool of potential buyers who were interested only because of their own infirmity or inability to afford the higher-priced options in the marketplace. What was worse, the remaining 100 units were considered less desirable, with the greatest potential cost to sell. Leslie had hoped the existing marketing manager would remain on board to help through the transition, but he had just taken a better offer at a more luxurious CCRC under construction a few miles away. The remaining sales team of two experienced agents and one novice was enmeshed in an internal battle over listings and commissions. Leslie thought it was a miracle that it had actually managed to sell 100 units. He knew he would have to bring in a new marketing approach that was targeted to *The Fairford*'s true customer, the medically challenged current city dweller who had $500,000 or so of assets in some combination of existing home, pension, and investments. This was going to be a tough sell, but, thankfully, it was only half of the total units.

Residents

William looked at the letter on his desk from *The Fairford* residents' council. Herb Thorber, the president of the council, was well known to be a rabble-rouser in the community. He had commandeered his place as president just a week after the previous president died of heart failure. Although most residents did not react to the potential acquisition with the vehemence of Thorber, or express concern about the issues he raised, Leslie recognized the importance of good relations with the council. On the other hand, despite the decisive tone of the letter, Leslie knew that the state continuing care laws specifically granted complete authority for operations to the licensee, so that he was not required to meet Thorber's demands. If he was in compliance with the regulations and legal documents and was meeting the residents' needs for care and supervision, he had met his obligation to them. Although residents' rights groups were sprouting up to insist on a seat on the governing board of the management company, for the time being, state law specifically prohibited residents from involvement in governance.

Leslie also knew of individual homeowner issues he would have to address in conjunction with *The Fairford* acquisition. In order to make sales, the original management company had cut some unusual "side deals" with individual residents, including waiving their requirement to join the group insurance plan. One resident was known to be running out of resources, and would not be able to pay the monthly fee. Her unit was owned in trust by her stepchildren, from whom she was now estranged. Another resident was causing significant disruption in the dining room, but had pledged a serious lawsuit if any attempts were made to control his behavior or evict him. His son was an influential attorney with a thriving private litigation practice. A third resident was conducting a not-so-discreet affair with her young dog walker, who was rumored to be very interested in her prized collection of Imperial Japanese artifacts. Just last week, this resident had accused *The Fairford*'s housekeeper of stealing four rare ivory carvings from the Tokugawa period.

Health Care

Health care was a serious deficiency of *The Fairford* project. The community was built to allow assisted living in every unit, but the fee structure made no provision for actually providing those services. Although the residents had been promised an on-site, assisted-living wing, the area that was to have been devoted as common space to the care center had been converted to condominiums when the original developer was seeking improved cash flow. Leslie didn't see how he could honestly offer continuing care without significantly improving what was currently offered.

The long-term care insurance was also fraught with problems. The insurance program that had been approved in the continuing care documents allowed for personalization of the long-term insurance program, depending on the needs of the resident and his or her existing insurance and financial resources. Some residents had coverage for partial assisted living and skilled nursing claims, some had coverage for assisted living or skilled nursing only, and some were considered uninsurable. The determination of eligibility had been made by a series of clinical nurses hired by the original management company, with an occasional, but by no means consistent, second opinion by a physician. None of the nurses had any experience in risk management. Their evaluations were based entirely on clinical judgment. It was an understatement to say that *The Fairford*'s current insurance program was confusing, difficult to market, and presented serious risk to the management company assuming an unknown level of liability. In addition, the medical records for half the residents had become illegible when a water pipe burst. They had been thrown away.

Leslie knew the state licensing agency would require the new manager to acquire all past liability from the previous manager; Leslie wondered what his insurance and legal counsel would have to say about that, or if they could craft some means to hold him harmless for this particular health care mess.

Residents' Services

For all of its faults, *The Fairford* staff did a better than adequate job in delivering service to residents. The services outlined in the resident documents were being delivered and the staff often made up in personal compassion what they were clearly lacking in training and management skills. The facility offered an engaging activities program both on-site and off-site, a regular round of scheduled transportation to points of interest, and a number of special events to mark holidays, seasonal events, and special occasions. Aside from typical issues about food, the residents were generally happy with the operation, although Leslie felt the efficiency of some departments could be dramatically improved. The biggest challenge was that improvement would require some increased expense, to which the residents were vehemently opposed. Again, Leslie wondered how much pride he would have to swallow to have his company associated with a merely adequate status quo property rather than an efficient showpiece.

Design and Build

The Fairford was well-built, with good safety standards and decent finishes, so maintenance would not be excessive and Leslie would not have to worry about the lawsuits all too familiar to contractors. But the spaces in the common areas and the individual units were poorly conceived at best. The original architect had been told to design an apartment building. When the CCRC market presented a better cash flow, the first developer had impulsively decided to convert the property, retrofitting for assisted-living regulations as best he could.

Leslie's ideal scenario was to convert all of the seventy-three unsold studio and one-bedroom units to two-bedroom units by knocking out walls and reconfiguring the spaces. In this scenario, there were significant plumbing and earthquake engineering issues to be overcome. He estimated that the conversion could cost approximately $10,000 per existing unit. He also knew the community would suffer from the lost revenue per unit, and doubling the fees for the converted units would be insupportable in the marketplace. Perhaps most importantly, the city would have to approve the conversions on an individual basis; the last request the community had put forth had been denied.

The common areas would be easier to redo. The issue was: who would pay for a renovation? The community had neglected to create any reserves, so the funding would have to come out of Leslie's pocket or a special assessment to all residents, who were against any increase in fees. Although Leslie knew he could make the common areas much nicer, he wasn't sure it would increase either the property values or his marketing success. He did know it would improve his pride in the project and his ability to establish his preeminence in the market.

These issues made Leslie nervous, to say the least. Would he have the ability to manage the operational and marketing problems in the midst of his acquisition? Could he clear them up before the acquisition went through? Most importantly, was the whole deal worth the known and anticipated aggravation?

■ William Leslie's Dilemma

It had taken William hours to organize the two projects into comparable formats, but a clear answer had not yet emerged in his mind. The two projects posed different kinds of risk, different rates of return, and different long-term strategic advantages for The Leslie Organization. His analysis had not resulted in a "right" answer so much as a series of questions against which to weigh his strengths, resources, and market opportunities.

William Leslie's Conclusion

Leslie stood up from his desk once more, and looked down at the lights of the city. The change of perspective suddenly offered an insight: He didn't have to select one or the other project. Although doing the two projects simultaneously was too taxing, a staggered approach might put both projects within his grasp.

Leslie quickly sketched out a timeline on a piece of paper. Assuming he could find a quick $14 million in financing for *The Fairford*, he could move ahead on that project immediately. This would keep his operations and marketing team occupied, but would not prevent them from contributing their knowledge to the planning stage of *The Hampshire* project. Meanwhile, his construction and architecture teams could be leading the charge on *The Hampshire* project, proceeding with the significant pre-development and predesign work that would need to be done before the project was underway. The operations and marketing team could contribute to *The Hampshire* enterprise team on a regular basis, with their overhead costs covered by their work on *The Fairford*.

Leslie knew the dollars would not work out exactly. *The Fairford* would be cash-positive in 3 years, whereas he would need a substantial amount of development seed capital for *The Hampshire* in about 18 months, and then construction financing to boot. But a lender was far more likely to provide bridge financing on *The Hampshire* with the collateral of *The Fairford* available a year later, rather than the open-ended risk posed by *The Hampshire* project alone. And, although *The Hampshire* offered a better cash return in the future, he could carry some of the development costs with his *Fairford* profits, and end up with two viable properties instead of one.

Staggering the projects would also provide a crucial learning curve for the organization, assuming the known risks of *The Fairford* before having to commit to all the details of *The Hampshire* project. *The Fairford* would provide a testing ground for his theories, and also provide ample examples of what not to do, based on previous developer and manager mistakes. Most importantly, he would have created a portfolio of two projects that would ultimately cover a broader spectrum of the senior market, with units ranging from $99,000 to over $1 million, serving a broader socioeconomic group. If the market shifted, he could potentially adjust the fee and service structure of either facility to take advantage of market growth, or at least to cushion against a downturn in the market.

Leslie's ultimate goal had always been a strategically selected portfolio of five or six CCRCs. These two projects offered an excellent opportunity to learn about a range of possibilities in the market, and then to make future acquisitions or developments in light of what he had learned. With this new vision for the two communities, he could venture into the CCRC market with pragmatism and great potential for success. This truly was the decision that made the most sense.

Notes

1. D. Porter. (1995). *Housing for Seniors: Developing Successful Projects*. Washington, D.C.: Urban Land Institute.
2. J. Harrigan and P. Neel. (1996). *The Executive Architect: Transforming Designers into Leaders*. New York: John Wiley & Sons.
3. J. Dewhirst. (1997). *Letter to American Association of Homes and Services for the Aging Members*. Washington, D.C.: AAHSA.
4. R. Heifetz. (1997). The work of a modern leader. *A Newsletter from Harvard Business School Publishing* (April): 4–7. R. Heifetz. (1997), *Leadership without Easy Answers*. Boston: Belnap Press/Harvard Business School Press, pp. 4–6. R. Heifetz and D. Laurie. (1997). The work of leadership. *Harvard Business Review* (January–February): 124–134.
5. W. Sahlman. (1997). How to write a great business plan. *Harvard Business Review* (July–August): 98–108.

PART I

CRITICAL SUCCESS FACTORS

There are three aspects of the CCRC executive strategy: insight, analysis, and method. In the following narratives, we gain insight from the experiences of the men and women responsible for the development and operation of two exceptional equity CCRCs—The Cypress of Hilton Head Island in South Carolina and The Stratford in the heart of the San Francisco Peninsula. When you drive to The Cypress, you travel through the lowlands and tidewaters of South Carolina and enter the verdant 4,000-acre Hilton Head Plantation. When you drive to The Stratford, you see the skyline of San Francisco, drive along the San Francisco Bay, and through the densely populated and highly desirable Peninsula. These are two entirely different settings. The Cypress offers the delights and pleasures of rural life, and The Stratford offers the excitement and opportunities of a cosmopolitan setting. Though different in many ways, there is commonality. Each of these equity CCRCs was conceived and led by exceptionally gifted and highly ethical people. Each achieves a standard of performance that returns sustainable profit to investors and brings to the elderly the opportunity to live with dignity, choice, and independence.

How do developers, architects, and health care and service providers duplicate these achievements in their own communities? What are the ideas that they can apply to their individual situations, within wide variations of the scale and resources? How can we find a way to help people turn the equity in their homes into a secure future home? How do we apply these concepts and address the social and financial issues facing the majority of middle-class Americans? The answers begin with the two case studies presented. We are providing a snapshot of the work of two of the best. The Cypress and The Stratford opened their books to us, made all their documents available, and encouraged their professional staff to cooperate with the authors as they worked to bring to readers the essence of an exceptional senior community experience.

The discussion and interviews comprising the case studies are helpful in many ways. People new to the equity CCRC concept will find practices and principles on which to build professional expertise. Readers who are highly experienced will find their best thinking confirmed. Social service, government, and political leaders will obtain a lasting impression of what must be accomplished to achieve and sustain the highest possible quality of life and services for the elderly. The elderly reader who is facing a choice for the future will know what to look for when evaluating options. In the interviews, leaders in the CCRC industry and experts with experience on major and complex projects talk about their experiences and plans for the future. The case studies are designed to help us understand the complexity of the retirement community challenge. Many of the contributors to this book note that the greatest challenge is to go beyond the commonplace and bring to the market the innovative thinking needed to meet ever-changing needs and desires.

The Cypress and The Stratford

The Cypress and The Stratford equity CCRCs exist as benchmarks for the retirement community industry because two individuals were capable of understanding the challenge in all its dimensions, formulating concepts, and managing a development that withstood assessment by investors, lenders, government entities, and prospective residents. They also surround themselves with the very best of people. James P. Coleman of The Cypress and John A. Raiser of The Stratford talk about themselves and their work from different perspectives. Essentially, both stories share a theme—what it takes to succeed as a retirement community executive and to provide others an opportunity for success.

■ James P. Coleman and The Cypress

The Cypress of Hilton Head Island is a "continuing care retirement community," but "continuing care country club" would seem to be a better description. Designed to offer a full range of services for seniors (the average age of purchasers is 74), The Cypress quickly became well established. The villas, apartments, and cottages sold quickly, as did The Cypress Bay Club, which was added to The Cypress to provide waterfront cottage sites. There are now a total of 196 apartments and villas, and 84 cottages. The Cypress includes all the basics—a continuum of health care services, maintenance of residences and grounds, meals, housekeeping and laundry service, most utilities, transportation, and a wide range of programs, from art classes to water aerobics.

James P. Coleman

The health center offers a wide range of services. As the director of nursing explains, "We are licensed for 77 beds of assisted living, skilled nursing, and Alzheimer's service, equipped and staffed to meet almost any need that might arise. Our experience is that approximately one-half of *The Cypress* members will, at some point, need the services of the Health Center." Typical feelings are summed up as, "We will live longer because we are here. Physically, we have the right diet and the right exercise. Emotionally, we have friends and companions, and financially, we know we are all set. It's not only fun living here, but the peace of mind we have gives us a serenity which is priceless."

Coleman's Executive Leadership

An appreciation of James Coleman's work is best gained by considering comments by others regarding *The Cypress* achievement. This retirement community has received honors and critical acclaim across a wide spectrum of professional organizations and publications. The Urban Land Institute awarded *The Cypress* the institute's prestigious Award for Excellence.[1] The jury chairman, James Luckman, when presenting the award, said, "*The Cypress* of Hilton Head Island has become a prototype for the emerging market of housing for seniors." Referring to the award, Charles Fraser, pioneer Hilton Head developer and previous winner of an Urban Land Institute award for developing

Sea Pines, said it was like winning an Oscar. "It's exciting. For *The Cypress* it's a seal of approval as something of value and providing a public service." This was the second major award in 1993 for *The Cypress*. Earlier, the National Association of Home Builder's Senior Living Council selected it as the "Best of Senior Living Communities" in the nation. In *New Choices*,[2] we find *The Cypress* cited as a notable part of the small but growing number of communities where the residents own their property. Speaking to the benefits of CCRCs, *New Choices* considers the biggest problem CCRCs face is their image. All too many people think these communities are nursing homes with extra grass and trees. Actually, the best of them rival high-quality adult leisure communities in their social and recreational amenities. The primary difference is what they offer in services. *Barron's*[3] cites *The Cypress* as an exceptional example of communities where retirees can spend years that are truly "golden." *Builder*[4] notes that *The Cypress* has received three national awards for integrating new living units, hospitality services, and health care options in a prestigious campuslike setting. *Urban Land Magazine*[5] finds the idea behind the country club ambiance of *The Cypress* is to assure purchasers that, although they may be downscaling their individual housing, they are not making life-style sacrifices. For an affordable price, *The Cypress* provides seniors with a community that is not only needed, but desirable and dignified. A detailed review of *The Cypress* appearing in *Hospitality Design*[6] walks the reader through the campus, pointing out the elegant touches that set apart this upscale retirement community.

A Concept Is Formed

We learn to appreciate Mr. Coleman's abilities when we listen to the story behind *The Cypress* achievement.

I'll just go back to the start. The company I was with had developed Hilton Head Plantation, a 4,000-acre planned-unit development. I had been here since 1974 as an employee for 10 years and then for another 6 years as part of the ownership group. It took 20 years to develop this community and this parcel was the last piece. We had plans for another subdivision and it occurred to me that there might be something grander and greater we could do with this last 100 acres. We had a little plane at the time, and so I hopped on the plane and went and visited probably forty different retirement communities, just to see what was going on in the industry. The Urban Land Institute had a conference about Senior Living. The National Association of Home Builders had an organization that was a resource. Another association called the National Association of Senior Living Industries, which is primarily consultants and management companies, had a couple of conferences a year, and so there was starting to be some standardization with terms. At that point, 1988, there was congregate care, continuing care, life care, assisted living, personal care, nursing—all those terms were really being misused. They've since become defined a little bit better. About the time we got started here, we finalized on "continuing care retirement community" and started using that term. I think most people in their 70s now know what a continuing care retirement community is. In marketing, you wish you didn't have to have the word "retirement" in your product, but if you don't, you don't communicate what you are. What continuing care retirement community means is independent living with health care and skilled nursing on the same campus. Full continuing care, where people have to be independent to move in, and then no matter what happens to them the rest of their life, they're taken care of.

What we're really all about is peace of mind. When someone signs up with us, we want them to know they don't have another care about anything. We wouldn't take them if they're not financially qualified. If someone is accepted for membership, they are not going to be asked to leave no matter what happens. We'll obviously take care of your health care needs. There's a skilled nursing center right here. If you want to stay in your home and have home health care, you can have that. If you want assisted living, we've got a wing for that. If you've got Alzheimer's concerns, we've got a wing for that, and, of course, basic skilled nursing. So, no matter what happens to you or your spouse, you, your spouse, and your children don't have to worry. We'll take care of you. We're going to serve nutritious meals. We're going to offer classes for exercise of the body and mind. We're going to give you opportunities for trips. So, it's really the total package that we're marketing. The continuing care retirement community really fills all needs and the other models, such as assisted living or congregate, do not.

As a master developer, our challenge was to not only maximize our return, but do something that makes sense in a full-service community. We've got people retiring here in their 60s, which is the main market for Hilton Head. So, we decided that a continuing care retirement community was logical as that population aged, and then went to school on the other communities. There are lots of management companies in this business, but there really aren't but a handful of developers who do more than one project. Hyatt has done several. Marriott has a few CCRCs, but they've decided to concentrate on assisted living now. There have been perhaps only a dozen others who have done more than one CCRC. And so, I saw an opportunity as a businessman with another 20 years of my career ahead that this would be a great industry to be in and it has turned out to be.

Listen to the Elderly

We had the land here and zoning was not an issue. It is in most markets, but we had the property. We knew our potential customers. It was very easy to do focus-group interviews, to find out what people wanted. That's the first thing we did here. We said, "We think we've got a good idea but let's go ask the people that we think we're going to sell it to." In the Hilton Head market, they were extremely easy to find because we'd already sold them their first retirement home, so we knew them personally. In *The Cypress of Charlotte*, our recent enterprise, it was not much more difficult because we have people here who have friends there, and they will go through the church directory, and go through the country club directory. We get people in their mid-70s and invite them to coffee and sit around the table with 18–20 of them and have a focus group. And they come at 10:00 in the morning, since they're not working. It's real easy to get feedback. That's what we did in both projects. We started out with a series of focus groups. We said, "Here's what we think is a good idea. What do you think?"

I'll tell you a little side story. I thought a really great name would be "The Senior Class." That was what I wanted to call this project and that was the working title when we started. I envisioned the marketing materials being an old annual from the '30s and the brochure would read like a high school or college annual. The name said "Class" and it said "Senior." I thought that was really a clever name. On one of the focus-group questionnaires, we had multiple-choice questions, and we had names. "The Cypress" was one of them, along with "The Senior Class," and "The Oaks," and "The Birch." We got the questionnaires back and not only was there not a single vote for "The Senior Class," but two or three people actually struck through it, and one person wrote, "No way."

Avoid Labels

I learned a good lesson there. And it really goes to the heart of the marketing challenge, which is what people perceive these communities to be. Even though they're proud to be seniors, they don't want to see any labels. As nice as we are and as well-known and established as we are, even on Hilton Head, people still say, "That's the old folks' home." They use the word "home," which has a negative connotation. That's the challenge of the industry. It's the perception that you're going out to "the home" because 40 years ago, there wasn't any place but "the home," which was minimally done, and usually had been church-sponsored and designed to take care of everybody. They really are downscaled in terms of quality and size with a charitable-type approach.

That's been our problem, and our approach from the very beginning was to try to have a country club environment. We've got health care on campus, but this is an upbeat, active, lively community, and in the past few years, this project, along with a few others in the industry, has begun to turn the image from acceptable to prestigious. That's really what we tried to accomplish and I think we have. When we started here, most companies were of the charitable type. It was acceptable to live there but people weren't proud to live there, necessarily. You weren't looked down on if you lived there, but, "Well, Joe's moved over to the home. That's okay." We've tried to take the image from acceptable to prestigious. Most of our members put a Cypress license tag on the front of their car. Voluntarily. We don't push them to do it. We just make it available. They're proud to be at *The Cypress*. We've really come a long way in the industry, when people wear a golf shirt with their community name on it, the same way they wear a golf shirt with the name of their country club on it, and go to the golf tournament or to the grocery store.

Serving a Need

The CCRC is an absolutely marvelous product—not just *The Cypress* but every community like this. Every one I've gone in, the residents are happy. Even the ones that are older and outdated, with 20–25-year-old small apartments, people are still happy to be there. They don't move out. It's very, very rare that someone says, "I've made a mistake. I want to move out." While occasionally someone will move because of a family situation, we've had nobody that has said, "I don't like being in this community. I want to move back to my old place." That just doesn't happen. Most of them say, "I wish I'd done it sooner." During the sales process, we hear from them, "I'm not ready yet. I'm not ready yet. I'm not ready yet." That's what we hear over and over again. They get here and they say, "Gosh, why did I wait so long?" As an industry, the market penetration that we've had so far is very small. The opportunity for this industry, throughout the United States, is just phenomenal. We still have a teeny-tiny percent of people in their 70s going into communities like this. There's lots of room, lots of opportunity for growth.

Starting the Enterprise

In 1988, we put together an investment group and raised $4 million. We bought the land for $2.5 million, which gave us $1.5 million for marketing to obtain presales. The business risk in these communities is the presales. You have to spend several hundred thousand dollars during the presales phase because you have to hire a sales force, do the marketing, and pay the architects and land planners enough to have a product to present. You may or may not have to go through rezoning, depending on your land situation. You've got to gamble and risk several hundred thousand dollars to sign up enough people to satisfy the lending requirement, and you have to satisfy the state requirements. Most states require a certain presale level, generally 50 to 70%, before they'll let you start building. South Carolina is one of the few that does not. North Carolina and Florida do, along with most other states. Those presale requirements usually fall right in line with the lender's requirements, and they fall right in line with what a prudent developer would require of himself. They're not onerous. They're prudent. Our magic number was 100 contracts, which was two-thirds of our Phase I of 150 units.

When we started, South Carolina had no regulations for CCRCs. The state has since passed legislation requiring what is really just a disclosure. They ask questions and you answer the questions. South Carolina doesn't really require anything of you except information. North Carolina requires much more detail. They must approve what you plan to do. The financials have to be very detailed and they require a third-party market study. They require certain presale levels before they'll give you the license and they require a certain number of closed sales before they'll give you the permanent license to operate. We work with the Department of Insurance in North Carolina and its thinking is consumer protection, like an insurance company. Show me all your financials and we'll analyze them. If it looks good, we'll let you sell that policy. In our case, we'll let you sell that condominium. Frankly, North Carolina's approach is more appropriate. No developer likes to go through any regulatory body, but it should be done. In fact, a new retirement community at Hilton Head that is struggling would not have been able to build in North Carolina or Florida or most any other state because presale requirements were not met before it was built. It opened less than half full and the operating deficits are huge. So, the regulations are okay. We're doing consulting on a project in Pennsylvania and we've done some consulting on a project in Florida. So, we have dealt with both of those regulatory situations, and in Pennsylvania, they had to rewrite the law to allow an equity condominium sale. They were successful in doing that. Florida is still a difficult state. The problem in many states for our equity model is that it doesn't fit into the regulations that were written for the entry-fee model.

The First Members of the Executive Organization

We're a real small company. When we started *The Cypress* in 1988, I was president of a big development company. We had several projects going on, so I was not full-time on *The Cypress*. But one business lesson I've learned is that you've got to have somebody good who is. You've got to have a senior person with nothing but that project to worry about. We were doing the Main Street commercial area, the Country Club of Hilton Head, and were finishing up several subdivisions. We really had a lot of things going on. We had talented people in our company, but, specifically for this project, I knew we needed to have somebody on top of everything. So we selected the sales manager of our brokerage operation to be the general manager of *The Cypress*. He and I together brainstormed everything. We went and interviewed the management companies and we visited the communities together. One thing that I never want to do in business is be a single practitioner. You've got to have somebody to bounce ideas off of. You need somebody to read your draft letter, read your draft copy, check your numbers when you do a pro forma.

My partner now in *The Cypress of Charlotte* came on board in 1990 right after presales and just before starting construction. He is a good partner, who really understands the whole picture. It's essential to have someone to brainstorm with but also for backup. People take vacations, they get sick, different things happen. A good partner can cover all bases with the banker or the customer, or the construction guy. It's nice to have somebody who can answer the question and keep things moving.

Most developers that build golf club communities start out operating the club. They just hire a manager, and they get involved with whether it's cheeseburgers or hot dogs at the cookout. Pretty soon, they make a mess of it. I had already learned that lesson. I didn't want to be an operator, especially with the health care. So, very early on, we knew that we had to hire that expertise. We interviewed lots of companies and selected Life Care Services Corporation. They operate over fifty CCRCs. In terms of strictly CCRCs, Life Care Services is the biggest operator in the industry. They have been in business for over 30 years now, and are really good. They consulted with us in the beginning and were valuable in putting together the operating pro formas. They were helpful in reviewing our plans for the health center, the clubhouse, and the residences. They brought in an executive director about 6 months before we opened and an associate administrator about 3 months before we opened, who started interviewing staff. Life Care Services provides those two people, and they get good support from the home office. The history of Life Care Services began with a construction company that built a retirement community, and the president of the construction company saw that it wasn't operating right. He couldn't find anybody to operate it, so he saw an opportunity and started a company to manage CCRCs. They're good with regulatory bodies in all the states. They're very skilled in operating the health center. Another advantage is that they have good buying power through purchase contracts for thirty to forty communities, for things like insurance, food, and cleaning and medical supplies.

The Staff

Once you open, there's always the challenge of getting enough good staff people for the nursing home, especially nursing assistants. It's a 24-hour operation, and getting nurses aides to work the midnight shift is never easy in any community. Other than that one area, however, we have no problem hiring top people. The employees really like working here. They get the satisfaction of serving residents. The residents are nice to them and appreciate the staff, as opposed to, say, a hotel that is impersonal. It's predictable. There's the interchange of knowing the residents and the appreciation back and forth. It's a warm, friendly environment to work in. Working in the health center is better than the hospital. In the health center, people are generally there for a time and you get to know them, whereas hospital patients are in and out in a few days. So, we're successful in getting good people

Profitability

If there's any brilliance in what we've brought to the industry, it's the way to make a significant profit and still offer the most attractive economic deal for purchasers. We didn't second-guess any of our financial structure. We didn't make any mistakes on how we structured the project. The condominium purchase equity plan, the not-for-profit club, and how we get paid, all of that worked out great. We wouldn't change a thing. Our structure was new. We were the first "condominium purchase with 90% equity." Members buy a condominium, we get a 10% membership fee, and they get 90% of the equity upon resale in the future. We take a 10% membership fee from each new purchaser. Our plan is better than a 90% refund because as the value goes up, they enjoy the appreciation.

Most CCRC communities are entry-fee with big bond issues. In Charlotte, we're going to have a $48 million bank loan that will be paid off when Phase I is sold. Typical CCRCs in North Carolina with a cost of $50 million would do a bond issue of $60 million. You literally add that much to cost when you do a bond issue for things like attorney fees and underwriting fees. So, if the cost is 50, they'll spend 60 for the same end result. Instead of selling condominiums for $275,000, they'll charge residents a $150,000 entry fee. From the purchasers, they'll get about $20 million, which leaves debt on the project of $40 million, which the residents have to pay for in their monthly fees. The residents may or may not get some of that entry fee back. Typically, there is a choice of options. A resident can pay $150,000 and get none of it back or pay $180,000 and get 50% of it back or pay $220,000 and get 90% of it back. There will be a mix of that, and they'll end up opening the community with $40 million in debt and each resident, in their monthly fee, is paying $400 or $500 dollars a month to service that debt. Conversely, we'll spend $50 million and we'll get $50 million from the sale of the units in the first phase, so we've got no debt. That's obviously good for the developer, but it's also good for the residents, because they aren't carrying any debt service in their monthly fees. With all of the common facilities built in Phase I, the profit margins in Phase II are significant.

The Future

For the future, I think where the industry should go is where we're going, the full-service CCRC, because we cover the entire continuum of care. If you go to a National Association of Senior Living Institute conference, or a conference in Washington where the bankers and lenders go, or you go to the trade shows, everybody's talking about assisted living. That's been the hot thing since about 3 years ago. I don't feel comfortable with assisted living because it only covers that one small portion of the continuum of care. Most assisted-living facilities don't have a skilled nursing component. Marriott has a nice prototype, and where they can get a license, they'll do assisted living and skilled in the same building. That works pretty well. They'll also do what they did in Charlotte near us, which is assisted living without skilled care. Under that situation, there is the dilemma of what happens when you need to go that next step. The daughter thinks she got mama settled in a place, and then she gets a phone call one day saying, "Come get your mother, she needs skilled nursing care." "But, wait a minute, I thought. . . ." "I'm sorry, we can't help you. She's reached the point where she needs skilled nursing. There is a place across town that we think has a bed." And by that time, mother's to the point where she can't help herself. The burden falls strictly on the child or strictly on the care giver. It's beyond mother being able to make her own decisions at that point. So that's what I don't like about assisted living.

I also think that assisted-living facilities are going to be overbuilt. By the nature of it, you cannot presell it. If you did, by the time you open the building, they'd be needing something else. So it's purely a speculative situation to build one, and by the time you build one and two other guys in town get the same idea, the market's oversupplied, so it's a dangerous situation.

I see the future with more and more upscale communities. Probably the average entry age is not going to drop. The age is probably always going to be in the mid-70s. I don't see us getting into the 60s. But people in their early 70s are now living longer, so the percentage of their lives that we're getting is greater. The 74-year-old lady who moves to *The Cypress* has on the average 17 years to live, and that's the equivalent of the time from birth until she graduated from high school. There can be 20–25% of your life after you move to a CCRC.

Over the past 4 years, the image of CCRCs has changed dramatically. The "old folks home" has become prestigious. Historically, retirement communities have been done by volunteer groups, church groups, and others that didn't really have a disciplined focus. The people on the committees may have been good executives in whatever business they were in and they were pulled together as a committee to try to make one of these communities work. In just about every case, the people involved had not done one before and would not do it again. They were trying to satisfy a perceived need in their local community. A lot of mistakes were made. Most of the developers back in the '70s and early '80s were "do good" groups. They wanted to develop a place for the elderly women of the church. That was the mind-set. That's all changed now. But, here at *The Cypress*, we are independent, fun-loving, country club type people (and I don't mean country club in terms of necessarily where they're from, but just from the activity level). That's the whole mind-set of who we are serving.

Extending the Concept

Some people wonder how far down in price and number of units we can take our concept. Can you get down to a $100,000 product? Or a $150,000 product? Our average is about $275,000. Looking at it from one aspect, you've got to have economies of scale, which dictates at least 150 units. The best value for the resident is in a community of about 250 to 300. You've got the same housing. In a community of 300 versus one with only 100–150, the monthly fees are going to be a lot less. I would not do one with less than 200. We have a broad mix here of product, from a $165,000 one-bedroom to quite a few homes right around $200,000, and cottages from $400,000 to $700,000. The projects of the '70s and early '80s made big mistakes with mostly one-bedrooms and studios. Those products really have trouble now, because nobody wants a one-bedroom. We've only got less than 10% of our mix in one-bedrooms. So you're dealing with a two-bedroom that gets you the minimum unit at 1,060 square feet. We could perhaps downsize to an average price of around $200,000 depending on what was paid for the land and the market. So it's possible to average $200,000 with 300 units and make a project go nicely. However, the absorption would probably be slower. We believe in a broad product mix and the nice thing about our product is that we appeal to so many different people that we get our sales rate up to a high level on a consistent basis.

◼ John A. Raiser and *The Stratford*

John Raiser is an engineer, architect, and a builder of buildings and communities. He founded The Raiser Organization because

John A. Raiser

he believes in the importance of a unified vision in the process of building, from design to completion. He believes that every property must be an asset to its owner, to those who use the building, and especially to the community. He believes that the process used to develop and build must have as much integrity as the structural engineering that holds every column and beam in place. This design/build capability positions The Raiser Organization to manage a CCRC enterprise through its entire life cycle, from concept to management and resale.

Mr. Raiser strongly suggests that this asset creation process of development must be a characteristic of every CCRC enterprise. As a model for best practices, The Raiser Organization creates and maintains assets through the design/build integrated process of development, design, construction, and management. The organization designs and builds buildings to be well maintained, to support and increase their value. Known for their strong orientation to service and swift attention to problems, with a cultivated network of skills and alliances, the organization created *The Stratford* with the needed mix of CCRC services to assure and sustain the investment of equity residents.

The Raiser Organization's benchmark achievement in the CCRC industry is *The Stratford*, an equity continuing care retirement community located in the heart of the San Francisco Peninsula. *The Stratford* defies every notion of a traditional retirement community, and provides a refined, forward-thinking way of life. *Stratford* residents assure their financial and medical futures, make their own choices, and live in their own condominiums. *The Stratford* stands apart for a variety of reasons. Each of the sixty-seven spacious condominiums is custom-designed and fully licensed by the State of California Department of Social Services for independent and assisted living. *The Stratford*'s prime location is a block from downtown San Mateo, a bustling city of 100,000 residents, with 16 acres of city parks and gardens just across the street. The state-of-the-art building combines European craftsmanship with the latest in California fire and earthquake safety. From the garden-fresh flower arrangements to the temperature-controlled wine cellar and the glass-enclosed swimming pool, *The Stratford* reflects an environment of quality. *Stratford* residents purchase their condominiums and pay an inclusive monthly fee for long-term care, dining, housekeeping, and services. The comprehensive health care program provides assisted living on-site and skilled nursing for life, at the location of a resident's choosing. Because residents purchase their *Stratford* condominiums outright, they leave their condominium equity to their estate, enjoying the benefits of the Peninsula's tremendous real estate appreciation.

John Raiser's Story

Let me tell you my story. It will help you understand how you must grow to gain the abilities to succeed in the CCRC industry. I grew up in Greece. My father, Leslie, was a noted and diligent architect and a builder in Athens. Throughout his 42 professional years, he built condominiums, hospitals, factories, bridges, and highways. He was concerned with infrastructure and how it helped people live better lives. He was the first one in Greece to have a pile driver, which was almost unheard of because Greece was not that advanced in technology, but he heard of a diesel pile driver in Germany, and he sent for one. He was doing some highway work, and tried to figure it out—how to make this thing stand up there on top of the pile. So, he designed a wood-frame rig with little steps for people to get up there and, with pulleys, they got this pile driver up and, sure enough, it worked. Later in his life when he saw a crane holding up a pile driver, like we do here, he said: "Why didn't I think of that?" But he was not afraid to improvise and to be a pioneer and do what he felt was best for the time and for the future.

So, I grew up with that environment, that thinking, and when I was 17 years old, I decided to come to the United States to study at Ohio University, where I spent 5 years in a program of architectural engineering. Marvelous program. Very practical. Very hands-on program. We had a distinguished professor of architecture who had retired from the Harvard School of Design. He was a true architect and an inspiration. But at the end of my last semester, I asked him, "You know, Professor Frost, I really appreciate what I've learned here. I feel very comfortable with design, with color, with architecture. I love the profession that I followed. But I am totally uncomfortable making a building stand up!" And he looked at me: "Well, sure you feel uncomfortable. We didn't teach you how to make it stand up! We taught you architecture. You hire an engineer to work with, and he'll make it stand up for you." Well, that kind of bothered me, so I went on to the University of Kentucky, and I got a Master's in structural engineering, so I could imagine how a building could function from a practical and aesthetic point of view.

A Career Begins

When I finished my degrees, I went back to Greece and worked with my father for about 3 months. I decided that that was not where I wanted to establish my career. So then came the question: Where do I go? At that point, I just enlisted in the service because I didn't want a draft to interrupt my career. Serving on a base in Missouri, I knew that Missouri was not where I wanted to live the rest of my life. I charted out where I would want to be. I looked at Boston, New York, New Orleans, and San Francisco. I visited all those places. In Boston, I decided that if you were not with an established family with long-time connections, you didn't have a very good chance. New York was too dog-eat-dog. It wasn't my style. I went down to New Orleans, and I saw some real opportunities there. But, when I came to San Francisco, I knew it was right. I liked the climate, I liked the culture, I liked the city of San Francisco. I liked the symphony, the opera, the museums. I liked the ocean, and I liked the temperate climate—not too cold, not too hot. And here I am.

But then, the next question that came up was: Now that I've learned how to design buildings and how to make them stand up, how are they going to get built? As a consequence, I decided I'd go and get a job in the construction industry. But nobody would hire me in the construction industry, because I was considered overeducated and underexperienced. For a whole year, I knocked around in the Bay Area interviewing with just about every company there was and no construction job. I was renting one room from a couple that had a duplex, and I had one shelf in the refrigerator, and I was working as a structural draftsman. Well, that gave me something to put gas in the car and get around, but it was very discouraging that nobody would give me a job in the construction field. Here, 7 years of college, and I thought I knew what I was doing! (I didn't know what I was doing.)

So, one day I was driving down Bayshore in Burlingame, and I saw a job shack going up on an empty lot. The next morning, I showed up at 7:30 in the morning at that job site, and I asked the superintendent if he had a job for me. He looked at me and said, "What can you do?" Given my interview experience, I withheld my background and said, "I'll do anything you want me to do. You tell me what to do—I'll do it." He says, "Can you write?" "Yeah, I can write." "Okay, I need somebody to be timekeeper and answer the phone, take messages. Can you do that?" "I'll do a good job for you." So, I was on, and the salary that was offered me was one-third of what I was getting as a structural draftsman, but I figured since I had 7 years in college, nobody ever paid me a dime when I was going to college, at least I was getting paid something. And here was an opportunity to get into the construction field and learn what everybody was telling me I was inexperienced in. Well, that was a marvelous job because I did get to learn a lot, and in 18 months, by the time the job was finished, I was superintendent. From then on, I went another 3 years as a superintendent on other field jobs, concrete jobs, what have you. Then I went back in the office as an estimator for a couple of years. Then, I decided I'd hang out my own shingle because I didn't like the way buildings were being built, and I figured there must be a better way. Like my father in Greece, I figured I could improvise.

Starting a Business

So, I started out on my own. It was a lot tougher than I thought. At that time, I had a wife and a little baby in a two-bedroom rented house, where the one bedroom in the daytime was an office and in the nighttime was a nursery. My wife was answering the phone, and somehow we patched it together where I was superintendent in the daytime of the jobs I could scrape up and, at night, I was the designer to try to design the next job. That went on for about 5 years. I never dreamed it would take that long. It was always a hand-to-mouth existence. My father, retired in Greece, came over. He asked if he could work with me. He was tired of being the chief after 42 years, and we worked very, very closely together out of a one-room office, which we finally rented because we were outgrowing the house. I finally thought I had hit the jackpot because I found a department store that was going to build four 60,000-square-foot discount department stores in the Bay Area. The first ones were going to be Mountain View, Sunnyvale, San Jose, and they were negotiating for the last site. I gave them some prices. I gave them some designs. Everything looked good. I went up to Portland, where their home office was, and we finally shook hands and they said, "You are our guy, subject to us checking you out."

Creating a Business Image

Well, I was on top of the world. They started checking me out and part of it was to come down to see our offices. Well, the office was a one-and-a-half room office—my father and myself. They came in and said, "This is your office?" "Yes." "And you expect to do this volume of work out of this office with your father and yourself, with your father semiretired? You don't have other people?" I said, "Well, no, I don't. But we can do the job better than anybody." So, they went back. They thought about it, and I lost the job. That was a tremendous blow. I knew I could do the job better than anybody, but I just didn't have the front. And that taught me a huge lesson: that people want to confirm the wisdom of their decisions. They want to be impressed.

About 3 days later, we decided that we couldn't keep going like this, and we rented an office with five rooms. Our staff was still my father and myself. A company had gone broke and they had left some furniture in there. I told the landlord just leave it where it is, I'll be happy with it. We put in a couple of lines of telephone and tried to put some pictures on the walls. And, lo and behold, about a week had gone by, where I was competing to build an automotive dealership for Chrysler Corporation. At that point, we didn't have any other work. We needed it desperately. One day I was in my car, I had an early car phone, and I was on the Golden Gate Bridge, and I get a phone call from this fellow. He said, "You know, your proposal looks good to us. We want to come out tomorrow morning." (This was at 4:00 in the afternoon.) "Are you free at 8:00 a.m.?" "Well, let me check my schedule. I'll make time. If you come out, I'll be free."

At that point, our whole business was on the line. Okay, now we had the office. Now, we've gotta impress these people so we don't have another Portland problem. They're coming from Detroit to see our operation, check us out, and less than 2 weeks ago we got shot down because we didn't pass that muster. So, here we had the office already somewhat furnished. I called up three of my good subcontractors. Told them, "Do me a favor. Would you pack up all your work, put it in your briefcase, come here and work in my office? Just be there!" So, they came and they filled the desks. The next morning, my wife was at the receptionist desk and put on a nice smile and, sure enough, a couple of guys show up and say, "Well, is Mr. Raiser here?" She says, "Well, let me check." My wife decided that it won't look too good if these phones weren't ringing, so she called my mother, who was instructed to call every few minutes to make the phones ring. So we put on a hell of a show, and then these people wanted to see our office. They walked around and they saw some bodies there working away, doing something, and they said, "Can we go back to your office?" We went back to my office. They said, "You know. We are very impressed. We like what you're doing but we have a problem. You've given us a price on this one dealership, but we need to build three dealerships. Can you handle all three of them?" "Well, we'll roll up our sleeves and we'll do it." It was the Hayward Dodge, the Concord Dodge, and the Redwood City Chrysler/Plymouth agency. They walked out of there with about a $3 million contract that they left behind them, and we were on top of the world. We were no better, in reality, than we were 2 weeks ago when we were shot down for a third of that much volume, where I didn't have the show. Of course, we had to have the right bid and be able to talk about it properly, but show has a tremendous amount of influence on people.

Twenty years later, when we were thinking about entering the retirement community business, we had to do essentially the same thing. We knew we could do the work, but we had to prove to bankers, potential residents, and state legislators that they could rely on us. So, Helen and I started doing marketing events ourselves, right down to the home-baked cookies, and personally meeting with state legislators and attending planning hearings. Trying to convince them of the wisdom of their decisions. Making them believe in us and, therefore, enabling us to do the work.

Selling an Idea

But, back to the early days. The next thing, as we went on, we learned how to broaden the whole building concept. After coming out of college, I was very frustrated that, when I was looked on as an architect, I was told that you must put your plans out to bid. When I was presenting myself as a contractor, I had to give the low bid to be considered. And I would tell my clients: "Do you want a low bid? Or do you want a good building that makes money for you?" They said, "We want both." I said, "Well, the way you are asking the question, you're not going to have both." So, I concentrated over the years to see that we have a building that has a long-term return on investment, a good place to live, a good place to work in, and the developer that owns the building has enough respect for the asset to maintain it properly.

That was a new education for the developers and bankers. It's a new thought to many of them. We found that the primary listeners were the institutions that had gotten burned holding property. To them a deed of trust was owning a building, but, probably, the head honcho had never visited the building. He just knew that he owned a building in San Francisco, or wherever the building happened to be. The building is a problem. And I would consult with them, and I'd say, "Certainly it's a problem. Because it's an asset you have not nurtured." They said, "Well, what do you mean?" I said, "The building is an instrument of value that has to be taken care of like any other instrument of value, but it's totally different from a share of stock on paper. When you own a stock, you depend on the corporation that issued the stock to have the management to do it. In buildings, usually, you don't have the management. The person that owns it is the management. If you haven't managed it, that is why the buildings are in trouble."

I found that there are two thinking processes in the bank. One is the credit thinking, and 95% of the bankers are trained in the credit process. They look at financial statements. The other 5% are the real estate thinkers. The real estate guys are the ones that understand the value in a building, but they are in such a minority that they can never get their idea across on the board of directors. When it comes to a vote of the board or a vote of the managers or a vote of the president, the real estate guys are the outcasts. In order to survive, they have to implement and improvise such convoluted methodologies for lending on buildings, that the buildings get into trouble. What we saw, the overbuilding of office buildings and apartment buildings and many other kinds of buildings in the last decade, was brought on by bankers that offered money because they needed to loan money to justify their own existence—otherwise, their job was going to be wiped out. And the banks had money, and nobody asked, "Does anyone need this building that we are loaning on?" All they would look at is the financial statement, and a lot of financial statements were not as stable as the computer told them they were. And, pretty soon they kept building buildings because the money was there. But the tenants weren't there. The weaker developers disappeared—the bar stool developers that will buy and sell over a drink and act like a big shot. And those buildings caused a tremendous amount of agony and, unfortunately, the taxpayer had to bail out the whole system with the savings and loan fiasco that cost billions of dollars. It broke S&Ls. It broke banks. It broke all kinds of people. All that because the bankers would not view the building as an asset to be managed instead of an asset to be counted.

Underwriting is the analysis of a building in banker's language, and that's a very important skill. Underwriting is looking at all of the assets of a building, starting with location, size, comparables, cost, and the financial return on investment that comes as a result—and those are terms I had to learn. I figured if I'm going to be in that game, and play with these numbers, I'd better not take somebody's word for it. I'd better understand what they mean, and how they are being constructed. If you're going to ask for a loan to develop a CCRC or other property, I would suggest to you to sit down with your friendly mortgage banker and try to understand what he does or try to take a mortgage banking course at the local college or wherever you can find it. The Urban Land Institute is a very fine association of professional developers. They have a lot of seminars on mortgage banking.

A Social Commitment

In an ordinary real estate development, how we decide to design, build, and sell is a business decision. That is what home builders do all the time. Now, when we get to assisting the elderly and designing, building, and selling CCRCs, the program should change. It comes along with a very strong social commitment to provide for the community. And that can be done by either teaming up with an operating company or doing it ourselves, as we have chosen to do.

What seniors are telling me, whether they are renting or buying in the facility, is that they are at the point in life where one of these days, they are going to need support. "I trust you to provide me with that support, and think through and manage the business necessities to provide this support. I trust you to select a nursing staff. I trust you to provide the type of long-term insurance I will need and fill out the paperwork on my behalf and make sure that they actually do what insurance policies are supposed to do in view of a constant flux of new laws, new regulations, new government, additions or subtractions from Medicare—it is getting to be too much for me, and, as a senior, I cannot follow the laws that govern the insurance companies and implement the business action to offset them. By buying or renting in your facility, I will trust you to do all of these things. I will trust that you have the vision to be there when I need you, which necessitates the commitment not to sell out after the first year." We have made a commitment internally in our family that we will not build and sell, we will build and operate in order to carry out the fiduciary and moral responsibility that we have taken on with these residents: service and good medical and financial security.

The Stratford: **Ground-floor entry vestibule**

The Stratford: **Ground-floor living room**

The Cypress: **Lagoon and apartment units**

The Cypress: **Bay Club cottages**

1.0 Enterprise Concept

Speaking with the executives of *The Cypress* and *The Stratford*, the operative word is "marketable" continuing care retirement community. There are many different types. One of the biggest challenges for everyone, whether you are a continuing care community of equity ownership or rental or total life care, is to dispel the typical nursing home or adult home image.

▮ Quality of Life for the Elderly

In this interview, John Raiser discusses the evolution of a CCRC concept.

Life expectancy is increasing, exceeding all the current actuarial tables. One of my doctors told me that humans were really expected, like all other mammals in nature, to live just a little beyond their reproductive cycle. And, for thousands of years, this held true because people were living to 40, 45, 50 at the most. We have somehow beat the system. Now, the question is, how do we provide the quality of life for those who are living such long lives?

And how do we make them productive citizens and how do we support them? The single-family housing that evolved from the pioneers out on the prairies with big ranches and big farms slowly got denser and denser to where we had tracts and then we had urban densities and now we have people on top of each other. Currently, we have as many people living on this Earth as all the people that have lived in the last 5,000 years. So, we took the population of 5,000 years and it's all alive today. This is going to double again very rapidly.

When people retire and they live 20, 30, or even 40 years longer, they have to be supported by either themselves, their children, the community, or society. And society isn't prepared for it and isn't equipped for it. This is a totally unnatural phenomenon. We have uncharted waters, but we have to address it because it is coming, and it will have to be handled.

Quality of life is the issue that we're trying to address in this business. The abilities of seniors are different than the abilities of younger people. A lot of people do not want to recognize that, at age 75, they cannot do what they did at age 30. As we get a little more frail, we need certain kinds of support. There are probably going to be a lot of solutions, and our business only offers one solution. I'm very aware that it's not going to be the only one.

I've come to the conclusion that the senior population at this time is divided into two major segments. On one level, we have the "young" seniors, in early retirement, 65 to 75 years old, who are fully functional and enjoy life, with tennis and golf and other activities. Their children are grown. They want to travel, and they are perfectly capable of doing that. Their life-style now is really very similar to the life they lived before, except they have more time for leisure activities. They like a home like they had before, perhaps smaller, as they no longer need the three bedrooms for the children. They are able to negotiate flights of stairs, to go down to the basement or up to the attic; they like a garden and a workshop to putter in. They can live in condominiums, in townhouses, and generally need very little support. That's a very enjoyable age in life, where you no longer absolutely have to report for work at 8:00 every morning. You can do things you always wanted to do.

Now the second group is 75 years old and up and is starting to have less ability to handle the responsibilities of a home. They have a hard time with outside work, mowing lawns, cleaning gutters, painting fences, and so on. At the beginning of this cycle, travel is still quite possible and enjoyable, but as people get into their late 80s they tend to lose the desire and the ability to travel or play eighteen holes of golf, or do a lot of other things they used to do. They may still be in perfectly good health, but they have distinct areas where they need assistance, usually for a short time. The flu can affect them more than it did 20 years before, or a fall can temporarily affect them. They need some help to recover, but they really are not candidates for the hospital or skilled nursing, except briefly. So these folks start with us as reasonably healthy people who want to live the life-style to which they've been accustomed, who need a senior community, preferably a CCRC, that can give them assistance as and when they need it. This group represents a new generation of longer-lived people that in the past were so few they were ignored. It used to be that seniors stayed independent until they died or rolled into the dreaded skilled nursing facility.

So we decided to design a CCRC facility that was customized for this "new" group of seniors. We wanted to give them the life-style they've been accustomed to, with all the amenities, such as fireplaces, comfortable living rooms, and full kitchens, even though at that age they want professional meal services, too. The presence of a full kitchen is psychological, primarily to the women. It tells them that they have not aged as much as the mirror might show. They can still do a bit of cooking themselves and they feel that, if they had to, they could still do a turkey dinner. As I've said before, our experience shows that when they have a kitchen, they don't use it. But not having it is an acknowledgment of a limitation that they are not willing to accept.

That brings us to the psychology of aging, and why seniors are generally reluctant to move into these facilities. CCRCs are a new concept and sometimes seen as experiments. It is not yet "the thing" to do. Renting or buying a residence in a senior community is realizing that they need help, that they do not want to disrupt their children's lives. It is very important to remember that all people, seniors included, are need-driven, not choice-driven. But it's important not to point out to clients that they need help. They really know it, but they don't want to admit it. We try to get people to come into our facilities in such a way that no one acknowledges that they are ready for it. We know they have to make a choice, and they recognize it.

There is one group of elderly people who will never go into a retirement community. They are the ones who use the cliché, "I'm not ready yet." They think they are the first ones to utter those words, but we hear it ten times a day. They don't realize that when they are ready, they may no longer be able to make the transition to an independent living community. So the "not ready yet" group will probably never move. Others are a little more direct, and say they want to be carried out of their homes "feet first."

We find that the residents of senior committees are more logical than the average senior. These people are willing to analyze their situation and face reality and plan for the future, as opposed to people who live in the past and never address where they will be 10 years from now. It is a very hard thing for someone to admit that 10 to 20 years from now they will need some help. So we are getting a more self-aware group of people who are willing to think through their personal circumstances and to say, "Yes, I will be where my father was when I get to his age, and I remember helping my father."

It's been demonstrated over and over that people who do move into a retirement community where they can have the periodic propping-up that they need, the fresh, well-balanced diet, and the emotional support of their peers, live a lot longer. We cannot promise that a retirement community will help anyone live longer; we cannot say that, but it is amazing, the average age of seniors in retirement communities is much higher than the national average. So, keeping the propping-up process in mind, we try to design a unit that provides the features they have become accustomed to, but also allows us to provide the support they need as they age.

Typically, new residents are in perfectly good health when they move in. They are independent and have all five activities of daily living (ADLs) under control. We find that, at various stages, people may need help with one of these ADLs for a week or two, but then they can get back to normal. When someone needs help with two or more ADLs on a permanent basis, we recognize that he or she can no longer live independently and needs to have an assistant or move to the assisted-living wing. If dementia or Alzheimer's sets in, we are very concerned. People who cannot recognize their family or surroundings, or who get lost easily, cannot live independently in their own homes, condos, or apartments, and if they were the "I'm not ready yet" or "feet firsters," we cannot help them because they are no longer insurable. In a CCRC with an assisted-living wing on the premises we can support a spouse in the same building as the husband or wife who needs care. We can, for instance, allow a wife to get a good night's sleep in her own condo, while the husband sleeps in the assisted-living wing, where he has nursing support. He can get up in the morning and go back to the condo, and they can have a fairly normal life, but support is only an elevator trip away.

From time to time, the need to be hospitalized is inevitable. Hospitals and doctors, recognizing the support available at CCRCs, tend to discharge residents prior to normal discharge. The recovery period is cut tremendously. The psychological aspect of being in a hospital seems to extend the recovery period, whereas familiar surroundings and the knowledge that you're well enough to be home—even if "home" is a transitional stay in the assisted-living wing—a diet you're accustomed to, and seeing people you know, gives a strong boost to recovery.

Taking all of this back into the design and architecture of the CCRC, we often see CCRCs or other retirement communities designed as spread-out villages with cottages. This is great for privacy, but not for security or assistance, and can be very difficult in inclement weather for seniors over 80. We find that a high-rise building with vertical transportation and short distances from the elevators to the residences works much better, primarily because that age group cannot negotiate distances very well. From time to time, they're using a walker or a cane, and a 300-foot trip can be monumental. At other times, they can't go a half-block to dinner because the wind is blowing, or the rain is coming down, or the snow is covering the ground. This group is served much better with a vertical high-rise environment where they're always shielded from the weather, transportation is provided with elevators, and the walking distances are fairly short. The need to drive is virtually eliminated, because you don't have to go to the drugstore to pick up a prescription or to the store for a loaf of bread, or whatever. It's here, or it's delivered, or someone can drive you. When a person doesn't feel well, a properly trained professional is at his side in minutes. This immediate response can make a critical difference.

In my mind, I've narrowed down what segment of the senior population the CCRC should try to deal with in the future, and that's the "middle" senior age. People must have the ability to adjust to a new life-style, and we've found that that process must take place before age 85. Somewhere between 75 and 85, because after that, people are less able to adjust to new circumstances. They give up. "I'll stay in my home." And pretty soon, that's the end. People who pick themselves up by the bootstraps at 75, and say, "No, I've got a lot of good years, but I just have to change my life-style and move into a CCRC," generally beat all the actuarial tables that we see.

The one area where we have not been successful is in helping people to remain useful citizens. Despite all the help, we see people who withdraw within their apartments, who withdraw from the life of the community, become very self-centered, and that is really not a healthy proposition. I'm looking for trained people who can recommend how we can augment and support the purpose of life for these people. They cannot do what they used to do. But there must be things that they can do, and I may be overly idealistic, but I think there's a potential solution that I have not uncovered yet. I'm looking for it.

A Market Opportunity

The president of Raiser Senior Services at *The Stratford* tells us that the equity CCRC will never serve more than a portion of the senior population for a couple of reasons.

One is that this is a middle-class or upper-middle-class proposition to begin with. People who own their homes are the only ones who can really think about having accumulated enough wealth to be able to spend their old age in comfort. The rest of the population is going to, unfortunately, be stuck on the government tax rolls and dealing with Social Security. But CCRCs are still appealing for a huge number of people. As our societal infrastructure breaks down and people move away from their families, the idea of the elderly taking care of themselves in CCRCs becomes even more desirable. It's going to be a luxury to be able to afford all the services that it takes to keep you independent in your home. You're going to need to have your own driver, shopper, housekeeper, and nurse. You see it all the time, where someone is barely functional in their home and then they break a hip, and the whole infrastructure falls apart because they don't have enough backup services to take care of that final eventuality, on top of their normal, daily concerns.

CCRCs are never going to be the best model where resources are limited, because they are always going to be too expensive. When you say "continuing care," you're making a promise about long-term care for life, which is labor-intensive, and, as people need more care, they need more labor and they run out of money, so it's a self-defeating prophecy. This is always going to be for people with discretionary income. Could the government coopt it into something that might work? I'll believe it when I see it. I don't believe that they're able to be market-oriented enough to actually do it. But there's a huge business out there. There are going to be a lot of poor providers who end up succeeding by sheer demographics, and then we'll end up with other kinds of problems. I don't think anyone can actually see past the coming boom. Nobody knows if the market is going to shrink after that, or what's going to happen, or what the alternatives will be, so I think growth has to be sustainable. It has to be sustainable for the labor market, which is going to shrink, and it's must be sustainable economically to carry these facilities as they start up and grow over the long run and make sure that they can renew themselves in ways that will take into account changes in Medicare, changes in health care, and changes in the labor situation. But, the good news is there are plenty of jobs for low-skilled, relatively low-paid workers. There's a growing number in that labor pool, and they're looking for better alternatives than flipping burgers. This is a better opportunity, so it does meet a lot of societal needs from a provider, as well as a social, point of view.

Legal Challenges

I prefer to think of our legal problems as our legal challenges. The law is actually your best friend. I can't say that enough. Anyone who doesn't choose to be licensed is crazy, because then the residents, not the providers, have the final control. The law protects the residents from unscrupulous developers and protects the developers from selfish and self-absorbed residents. So, it's a good thing. However, your legal documents need to be airtight in giving you full discretion, in taking into account unanticipated medical advances, unanticipated technologies, unanticipated eventualities in such a way that you have an escape hatch, so that you have the ultimate right to evict a noncompliant or disruptive resident, so that you have control over where the money is spent if you're making a promise. And you have to be able to take into account that the state laws are going to change. The federal laws are going to change. You're stuck with your old legal documents, and if you haven't provided for some of those changes, you're just out of luck. It's out of your pocket and your hide. You have to deliver to the customer what was promised, regardless of what the market conditions say, which is why the one thing your legal documents have to assure you of is that you can raise the prices to accommodate market forces. If you don't do that, you're out of luck. Money will take care of a heck of a lot of things, but not if you can't raise the fees. I mean, right now there's a cockamamie law that a resident group is trying to introduce, to limit the increases in continuing care fees to the cost of living. Well, if they would limit them to the cost of health care, I'd feel a lot better, since that went up 35% last year, but limited to the cost of living is absolutely ridiculous. The customer base, the residents, are not buying consumer goods that contribute to cost of living, they are not spending their money in the same way that people who create the cost of living are spending it, and they're spending it disproportionately on things that are much more expensive, like health care. So, if something like that happens, we're all in trouble, and then it's time to get out of the business.

The End of the Nonprofit Advantage

It used to be that the nonprofits had huge advantages. People trusted the churches. People felt that because serving seniors was a charitable endeavor, they would be well taken care of by nonprofits. Those advantages have gone away. Nonprofits have to operate like a business, they have to use residents' money as wisely as for-profits. They certainly have a better cachet. I mean, we're still seeing a certain cachet for nonprofits, in terms of marketing. "Oh, that community must be good because the Episcopal Church is building it." They're getting tremendous spin. But, I think the distinctions are becoming blurred, and I think, in the state of California, the new law that actually requires facilities to maintain their profits within that facility and not transfer them to the development of another facility is going to completely stop the development of not-for-profit facilities of any size, unless there's another source of revenue. The disadvantage of not-for-profits is that they have no incentive to run the business effectively, if they can't take the money out and use it to help more people. So, I think their incentive is going to dry up.

Expansion

Reasonable for-profits are able to expand for a couple of reasons. One is that the equity model doesn't depend on the profits of one community to fund the next one. Second, we're seeing a lot of opportunity in the acquisition arena of underperforming facilities where someone has already taken the risk and lost. A lot of companies get into this business and think they're going to get paid back very quickly and end up getting driven out of the business. That's when it's bottom-fishing time. There are facilities that someone is willing to unload just to get out of the business, after taking their losses, and there's a real opportunity there. There is reduced potential, because you're taking used goods, and you're trying to make it as good as you can. It's very different from taking an enterprise concept and developing it from scratch, but you can still apply most of the principles of the enterprise concept to the acquired facility.

■ *The Cypress* **Strategy**

I think *The Cypress* has been so successful because we have analyzed our market very carefully. This market is educated, they have the means, they want quality in their lives, and they want good services. We found out how to deliver that product. I think where other communities fall short is that they underestimate what someone will invest in a good product. In the least favorable situations in care communities, a 75-year-old couple is being asked to turn over $200,000 and not get any return. That's not necessary. *The Cypress*, on the other hand, is an investment for one's future and for one's children. People want that. These are smart individuals who have worked hard for their money and the reason they have money is that they know how to invest.

A Marketable Product

A *Cypress* marketing executive addresses the challenge in a way that shows that concept and marketing are one.

As far the success of our marketing, it's very simple. We came up with a marketable product. A product could be marketable but be flawed and those flaws may not be seen until later on, maybe 5, 10 years down the road. *The Cypress* concept is a product that is going to last a lifetime, and ten lifetimes. It's going to be something that continues on with financial prudence, resort living and the sort of "country club" atmosphere. None of that old narrow-hall, dark-corridor image of nursing homes. We offer excellent services, hence we have wonderful resident referrals. We don't have to spend a dime on advertising here, now that we're in our fifth year, because we do get so many resident referrals. We have established a good name. Now as far as *The Cypress of Charlotte* community, what I've learned and what I've noticed is that before assuming anything, let's go out and ask them what they want. They're paying for it, so let's provide them what they want. And the best way to do that in the initial marketing stages is with focus groups, in asking the questions. So many other communities don't do that or just assume that they want one meal a day. Let's ask them how they feel about meals and linen service and things like that. Maybe there are things that the community at large doesn't want. Let's ask them. Finding a desirable location, obviously, is important. And communicating to those folks in the initial stages that this is not like any other old folks home. You invite them to focus groups and they share their input. Because let's face it, everyone likes to be asked to help.

The monthly fee at *The Cypress* is a great value, especially as it pertains to the use of the Health Center. Here at the *Cypress*, we distributed the risk, which is an excellent idea; so if you use it, you get a discount. So it's beneficial for someone who's going to use it for a short time or anyone who's going to use it for a couple of years. Members receive 90 prepaid days of nursing care. That's the privilege of being a member, a part of their monthly fee goes toward that. When they're considered permanent residents of the Health Center, then they pay 50% of the daily rate. And talk to anyone who's paying full coverage, it's a phenomenal benefit. Then when they sell their home, and that home has built up equity, that equity can be used for long-term nursing care expertise if necessary. Long-term care insurance can cover the remaining 50% that a member has to pay. But remember, long-term care insurance is going to have a deductible, too. It's usually 90 days. We cover the 90 days. Long-term care insurance typically covers 60% of nursing care. We already cover 50%. So long-term care insurance is not needed by *The Cypress* residents. And Medicare doesn't do a very good job at letting these folks know that it doesn't cover nursing care, only a nominal amount.

This community was established initially with cottages and apartments, the apartments ranging from 810 to 1,500 square feet. Then we decided to introduce another product that would bridge from 1,500 up to 2,000 square feet and more that's being offered in the cottages. We labeled that new product "villa" to differenti-ate from our existing apartments. We offered balconies and a few more amenities. Consequently, we now offer sixteen differ-ent plans and our average price now is over $250,000.

Several of the communities that I've had experience with have had monthly fees that exceeded what folks could spend. That's a marketing nightmare. Both charging too much for the monthly fee and also offering a product that is too small, along with not offering enough choices, enough options. Here at *The Cypress*, if you want to move a wall, because you own it, you can move that wall. Most other communities do not allow you the option to choose different colors of carpet and paint, move walls around, make it your own. People like the pride of home ownership and when you take that pride away, they don't have a feeling of control. I have seen poor advertising still reflecting too much the importance of total life care or nursing care. We're all glad it's there when we need it, but do we have to look at it, be reminded of it? No. Again, looking at the *Cypress* and Charlotte, marketing a country club, resortlike community is definitely a bonus. Marketing nursing care, I question how effective that is. I've seen some overdo that.

Each CCRC Is Unique

Contributing to the discussion, another *Cypress* executive offers her favorite saying: "Once you've seen one CCRC, you have seen one CCRC."

Because they are all so different. In most church-related com-munities, for example, there is no bonus program or commission program. They are not "selling." That's the biggest mistake I've seen. They didn't train their staff for "sales." Ten years ago, I don't think there were too many organizations out there that were getting into this business. Now the demographics are clear to everyone. So the industry is moving toward servicing the elderly, or adult seniors—and they have not trained their sales staff, they've been complacent, and said, "Okay, the job pays $20,000. Basically you just need to be a tour guide." That's where I've seen the problems, where they have not trained sales people and given them the respect that they deserve.

The CCRC Incentive

Someone did a study at Duke University a few years ago, because Duke was building a retirement community. Why are you choos-ing a continuing care community? What are your reasons? And the study showed that the number one reason is peace of mind. Knowing that if something should happen, I can get care, primarily because I don't want my children to worry about me. And, let's face it. Unless this nation gets back to getting families back together, closer together, and I don't see that happening, senior parents will always have to rely on someone else to take care of them. So having that peace of mind was the number one reason. The second reason was maintenance-free living. Wanting to be able to shut the door and travel and know that everything's being taken care of. Where else can you get that but in a continuing care community? Health care and food service were also high on the list.

■ Thoughts About the Future

John Raiser suggests that we can drive the equity CCRC concept to everyone who owns a home that is pretty well paid for. In some parts of the country, that home may only be worth $150,000, and in other areas, it may be worth a half million dollars, but the equity concept still works as a direct exchange when in the same or less expensive area. The middle spectrum of retired people who do not own their own home reasonably free and clear are relegated to a rental type facility, which may offer fewer amenities and less security. The third category is the one that is subsidized by the government—smaller rooms, more communal services, but there's a great need for them. Our Rotary Club owns and operates an 82-unit retirement community. That retirement residence is really nothing but an apartment building. We built it with tax credits from the U.S. Treasury, and we're keeping the rents under $400 a month, which is affordable for those whose sole income is Social Security. We can apply what we learn from high-end CCRC to Social Security recipients and accommodate them a dignified way.

The CCRC Industry Is Risky

CCRCs are in uncharted waters. We are dealing with medical care and coverage that is constantly changing, including Medicare's contribution, and medical conditions that are constantly changing. We are also dealing with the real estate risk of a developer building a building that has a fixed overhead and fixed demands, to service the debt and pay taxes, and pay the utilities. We're also assuming the hotel risk, although that risk is somewhat minimized. We don't have to worry about acquiring new tenants every morning, but we do have to worry about providing all the services of a hotel. So, there is a little risk adjustment. The developer risk is the biggest risk. The second biggest risk is marketing—to constantly keep selling the original units and handle the resales as they arise. Because as units remain vacant, the income, the cash flow, diminishes, and that presents a big risk to the developer and the community.

Very few people want to undertake these risks, and this is really the problem. The developer must have the ability and the knowledge of a developer, and also have an altruistic mentality of community service, to make a truly beneficial community. We have found that the highly restrictive, regulatory restraints are really keeping people back from taking the risk of building facilities. On the other hand, when there are no restraints, there can be a lot of exploitation of the elderly. It is not a very straight, easy way to make a living, so you must have a dual agenda—profit and service to the community, with neither getting out of balance with the other.

Working with Hospitals

Can alliances be built with the hospital groups to provide more senior retirement communities? We have tried in a couple of instances without much success. In one instance, we had tried to forge an alliance with our local hospital, and that did not get consummated because the thinking of a hospital is so very different, and to this day, I'm not quite sure why. Then, we saw the issue arise with *The Carlisle*—a CCRC we are now managing in San Francisco—which was being managed by a major San Francisco hospital. Before our arrival on the scene, its idea was that the hospital should, as a natural extension of its service, get into the CCRC business. After 2 years, they had to throw in the towel and pull out. They found that CCRCs are very different businesses, and there was less synergy than originally imagined. There was no leverage in their expertise. They did not understand the hotel-type services, the more upscale food services that were provided, and the insurance elements that are part of a CCRC. The hospital is accustomed to collect on insurance but not in providing insurance. They are actually providers, but they're providers of a different kind of service. And, having talked with three other hospital directors, their attitude is, from all we have heard and all we have seen, we don't want to get involved in retirement communities. Keep us out of there. You send us your sick people. When they become sick, we'll take care of them. But don't try to put us in the retirement community business.

2.0 Executive Organization

Throughout these interviews we gain a sense of how to create an executive organization. John Raiser suggests that the concept and the organization should evolve at the same time.

■ Creating an Organization

Let's say that a developer has a plot of land, and a concept for a continuing care community. It's just an idea, but you're going to have to hire this whole cadre of people, sell them on your idea, revise your idea to meet their expectations and mesh with their experience, and then develop the concept out of that. Ideally, you'd have either members of your own organization or other people you know in the industry that you could use as part of your concept team, because it's going to be very hard to just start off and say, "I'm one person. I have a good idea. I'm going to hire an architect who shares my idea and an engineer who shares my idea," and so on.

So, let's assume you have some people in your organization already who share this idea. Because to learn the business and to learn about each other at the same time would be excruciating. As you look at your organization, you may say, "Okay, we don't have all the pieces here," and you may need to infill with consultants or to hire some people. You may not need to hire your executive director 2 years before development. I mean, it's a nice luxury to have, but I'm not sure it's a necessity. But you need someone who represents the point of view of operations, and a person who is sufficiently experienced so that other people will respect his point of view.

As you create an organization, you have to identify where people can best contribute. The example that keeps coming to mind is a chef. Whenever you design a kitchen, never have your first chef participate in the design, because every chef afterward comes in and says, "What the hell do we need this machine for? This is all wrong. We need to move this around. The shelves need to be here." Because cooking is such a subjective thing, people have their own rhythm, and they've worked with different equipment, so that they prefer certain equipment and layouts. At *The Stratford*, we hired this famous kitchen designer, but very deliberately we didn't let our hired chefs start messing around with the design. Sure enough, the first chef we had went directly to the maintenance guy and said, "Fix this, this, this, this. Move this. I want this over here." Did exactly what we were talking about and then left in 18 months, so that the next person who came along felt it was all wrong, and the maintenance guy had to redo it all again, until we got involved and put our foot down.

A State of Flux

What we also see is that executive organizations are always in a state of flux. This reflection by a *Cypress* executive is a prime example.

When our new director of nursing came on board, we sat down to get to know one another. That's a little awkward because all of a sudden, you're thrust into this working relationship and you don't know the person you're working with. We have worked very hard at trying to find out about approaches and styles and what's important and what is less important to the two of us. My words to her the first couple of days that she was with us were, "I consider the two of us more of a team than a supervisory relationship. I think more can be accomplished with the two of us working on the same agenda together."

■ Career Opportunities

Certainly, the CCRC industry needs effective executives, as the president of the Raiser Senior Services suggests.

Considering what we see at *The Stratford*, and I'm sure this applies to *The Cypress*, there's going to be a huge demand for good managers and executive directors. I think directors who understand how to motivate and train staff, as opposed to how to direct them and control them, are going to be more success-ful. I think it's going to be a woman-dominated industry, although, ironically, men succeed better with residents because residents respect men. This generation of seniors respects men more, but hopefully the next generation will respect both gen-ders if they do a good job. So, women really have to earn their stripes, but I think it's a viable career. The problem is going to be burnout and repetitiveness, and the way to mitigate that is to make career moves, either within an organization or beyond an organization to progressively either more interesting or more creative communities. You stay at one community for 5 or 7 years, and then you move on. And then, financially, you expect a salary that's more than reasonable and then you make sure that as you become more valuable to the organization, you get some form of profit sharing, something that ties you to the com-munity and makes you invest in the long-term viability of the project. Many executive directors focus on making the current residents happy and don't really worry about preserving the equity of the developer or of the residents or whoever it is that stands to benefit. They end up doing the organization a disservice, and that's very typical because executive directors aren't generally rewarded for that long-term vision.

A Healthy Skepticism

The authors note that all of us strive to become exemplary executives. We pay attention to management theories and listen to what those in the retirement community industry and related professions have to say. This information and knowledge, however, no matter how valuable it appears, must never be considered sacrosanct. Everything we read or hear is worthy of study and intense critical analysis. In *The Witch Doctors*, Micklethwait and Wooldridge[7] point out that the business world is overrun by fads, where each management guru promises a cure for what ails corporate America. Their comparison of offered advice with results shows that we have every reason to be cautious about what we buy into. Theorizing is often superficial and considers the organization's situation in a simplistic fashion.

3.0 Finance and Law

This critical success factor has a direct bearing on the soundness of the CCRC enterprise. It is obviously a primary concern of prospective residents. CCRC enterprises must therefore be formed with an exacting financial and legal structure that precisely documents how all legal, financial, and regulatory requirements are to be fulfilled. It is essential that enterprise participants never lose sight of what must be done to protect the rights of residents, developers, and lenders. It is also essential that participants adhere to local and state government licensing, regulatory, and disclosure requirements. The following interviews alert us to many aspects of this process.

▧ *The Cypress of Charlotte*

The Cypress of Hilton Head Island now has a sister development, *The Cypress of Charlotte*, which continues James Coleman's work to establish a new standard for continuing care retirement communities. Similar to *The Cypress of Hilton Head Island*, the new enterprise offers the same high-quality country club atmosphere and the same level of service excellence in a traditional Charlotte setting.

In *The Cypress of Charlotte* concept, retirement should be both worry-free and exciting. The services and activities covered by the monthly fee include dining, with three meals daily in the Clubhouse; bed and bath laundry service; weekly housekeeping; transportation for groups and individuals to shopping, appointments, special events, and outings; activity and education; valet service from parking to hanging pictures; and complete exterior and interior maintenance. Security begins at the gated entrance to the campus. The on-site health care facility offers assisted living, skilled nursing, Alzheimer's care, and a wellness program focusing on diet, exercise, and personal and medical concerns.

The Cypress of Charlotte is owned by the members through the Cypress of Charlotte Condominium Association. All of the common facilities including the Clubhouse and Health Center are deeded over to the Condominium Association. Once construction financing is paid off, the community will remain debt-free and will operate on a not-for-profit basis. Although the developer retains ultimate responsibility, residents are active in providing guidance for financial and operational issues through a variety of committees. The Cypress Company's commitment is that the community will remain financially sound and that monthly fees will be kept at a reasonable level. The management team for *The Cypress of Charlotte* is the nationally recognized leader in CCRC administration, Life Care Services Corporation, whose goal is to promote the finest quality of life possible.

Disclosure Statement

All of the preceding features, amenities, and services require specification in legally constructed documents. The legal and financial standard here is "disclosure." A primary document for the enterprise is the Disclosure Statement (Information Booklet), which explains to prospective residents, their families, and their advisors who and what is involved in the operation of *The Cypress of Charlotte* in nontechnical language. The companion documents are the specific Purchase and Sales Agreement and Membership Agreement signed by the resident. Also available to a prospective resident or his legal representative with a general power of attorney is information regarding reserve funding, experience of persons who will make investment decisions, a current actuarial study, and information regarding persons having a 5% or greater interest in *The Cypress of Charlotte*.

Financial Statements

For an enterprise like *The Cypress of Charlotte*, it is common practice to offer balance sheets containing statements of operations, net assets, and cash flows as projected for 5 and 10 years. There is always a disclaimer that anticipates differences between forecasts and actual results because of events or circumstances, and notes that these differences may be material. This work encompasses every expenditure: assets, liabilities and net assets, revenue, expenses, and operating income, net operating income after taxes, net assets at the beginning of each year, and net assets at the end of each year. The financial statement includes a statement of the accounting policies required by law and how assumptions regarding the financial disclosure were derived.

■ Legal Considerations

When attorneys work to identify the regulatory and licensing requirements that must be met and to characterize the mandates for safeguarding the rights of investors, lenders, and homeowners, the results set a performance standard for every deliberation. Consider that you are already competitive in the senior living industry. You have an extensive knowledge base, expert staff, alliances in place, and a market situation that you fully understand. What you need to know is how to safeguard the proposed investment. This is the primary objective of legal research. The following discussions range from the study of regulatory statutes and licensing requirements to the development of homeowner contacts and homeowners' associations. The first conversation, with Paul A. Gordon[8] and Allan D. Jergesen of Hanson, Bridgett, Marcus, Vlahos & Rudy, LLP, Attorneys at Law, San Francisco, two of America's foremost retirement community legal experts, stresses the essential need to have someone who is highly experienced identify, review, and respond to the licensure laws that vary dramatically from state to state.

PAG: If you're looking for things, big mistakes that people have made in this industry, I've seen a few of them. The one that comes to mind is a project where an experienced CCRC developer, one of the largest CCRC developers in the country, came to California to build their first project. They didn't realize that, unlike a lot of states, California requires you to get CCRC certification, even if you don't pay for people's care on a kind of insurance basis. So, they went ahead and they built this residential apartment, and they put a nursing facility next door to it, and they promised people that they could move into nursing if they needed it, but they'd have to pay fee for service. And then, after the building was built, in fact, around the time that I first heard of it—the building had already been filled with people—they discovered that they had to be licensed: that their residential units had to be licensed as what is, essentially, an assisted-living facility, even though the people in there didn't actually need assisted living just then. But, because it was attached to a nursing facility, because there was this ability to transfer over to nursing, the whole thing had to be a continuing care facility, the residential building had to be licensed as such. So then they dutifully applied for the license. The Department of Social Services sent a form down to the fire inspector to have the building receive fire clearance. Turns out the building could not pass the fire inspection. It was built to the wrong code because a different code applies to licensed buildings. So, they had gotten all the way down the track, built the building to the wrong code, and had received— the day that I got the phone call—a notice from the state that they had 10 days to inform all of the residents that they're entitled to have all their money refunded and to move out of the facility, and that the state had filed a lien against the entity, and against the building, and recorded it with the county recorder to secure the rights of the residents under their contracts.

Now, that was ultimately solved by a lot of panic-stricken negotiation and so forth, but the point is that there was somebody who is experienced but who didn't do enough homework, apparently, about the licensure laws in the state. And the licensure laws for CCRCs vary dramatically from state to state. Some people think that you have to have an entrance fee in order for the project to be considered a CCRC, and that's not true in all states. In California, for example, it is a promise of care for more than a year; whether there's an entrance fee or not, it's going to be considered continuing care.

A Regulated Industry

ADJ: We had another developer, equally as sophisticated, a national company, that came in, and they had their own legal counsel, central legal counsel out of state, and they knew, or they sensed, that there were some licensing issues, and actually made contact with the state and received informal assurances from the state—the person who was probably in a position to give assurances—that their facility was not licensable, or did not have to be licensed as a CCRC. It turned out the guy was wrong, and they came to us a few years later, when the thing was in the process of actually being built. It was because there had been a change in personnel at the state level, and the state people were saying, "You should have come to us in the beginning." And we had to honestly tell them they should have as well. And so, that was also a very long series of negotiations in which the entire form of the project was, in a way, warped, because certain things then had to be done that hadn't been planned, and they had to change things and really adapt what had been a purely real estate project (this was actually an equity project—a cooperative-type project), they had to turn it into or modify it into a continuing care project. So, I guess, the moral there is find the experts. And then, also, get some pretty clear guidance from the state at the beginning. Don't think that it's to your advantage to escape, say, a system of regulations based on an assurance in a phone call from somebody because that can come back to haunt you. Better to know up front.

PAG: Another thing about regulation is that a lot of people getting into this field, particularly those coming from the real estate development side of things, as opposed to those coming in from the health care side of things, aren't used to being involved in a regulated industry. Of course, CCRCs are a rather heavily regulated business, and so they often try to avoid regulation. Real estate developers are kind of notorious for hating regulation. And with good justification. The problem, though, is that in this field, I find myself trying to convince clients that regulation can be something of a safe harbor, because if you're not regulated as a CCRC in the particular state, but you're doing something that is very close to CCRC activity, it could be one of a number of other things that is much worse than CCRC regulation. You would be in the business of selling health insurance—something you don't want to be in the business of doing in most states unless you really have your act together and intend to do a high volume of business. You could be a health maintenance organization, or you could be selling securities. In fact, in the old days—which I guess was the '60s, maybe the early '70s, some people were getting in trouble selling continuing care contracts in the Midwest in states where there were no CCRC statutes. They ended up being prosecuted and convicted of securities fraud, because they were found to be selling securities as they were milling around and trying to collect deposits for the purpose of building a new retirement community that then eventually failed and people got sued and there were allegations of fraud. We had a client once who made a very good faith effort to try to characterize their CCRC look-alike as something else and tried to structure it to avoid the CCRC laws, and so they went dutifully to the state agency that controls the prepaid health plans, which is basically the same one that governs HMOs. They got stonewalled for a year because that agency didn't know how to deal with the actuarial aspects of the CCRC, which, of course, are based on the person's life expectancies, whereas HMOs and prepaid health plans work on a year-to-year, premium-type basis. And so, after a year of essentially being stonewalled, they finally relented and decided, yes, we have to be regulated by the CCRC people, or we're never going to be able to move our project forward.

ADJ: To follow up on that, I think the most foolish developers are those who go in with the attitude of, "I'll do as little as I have to," in terms of submitting to regulations, say, an anti-regulatory attitude. This may vary from state to state, but we found in California, and I suspect it's fairly typical, that those are the ones who may get a little bit in the beginning, because they can take some shortcuts. But these are very visible projects, and the state agency, even in a large state like California, will find out about them very quickly. If nothing else, their competitors will tell the state agency. And then what you have is potentially an atmosphere of irritation and friction from the very beginning. And the attitude of the regulators makes a big difference. I can tell you a tale of two facilities—they're both luxury equity projects within a few miles of one another. In one facility, the developers decided that they didn't need to deal with the "bureaucrats," and had an attitude of resistance. The legal bills of that facility were horrendous, year after year after year. In the other facility, the developers went to the state as they were planning the project, and said: "Here's what we're thinking of doing," before anything had happened. "What is your advice? What can we tell you?" The atmosphere to this day has been one of cooperation, and, in a way, the second facility can get away with a lot more than the first facility. In the first facility, if one little thing goes wrong, a resident complains, the state regulators are down there. Now, the other facility, where the same resident complains, the state is likely to say, "Oh, well, why don't you just work it out with the developer." I'd say go in with that attitude, and, also, find legal counsel who go in with that attitude. Not the "take no prisoners" or "we'll find a way of getting around everything for you."

Equity Communities

PAG: Most states have at least an escrow requirement for pre-construction deposits from prospective residents of the facility, so that at least there is some assurance—there is never total assurance—but there is little bit more of a safeguard of that resident's funds, first of all; and secondly, many states will have the requirement that a certain number of deposits be received before construction commences or before the facility is certified to enter into continuing care agreements. The purpose of that is to prevent facilities from being built that have an undercapacity of people. So few people actually sign up that the people who are in there, who have sold their homes and made possibly an irreversible commitment, aren't alone, rattling around in the facility without sufficient residents there to pay for the costs of operations. These facilities are not easily convertible into other types of uses because they usually have at least one and maybe two or three levels of care, and so a continuing care facility, just the physical plant itself, tends to be not very easily converted to other uses if it fails during the fill-up period.

The equity type of facility is quite a bit more rare, but we think it is a better mousetrap. This type allows residents to have an equity interest in the facility, so that if they decide that they need to move out sooner than expected, maybe they don't like living in that facility, or for whatever reason, perhaps they die a lot sooner than is anticipated, their heirs have something there that can be sold; whereas, in the entrance-fee facility, most of them, at least the traditional ones, you're basically paying less money as an entrance fee, but you're betting that you're going to live your life expectancy or longer. If so, you'll get your money's worth, essentially. But, if you die sooner than expected or you want to move out for some reason, sooner than your life expectancy, the pricing structure is such that you would end up losing some money out of the deal. Another thing about the equity-fee structure is that when a person moves out of a residential unit on a permanent basis and goes to, let's say, a skilled nursing facility permanently, he can be required to sell the condominium or coop unit, and put those monies in trust to help pay for nursing care. This is also a nice form of security, and I think it makes the project overall a lot more stable.

The problem with equity communities, I think, is when developers structure them in such a way that they give too much managerial control to the residents. This is, after all, a service-oriented business, and anyone who has dealt with homeowners' associations knows that homeowners' associations are not always good at doing even the simple things, like repairing leaky pipes and determining what color the carpet ought to be in the lobby. And when they, then, are left with all of those issues to contend with, plus when Mrs. Jones has to go to the nursing facility or how we're going to allocate fees for assisted living or for dining among the various units, you know, on a square footage basis, on a per capita basis, or on a per unit basis, everyone involved in that decision has a conflict of interest, potentially. Let's face it, who wants to retire, and, at age 80 or 85, be running a complicated business with a nursing facility and assisted-living facility and a dining service. So, we think that when the equity facilities are structured, they should be structured in such a way that the resident gets all of the tax and real property benefits of home ownership but none of the management powers that would normally go with the homeowners' association. That should be left with the facility's developer and operator.

Legal Understanding

ADJ: Whether you're dealing with an equity project or a non-equity project, you have the prospective resident—say, the 80-year-old person. Relatively few can understand the details of CCRCs, no matter what kind of project you're talking about; whether you're talking about a more traditional one with an entrance fee or a newer type, the type just mentioned, of equity. I think you've got to do several things. First of all, you want to make certain that the legal documents, which are going to be complicated anyway, are written in plain English. There is absolutely no excuse for documents that look like old-time bills of lading or new-time insurance agreements. They may have to be long, but they should use simple words, no legalisms like hereinabove or wherefore—no excuse for that at all. They should be consumer-friendly. Now, having said that, I suspect that your average prospective resident will either be asleep or in a state of total incomprehension by the third page. It's just that these are legally complicated things.

So, I think, two solutions there. One is our best clients encourage prospective residents to show the agreement to family members, advisors, accountants, lawyers, and get their advice. Now, a further caveat—very often the people who you might hope would provide the best advice are not, quite honestly, in a very good position to do so. The classic case is the family lawyer in an equity project. The family lawyer will call one of us and say, "I've gone over your papers and I just can't believe you're really doing this." "Well, what do you mean?" "Well, how can you have a condominium where the residents have no say in the management?" Or, "How can you have a condominium project where, following death, the estate doesn't collect the entire sale price? It will give a portion of the sale price following death or, indeed, if the person leaves during their life, to the developer?" These things then have to be explained. And I think the better family advisors will engage in the dialogue. The worst will simply not understand, and create further problems.

An Informed Marketing Staff

ADJ: This leads to the second thing that ought to be done. And that is a very close relationship between the marketing and legal folks. There is often a divergence of interest. We lawyers worry about bad things happening. We warn. We caution. We set limits. The marketing people are looking toward all sorts of good things happening. They encourage, they push on, and, so, each can be guilty of being in their own world. They've got to get together, and what you need is lawyers who are mindful that what you're trying to do is not just to protect and scare people away, but to sell—to sell in a conscientious and honest way. You need marketing people who are not just prone to try to sell regardless, and I would, by the way, look at their financial incentives. I think that's very important. If they're prone to sell regardless, then that's what they're going to do. If there are incentives to sell intelligently, then that's what they'll do. In any event, to ensure that the lawyers and the marketing people get together, it often makes sense to have a second set of documents that are not, strictly speaking, legal documents. They summarize the main aspects of the project in a way that a layperson, possibly not the resident, but the resident's advisors, can understand. It gets them into it, and then they can then move from there to the actual legal documents. Final comment about that. You have to be very careful because the descriptive "nonlegal" documents, although not formally a part of the contract, can become a binding part of the promise. So, if they go a little bit too far or fill in something, then you have to assume that that's what you're going to be held to.

PAG: I agree that getting the marketing staff to talk to the lawyer who drafted the admission agreement is really a very important thing to do. A lot of times, the marketing staff really doesn't understand the agreement. The terms of the relationship between the resident and the provider of services are not really understood. You'd be surprised. Many may not have even read the entire agreement. Sometimes, the agreement isn't even fully formulated at the time when the sales staff is out there making pitches and representations about what's going to be offered. So it's important to at least have a draft of the admission agreement—everything subject to change over time during the development period—but at least to have a draft out there for the lawyers to explain to the marketing staff. Some of our better clients have actually invited us down to talk to the prospective residents when there are enough of them to gather together to make it efficient to do so, to explain to them, and to answer their questions about how the project is going to be run. "What if I die on this particular day?" "What if I have a health care need while I'm traveling in Europe?" You get all kinds of questions that usually the lawyers who draft the agreements can answer, and usually those issues are addressed in the agreement.

ADJ: Just following on that point, I think all of the promotional materials really have to be viewed by the attorneys, not just as pure legal documents, but also as marketing materials. One example: We had a facility that, in its promotional documents, told residents that they would receive unlimited nursing services on-site at the facility. What it meant was that there would be no limit on the number of days that would be covered by the regular monthly fee. Well, what happened was, very early on, some residents started showing the signs of Alzheimer's disease and dementia. And it turned out that the nursing facility was not set up to deal with that, and it felt that it had to transfer these people off-site. And there was language in the contract that could be interpreted as allowing that. But one of the things that undercut that—and this was pointed out by the residents and their families—was the language about unlimited nursing services. To them, that meant nursing services, regardless of what the underlying condition was. So, I think it would have helped to have it reviewed by an intelligent legal counsel, and it would also be essential that intelligent legal counsel understand marketing terms like "unlimited" or "whenever you need it," things like that, that have to be looked at very closely.

Disability and Racial Discrimination

PAG: We're touching on the issue of disability discrimination, which is a very big issue for CCRCs because, as you can imagine, when you're dealing with a population where the average age is 75, 80 years of age, you have a lot of people who have a disability or are going to become disabled. And you, as a CCRC provider, will be doing health care screening in determining whether to admit them or deny admission, you will be doing health care screening in terms of determining their placement within the facility, when they should be transferred from one level of care to another, and when they should be discharged from the community because you can no longer care for them. All of these are disability discrimination issues. We advise our clients to have legal review of all admissions screening documents and health care screening documents. And about advertising. One of the words that is somewhat suspect in advertising for CCRCs is the word "active." You often hear about "active retirement communities," and sometimes you'll see the brochures with the white-haired couple playing tennis or whatever, when, in fact, the age of the group is a little bit older than that. But "active" is a word that is used by many as signaling discrimination against the disabled or a preference for physically able people. We have generally advised our clients that instead of trying to describe the kind of person that they want to have come to their facility, they should describe the activities program that they have at the facility. But don't say that the person who we want to have live here must be active or must be able to participate in the activity program. And we have also advised that use of words like "lively" and "vibrant" is better than words that might signal a physical condition.

ADJ: Just another thought about brochures; the government has gotten into the question of implied racial discrimination—just from a brochure. If you have a brochure that purports to show either how an existing facility is or how a facility we're planning may be and, for example, there are five pictures and, say, one to five residents in each picture and they're all white, there is an issue. The government says that you have to show something that's more representative. So, something as simple as the ethnicity of the models that you used could be a source of problems.

Ownership, Development, and Operation

PAG: Well, a lot of times we see clients who do all three. And, frankly, I think that some of the better products that are out there have come from companies that try to do all of it and that eventually gain and have experience in ownership, development, and operation. That doesn't mean that it can't be done well having separate management and separate development and ownership. But, obviously, it requires more coordination. There are issues of who takes the lead. I think that, since this is such a service-oriented business, whoever it is that is going to be providing the services ultimately ought to have a very strong say in how the project gets developed. What the service program is going to be. What the interior design looks like. What kind of architecture. What kind of sites are used, and so forth.

The problem, though, is that if you have an owner and developer who doesn't have that operational experience but who is, nevertheless, involved in the project, they, obviously, are the ones who are going to be getting the financing, who have the land, and who are really controlling the project in its early stages. Hopefully, this owner and/or developer are going to be smart enough to realize that they don't have the operational experience, and if they're smart enough to know that, and you get a good manager in to listen to them, I think that can be a fruitful relationship. It's important when you have a relationship like that, though, to have the operator have some long-term interest in the facility. This isn't the kind of project where you want to have an operator on a short-term management contract because these are contracts for life, as far as the residents are concerned, and operations are going to be very important. That's why I say that a lot of the better products have merged together ownership and operation. But, if you have separate entities, I think the operator ought to have some kind of a long-term interest. Maybe some kind of a share in the equity or profit, if there's profit, or net operating income—something that keeps the operator there, keeps them involved, and makes them feel that this is a long-term proposition because that's what it is for the resident, and if the project is going to be successful, it must be successful for life.

It's fairly common that a developer, or an owner and developer combined into one entity, will build a turnkey product and then turn it over to another entity that does the operation. That's probably the most typical way for an owner and developer to "get out," as they say. And, in fact, there are some companies that specialize in it, that design and build. There's one that I'm thinking of that has carved out something of a niche in the retired military officers' market. This company has done several projects and they know the business very well. They know the design, they know the marketing issues, the feasibility studies, and so forth. They help a local group set up a not-for-profit organization that will ultimately be the manager of the facility, and they set it up, build it, and, essentially, walk away from the project when it's done. Now, I think, though, that they will also bring in management expertise, and so forth, through a third party, oftentimes.

Operational Philosophies

ADJ: You really need the management expertise up front, because knowledgeable seniors are not just going to subscribe to a facility based on a developer who candidly is not going to be there, is going to turn it over. And if the developer leads them to believe that he is going to still be there and then sells it, there could be potential licensing problems. It comes full circle. This is one of the things that the licensing folks are very, very concerned about. They say, "Who's in charge?" And that means who owns it and who runs it, and so you want to be clear from the start where there is divided responsibility about who is involved and what their relationships are and ensure that the prospective residents understand that.

PAG: There are firms that go around and buy projects, tend to find projects that are in trouble, that are having problems getting filled up or they're having pricing problems. Generally, the acquisition market is in troubled projects. There are, certainly, management companies that will come in and manage a start-up project on a contract basis, and get involved in the development period. In terms of people building projects, let's say, on speculation for sale of the entire project, that's a very unusual thing to do because it's so market-specific that I don't think the industry has quite come to the point where it's a fungible-type product that you can build and sell. If you're investing in it, I think you have to be in there for the long haul, unless you're doing a turnkey project for somebody else who has essentially hired you to do it for them. Then that somebody else, hopefully, has been involved from the beginning and probably represents some kind of either a nonprofit group or an affinity group of some kind that survives after the developer gets out.

I don't think changes in ownership have happened that much, and when they do, I think it can be somewhat unsettling for the residents. I know of one case now where there is a project that was developed on a not-for-profit basis by a nonprofit, religiously oriented provider, and that provider has had some problems making ends meet financially. A for-profit company is looking at it, sees it as a somewhat distressed property, and wants to go ahead and buy that property, and they're going to do that. I don't think the residents have so much of a problem with it, but, interestingly enough, the fund-raising arm of the local community that has been raising funds for many years to help support this institution is very concerned about it being transferred to a for-profit entity, and this is a phenomenon that is taking place in the larger world, as well. In the health care industry, you see large for-profit companies going around and gobbling up not-for-profit hospitals to the point where government is starting to get involved and starting to require review and approval of sales of health care institutions from nonprofit to for-profit ownership.

ADJ: What happens if a project is developed and marketed, say, as in this example, by a nonprofit, and the prospective residents are told this is a nonprofit organization, perhaps religiously affiliated? In any event, they are told that will be run on a nonprofit basis. And then, for whatever reason, it seems to make sense to bring in a for-profit. Do the residents have an argument that the deal has now changed? Or that there should be some sort of limit on the profits that can be made? Or that the for-profit must run it on a nonprofit basis, if that could ever be done? You want to think about these things early on, and the point is that these are not like other businesses, like hotels or restaurants, where you're just dealing with a clientele that comes and leaves, and if you change your mode of operation, you let the market take care of that. You are making promises from the very beginning to elderly people who will be there for the rest of their lives, so you can't just switch operational philosophies, turn on a dime with them. And, indeed, depending on which state you're in, probably the regulatory authorities will not let you. They will exact a price. For example, we're going through this right now, in a different case, where a nonprofit was set up and now it appears reasonable to operate it as a for-profit. The state is saying, "Well, if you do that, at least with the current generation of residents, it must be operated on a nonprofit basis, because you said that in all your marketing materials."

Sustained Profitability

PAG: There's one case that is the granddaddy of all CCRC failure cases, a bankruptcy that occurred in the mid-70s. The facility got into some financial difficulties, which were due, in part, to the fact that it tried to limit its ability to increase the monthly fees as a way of showing a sense of kindness. The contract had some limitations on its ability to increase fees, and, of course, in the '70s, we had double-digit inflation in the health care sector and in other sectors, and the fees just couldn't keep up with the cost of doing business, and so, eventually, the entire corporation went into bankruptcy. There was a lawsuit filed that involved the State of California, all the residents, and the sponsor. It went up to the United States Supreme Court on the issue of whether the religious sponsor was an entity that existed and could be sued. There were issues, also, about whether the church had financial responsibility for this corporation, which was a separate corporation, which the church sponsored but did not actually operate. As a result, there were some changes in California law regarding what you could say about your sponsor, who is your sponsor, and the ability to refer to a sponsor that is not financially liable, what kinds of disclosures you have to make, and so forth. The cardinal rule that came out of that is never limit your ability to increase fees, even if you're doing it out of a sense of kindness or charity.

The other thing that I would say that's related to this (and this isn't a case example, but it's something that a lot of people get in trouble with in new CCRC developments), and that is, in their zeal to sell the product out, they lower the prices at the front end. They keep the fees down very low—the monthly fees and the entrance fees, whatever it is—in order to sell the project out. Then, once the project is running and open for a couple of years, they look at their financial statements and realize that, "My, goodness. We're going to have to increase fees 10% this year, 10% next year, and 10% the year after that, just to break even or to catch up." What ends up happening, of course, is that the residents go ballistic because they can't afford a 10% fee increase per year, or 15% or 20%, whatever the number is. The problem is that if the pricing is unrealistically low, it catches up and bites you after a couple years of operation, and then you have a real managerial problem on your hands, and sometimes, if it isn't handled well, it can lead to class-action litigation. So, it's a real problem. The biggest problem is not filling up the facility in the first place. The second biggest problem is filling it up and having the wrong pricing structure.

A Legal Representative of the Residents Speaks

Arthur H. Bredenbeck, a California attorney with years of experience working with the elderly as they plan their futures, suggests that when the elderly consider retirement community life, they are looking for security, peace of mind, and for an exceptional quality of life. At the same time, he thinks people considering a move into a retirement community are concerned about giving up their independence and becoming dependent on a system.

I have watched this industry develop and watched clients of mine move to (and some move out of) retirement facilities, some of which are known to their residents as "The Prison." I think that's the danger and the promise of the industry—to allow residents to feel secure, feel safe, feel provided for, but, at the same time, to maintain the feeling of independence that they have had all of their life, and that becomes even more important as one goes up the economic scale. One very upscale community, as an example, has attracted a number of people who were leaders of business and industry in their working careers, who retired from that position, and, in many cases, took on community leadership and responsibilities. They moved into the continuing care community and were suddenly at sixes and sevens because they didn't feel in control and in charge any longer; that created tension and problems for the operators because there was nothing for the residents to do. That's part of the plan of the community—to provide all of the needs—and, yet, there was a need for the residents to have a position of power and influence, which was what their life history had been about.

Provide a Complete Picture

If one looks at the early examples of these communities, many of them took on, over a period of years, an institutional quality, and while they've been successful and sold out and are busy, there has been a sort of concern amongst residents that I've met with that they were treated as numbers, rather than as individuals. With the newer communities, the balance has certainly shifted away from that. I think the residents need to be given a rather accurate and complete picture of what they can expect before they move into one of these units. They have their fears of giving up freedom, they have their hopes of gaining more freedom and less responsibility and more protection. One of the worst things I've noticed is that, as the sales brochure is developed, promises are made or at least insinuated or perhaps could be read in by a prospective purchaser; then, a year later or 2 years later when reality strikes, the residents are unhappy, and that creates conflict, particularly if the project isn't completely sold out by the time the conflicts arise. The worst things for any developer is to have a group of unhappy residents telling their friends, neighbors, and the community that things are not as expected.

On the other hand, giving a complete picture of what it is going to be like to live in one of these communities to the prospective purchasers may be the most freeing thing that can occur because it allows the resident to see the vision, the hope, the freedom, the availability of activities. Amongst my older clients, one of the realities of their lives is that their friends are dying, their friends are getting sick, their friends are no longer able to drive at night, their friends are beginning to drop by the wayside. The attraction of the continuing care community is that there will be a group of friends (in many cases, new friends) who can have activities together without the need to go out at night, to be at risk in a strange restaurant, to need to arrange for transportation. As a developer can begin to show how those needs will be met, being sure that they're then able to deliver on those promises, the issue will go away.

I've not had the experience of people being so enthusiastic about moving into these kinds of communities that they just signed up without understanding. I think the danger is the other side. People are worried about giving up their freedom and want to know how the community is going to operate. The tension is between the sales staff, who needs to close sales, and the disclosure responsibility of being sure that the prospective residents understand what they're getting into. I think that becomes, in this kind of community, the responsibility of the developer, and you have to be sure that the prospective resident has taken the time and has the understanding and has a concept of what it's going to be like, so that there is not disappointment but, rather, excitement as the process develops.

Certainly, the idea of having meetings for prospective residents and having discussions about what it's going to be like, having visual presentations of the ambiance of living, the arrangements—this is difficult when the project isn't yet built. But to try to create some kind of physical depiction that is similar to what the residence is going to look like may become a very important issue, so that there is a realistic expectation. On the lower end of the economic scale, this is probably a lot less important because the person is likely to be grateful for the protection. On the higher end of the scale, the tension is greatest between the desire to be safe and protected and the desire to be independent—because there has been more experience with independence and more ability to pay for independence in the outside world.

Basic Challenges

The real issue is that if you're buying security, you want to know that you're going to be provided for, presumably in the same complex over the rest of your life, no matter what happens. The side piece of this, which I think most of the developments have created, is that the residents become the most segregated group because they don't want to be reminded of their own mortality, and so they don't want people in wheelchairs or walkers in the dining room or the common areas. They want those people hidden from view. And yet, what they've all bought into is the concept that they want to stay in the same complex, and that's a tremendous tension that I'm not sure anyone has satisfactorily resolved. At least, I have not seen it resolved in any institution. The older institutions put the assisted-living and skilled nursing facilities in a separate building, basically created a wall, and you are in one or the other but not both, so that the more healthy residents can go visit the people in the assisted-living areas but those people are not encouraged to come back to the independent living. That seems harsh, but it seems to be the way that it has been dealt with successfully.

I'm particularly concerned that, as we build more of the CCRC projects, as these become more mature, we're going to have a higher number of people who are in the end stages of life and who may have not just physical frailties but some form of dementia, which makes them disruptive to a community. If they're alone, one can, in some way, segregate and isolate those people and provide for them at whatever level of independence they can have, but when it is one member of a married couple, how do you split the couple, how do you create that kind of division and do it in a humane way that retains the sense of community that these institutions must work hard to create? This is a real challenge that has to be thought through—how one creates separation but togetherness at the same time.

I think there are solutions. The problem is that a new community is embryonic enough that, obviously, in the first 5 to 10 years of a facility, you don't face a lot of those situations. They are going to come later, as the initial buy-in group reaches the end stages of life, and whether that's 7 or 10 or 12 years out, there will be the problem, and I'm not sure that anyone has come up with "the solution." Again, I think the issue is to be sure that there has been a full disclosure and a plan, so that it doesn't become a surprising issue. We know it's going to happen. There has to be a solution. The people have to understand what the solution is going to be because, again, we're back to what is the resident's expectation. Whether there are going to be complaints to a licensing authority or something for inappropriate treatment. There is a retirement residence in this community that got some very, very bad publicity 6 or 7 years ago when they barred walkers, crutches, and wheelchairs from its dining room at the request of the residents, and the newspapers picked this up, and it became a major issue. I don't remember reading what the resolution was but, certainly, there were several weeks where the residents in question had major bad publicity in the community press. This certainly would have had to depress future sales, and there were units available in that community at the time.

Certainly, in the lower economic markets, a larger scale is going to be necessary in order to keep costs affordable. And as one builds a smaller project, since you still are going to have to have 24-hour monitoring, you're still going to have to have some kind of assisted living with 24-hour availability of qualified care staff, the costs are going to go up. But at the same time, most people, given a choice, in my experience, will choose the smaller unit because it's more of a family place, more of an apartment, more of a condominium style than is the large institutional structure that is serving 500 or more units. In my experience, having visited several of these communities in the Bay Area, the places where the staff knows the residents by name and can deal with them individually as human beings rather than as residents in a large complex is one of the keys to resolving the problems that we all know are going to occur in the relationships between the institution and its residents.

Appropriate Safeguards

I have been fortunate in not having any clients who have been in inappropriately operated facilities where someone actually took advantage of them and where one needed to use the legal system to get in and correct the problem. I am aware that that has occurred, but it is not in my own experience. I think the biggest issue has been that the regulatory authority is groping for answers to the questions and standards that are still being developed, and that the authority's response has not been as excellent as it might be. Again, the issue is to get the resident—the new resident in the facility—happy and comfortable, so that there are no complaints because the complaint process is frustrating. And when the resident doesn't feel that he or she is getting redress from the operator, there will be more frustration when dealing with the government regulatory authorities, who are really there do deal with the crooks who have been occasionally in the business.

I've found families to be very supportive of the equity concept of ownership and actually encouraging their parents and older members into these types of facilities. The issue there for a long time in the life care contract, where a flat sum was paid up front and was forfeited at death, was that it obviously worked against the interests of the remaining family who were going to lose some piece of inheritance. The more modern plan of providing for some return of the buy-in if the resident dies within a certain number of years, or some other means where there will be a return of the benefit to the family in the event of a premature death, seems to have solved that, although, again, the greed factor does come in. The materials need to explain why this is an advantage. I've had less problem with the family than with the resident, because we are dealing with older people, and their demands may not be as rational as one would hope that they would be.

Challenge and Opportunity

Well, the first one is that, unlike almost any other style of construction project, this type has no end. You build it, and in most states (California in particular), the developer needs to sign a continuing care guarantee, and is responsible for the project basically in perpetuity. The developer is going to probably not have a high profit margin on the initial buy-in, and the profit comes over a period of resales because, in most of the developments that I've seen, some part of the appreciation or value of the project is recouped every time that the project turns over. So, this is not going to be a get-rich-quick scheme. It's going to take some personal involvement because, obviously, in order to maximize the value of the project, you have to have satisfied residents who are communicating that this is a good place to live, this is a good community to join. Then there will be a market and, perhaps, a waiting list, which will let the price of the units appreciate, assuming that a good portion, if not all of the appreciation, is going to accrue to the benefit of the developer.

This is also a fast-moving market. There are more and more projects coming on-line, and the question is: Are we going to end up with too many projects and not enough people, or are we going to end up with too many people and not enough projects? We assume that the former, at least at some point in the future, will come true. To be modern and upscale and to meet the needs that are going to be identified 10 and 20 years from now is a real issue. I think definitely there is going to be a different kind of client for these institutions, but it's going to work to the advantage of the institutions. Ten years ago, in my own practice, I would meet with people who were in their late 70s—not old by a practical definition, so much as old by any outside vista—with whom I would raise the idea of moving into some kind of a congregate living facility and the answer was, "Oh, no. I'm not old enough." By the time these people got old enough, they were no longer mobile enough to move into these facilities and, therefore, ended up in skilled nursing or some kind of a very institutional environment.

When Should You Move?

Certainly, my experience in the last 3 to 5 years has been that younger people are willing to consider the move to some kind of life care community because we are all experiencing more and more old people in our lives as longevity increases. As people spend more time in retirement, we're seeing the people in their 80s and 90s who are still alive, and who are not capable of being independent. Whereas, 10 years ago, the clients I would suggest congregate living to would say, "Oh, no. I'm not nearly old enough. I'll talk about it in 5 or 10 years." The same clients today will still tell me they're not old enough but they're going to look at it in a year or two. The time horizon of the recognition of the need for providing security for true old age is there. I listened to a gerontologist not too many years ago talk about old age, and he said the biggest mistake any of us make . . . we think that age 65 is the traditional measurement of old age. His position was that 65 is the beginning of mature middle age, and you're really not old until 80. And when we look at people in their early 80s, they're still active. It's in the mid to latter part of the 80s that we're seeing the decline.

The thing I'm impressed about amongst my client base is that very few of them, as they grow older, want to live a particularly long time. They want to live healthily as long as they can live. I think one of the attractions of the CCRCs is that the statistics all seem to indicate that people living in a somewhat protected environment, where nutrition, medical needs, recreational needs, and activity levels are maintained on a higher level, do tend to have more years of an active participatory life than people who live alone and for whom the burdens of cooking meals become significant, and Wheaties three times a day is the meal of choice.

The personal relationship between the older person and the physician or medical provider is critical. I think, particularly in California, the day of the small medical practice has gone. The challenge for the medical industry and for CCRC operators is to find in the HMO style of practice, in the large clinic practice, a way to have a relationship between the patient and some provider. We're beginning to see, in some of the HMOs, a nurse practitioner becoming that personal connection who can spend the time giving help and advice and express concern. One of the huge advantages that CCRCs can provide is that they can build a more personal practice amongst older people within the walls, and my vision is that we will see in the next 10 years, at least in the larger communities and perhaps by banding together some of the smaller communities, a practice that will emerge designed specifically for people in the institution. Obviously, the challenge is going to be that most residents, when they move into the institution, don't want to, at the same time, change their medical care provider. I believe that will change over the next 5 years as the medical care provider becomes less personal. There will not be the bonds of loyalty, and it will be easier to provide care on a personal basis within the institution.

This goes back to the whole concept of continuing care. Most of my clients today don't want to die in an institutional setting. They want to die in some kind of a residential setting. Obviously, we can't provide that always in somebody's own home or in their own apartment in a congregate living facility, but it is important to provide hospice-type care in the last days or hours within the institution, and to have the provision for having family close, which means some kind of guest rooms, if family is coming from a distance, so that the family can be together in those cases where there is family who is still interested in doing that. In cases where there is not, it may be provided in an institutional setting that feels like a private home setting. I keep being surprised at how few of my older clients really fear death as much as they fear the loneliness and isolation of impending death. So, finding a way to care for people in their last days and weeks surrounded by a caring community is something that is a real challenge to the developer today.

Food Service

Probably the one major issue, and it should be obvious, and it should be unimportant, but it takes a major role in every situation I've seen, and that's food service. I think as I look at my older clients, food becomes a more and more important part of the daily routine—(a) you've got to eat and (b) you get your energy up for those mealtimes. And, so, to create both an ambiance in a dining room facility and, secondly, to provide food that is attractive and gets compliments, rather than the institutional food, are important issues for any developer. I've heard more complaints about food service throughout the industry from clients of mine than almost any single other issue, and so I think any developer needs to give a lot of thought to how they're going to create an environment for food service and then provide quality food that is attractively presented and enjoyed by the residents.

I am thinking here of two clients of mine who live in the same facility (both of whom are frail elderly), one of whom, at least according to her, is on doctor's orders to minimize fat and calories, and wants everything cooked very plain and very bland. The other is a gentleman who really only likes to eat steaks with baked potatoes and sour cream for dinner. There is no way that a limited menu provides both, and, yet, one of them is going to be unhappy. I can always tell when the food service has changed in the residence where they live, because I will get a call and a complaint from one of them that either the food is too fat or the food is too lean, and that tension is going to be there. Whether we have vanilla ice cream or chocolate ice cream is a major issue. I sat through a homeowner/resident council meeting where the big question was what three flavors of ice cream should they stock because that was all that the freezers would hold, and they could not agree on which three flavors.

Working with Residents

How well the operator and the board work together is very much dependent not only who is on the board, but the skill of the operator of the facility in managing those meetings so that the residents do have the feeling that they're being listened to and responded to, that there are answers to the issues, but not to let the resident council meetings become just gripe sessions where one gripe after another is listened to. The most successful operator I ever saw do this was one that had the list of gripes presented, had the resident council rate them, and then list them in priority. That took a lot of time, during which we couldn't hear new gripes. But the commitment was that the operator of the facility, then, would try to deal with the top three each week, and each meeting began with a report on the success of resolving the last three. There was a feeling of shared power. There was a feeling of shared enterprise. There was a feeling of accomplishment and, yet, the little complaints that were isolated by residents never made it to the top of the stack. That was not the operator's doing; it was the residents' council itself beginning to monitor the complaint level.

Activities

I think for many residents, the most important thing is the availability of activities, not the participation, and the fact that there are five things on the agenda that one can do. If one chooses not to do any of them, that's okay. I don't think new activities are terribly desirable for older people. They like the tried and true. They enjoy doing the things that they've done through their life, and to have them available and not to worry about participation is the key. But to show a variety—the walking club, one of the easiest things to put on, has proved to be one of the more popular amongst my clients, at least. It may only be around the block, but there's a group doing it together, so it's not lonely. And, most certainly, the card games and the movies and anything that gets people together to share space (as long as they serve food) will keep the residents happy.

The Carlisle, San Francisco

The Cypress of Charlotte: Residential cottage

The Cypress of Charlotte: **Apartment units**

4.0 Marketing and Sales

James Coleman observes that, in the early stages, dealing with high-risk equity cash, we spend a disproportionate amount of money on marketing. We spend the absolute minimum on planning, architectural services, and construction estimating, and put most of our resources into marketing or we don't have a project.

■ Marketing Experience

It's not hard to find good salespeople. They can learn the product. They need to be full-time, just on that project. There's one master community developer I know of who is trying to market a CCRC by using its regular sales force. It has a planned unit development with a multiple product sales force and it's trying to get the sales force to sell the CCRC as well as the other products and it's just not working. Why? Because those second home and home site sales happen quickly. The CCRC sale is much slower with lots of hand-holding and nurturing. We pay a salary with a bonus per sale and everybody's on the same team. If you've got three salespeople, they all make the same amount of money per team sale. If a sale is made, they all get the same commission, because it is very common to be dealing with somebody else's client. The last thing you want is a salesman thinking, "You're not my client and I'm in a hurry to get rid of you." Good salespeople need to be patient. It is a hand-holding, long-term relationship. Traditionally, the best profile is a woman in her 40s or 50s because that's about the age of the daughters of the people we deal with. We've been very successful with two men on our sales force. In Charlotte, right now we've got two men and one lady and the two guys are great, they're mature. Most 25–35-year-olds are a little too anxious. Because you've got to sit there and talk and you've got to listen. This market loves to just talk about things that aren't related to the sale. They just want to talk, and you've got to have patience.

We do our own marketing. It is the most critical part and I really am hands-on. Everything else will fall into place. Everything else can happen in time, but nothing happens unless you've got the sales. I conduct the focus-group interviews. I lay out and write the brochures and the ads. I write the direct mail letters. From focus groups, we advance to presentations. Now come see what you've decided you want us to do. And we present it that way. "Thank you for coming to our focus groups and now we unveil what you told us you want." We bring that core group along. We let them feel part of planning the community. They appreciate that. And you get some real leaders because the key to this thing is referrals. After you get that core group, it's referrals that's going to make it work. And the profiles of the people that live there. Every chance we got, we would list our members in the newspaper. "Thank you to the Founding Group," and we'd list them. (We'd always ask their permission.) During fill-up, we list who's moving here once every quarter. We run an ad saying: "The following people have moved to *The Cypress*" and list their name and hometown. I think it has to start with a local group. Now, about half our people are from Hilton Head, and about half are from other places. Usually, there's a Hilton Head connection for them. Either friend or family member. Maybe their children live on Hilton Head. In our first wave, however, of the first 150, about 85% were from Hilton Head, because they knew us, trusted us, and would buy it in the predevelopment stages. It's really difficult to get secondary markets to buy in the predevelopment stage. So, you've got to start with that local core group. And they're usually within a 5-mile radius of your project. You know who they are, you sit down with them, and you try to convince them to sign up early.

The penetration rate for CCRCs in every market is very low. We almost lost the project because we sputtered in our presales. Hilton Head is a relatively small market. I mean, it's a small town here. The population is only 30,000. It's nice to be in Charlotte now with a million person metropolitan area. There's another community on Hilton Head that has copied us that stubbornly proceeded without adequate presales and opened with less than half their units sold in their first phase. They're running a lot of red ink. We did everything we could to try and convince them not to go ahead, because we didn't want them as competition, but we also knew they would fail because this is a small market. Sure enough, they built it, spent a lot of money, and they're struggling. That's because of the low penetration rate that CCRCs currently get. Even in Charlotte, there wouldn't be enough room for two of us right now. We got 120 contracts there in our first 5 months of formal sales. This is a very fast pace that will probably drop down to a rate of six to eight per month.

What happened to us here was that we went over 2 years with our premarketing. We signed up people and then 2 years later, we were still premarketing. One of the reasons for that was the terrible recession in 1990. That was really a tough real estate recession, and people got scared that they couldn't sell their homes. Also, we probably didn't push it fast enough in hindsight. We already had the property and no interest clock running. We needed 100 sales for the bank construction loan. We had a groundbreaking ceremony with about 85 sales. We didn't really have what we needed to start, but we had to act because people started saying, "It's been 2 years, and you haven't started yet. I've gotta do something." So, we had to make it happen or not, so we forced it. My mother bought a unit and we got some of the investors to sign up for a home, and we somehow came up with enough to satisfy the bank and start. It was nice and steady after that. Six years later, we've got 320 units here, and we've sold them all.

We've got about 80 people on our waiting list. We ask people to give us $1,000 refundable, $100 nonrefundable. We ask them to be within at least 3 years of moving in and to go ahead and fill out all the paperwork and qualify. So, they're doing something. Some waiting lists are too easy. To understand how meaningful a waiting list is, you need to understand what salespeople are saying. Our people are pretty good, because they don't want to overload it. With 80 people on the waiting list, sixteen different plans and prices, from $160,000 to over $700,000, we still might get something that nobody on this waiting list wants right now. Usually, anything that comes up can be placed right off the waiting list.

A Lesson Learned

What have we learned? For marketing, we learned to really analyze the focus groups, to really find out how sincere people were. One risk in this business is that you get a lot of cheerleaders. You must watch that because everybody wants it to happen because they might need it someday. So, everybody's going to say, "Well, that's a good idea." And then you say, "Are you ready to sign up?" "Oh, I'm not ready yet. But I want you to build it, because I might be ready in 5 or 10 years." And those people are helpful, but they don't help you get your presale requirements. So, you can really fool yourself, and I've seen developers fall into that trap. First of all, you've got to make sure they're 75 and not 55. Or they're not 65. Because they're not ready at 65. If they're 75 and 80 and they're saying that, then that's one thing. But if they're 50 and 60, 65 years old and saying that, then they aren't going to buy from you for 10 years, may not help anybody. So, you have to be careful there.

■ The Sales Challenge

Speaking from what has been learned at *The Stratford*, the president of Raiser Senior Services answers the question: What do residents want?

Well, before they move in, they want what was spoken about in marketing. After they move in, they couldn't care less about marketing. Once they've bought, they don't really care if anyone else buys. They want to make sure they're getting what they perceive they were promised in marketing. Another comment back to marketing is, make sure anything you put in writing, you're prepared to live with for the next 15 years. Because they will save it, and even if it's unreasonable, even if it changes the cost structure, if you promised it, if you said anywhere in writing or even verbally that you will do this, it'll come back to you. And a court's always going to take the resident's point of view.

That's why you'd better trust your salespeople. That's why you're better off involving your salespeople in the process. It's very hard to work on commission if you have a 2-year time span to make each sale. You're going to get bored and frustrated before that ship comes in. And, second, you need to understand that the typical buttons that you push with a younger person are often antithetical to what you want to do with the elderly. They want to take a lot of your time, they want you to hear their life story, they want you to give them the features that they feel they need, only when they're ready to talk about it. If you're a good used car salesperson, you're going to be a terrible continuing care salesperson. Our best luck with salespeople has actually been with people who are outside the industry who have had some sense of business and sales but who aren't necessarily directly in sales. Our worst experience has been with people who sold straight real estate, because this transaction is so different. It masquerades as a normal real estate transaction but, in fact, it's a health care and relationship transaction, and it takes much, much longer, and the commission structure is different, and the legal requirements are different.

You want a salesperson to be able to make between $30,000 and $60,000 a year, all totaled. Whether you do that with a base structure, plus incentive, or if you do straight commission, you need to have enough of a flow. Salespeople are not marketing people. Salespeople are not going to go out and get leads to come through the door. Your marketing has to do that. Your special events have to do that. Your ads have to do that, as much as they can. Word of mouth. Salespeople are going to take care of your prospects once they walk through the door, but you need to assure them of a steady enough flow to make that compensation even viable. The worst thing you can do is have a revolving door of salespeople. The best thing you can do is have the same person there who is good, and who doesn't misrepresent you year after year after year, so that people know they can come and find the person that they became comfortable with. Our experience with another facility we manage is that having to reestablish those relationships with new prospects lost us some time and, I think, lost us some prospects. We were in a position in that case where we had to replace the salespeople because they were misrepresenting the product. There was no question they had to go, so we chose the lesser of two evils, but it's been a hard reestablishment of our sales momentum because of that.

You can't let go of the marketing, even when you're sold out. You have to figure out how you're funding your marketing because even when you're full, you've got to be like the butter company in World War II; you've got to be advertising, even when there's no product available. So that when rationing stops, everybody goes and buys your butter. And, you know, I think our friends in the industry have discovered that. I know of one facility that now has seventeen units on the market. And they were fat and happy for a while because they were all sold out. No one had anything to worry about, and so everyone forgot about investing in the future. When they started, and there was no one else in town, their waiting list was easy, because all they had to do was call someone and say, "We have a unit," and it filled up. Now, everybody goes and checks us out, they check them out, they go and look at the alternatives. It's a lot harder. Your product is older. We learned from their product, so we improved on their product. We figured out what the customer most liked about their product, and someone's going to figure out what the customer most likes about our product and one-up us. The most recent kid on the block is going to be the standard by which everyone judges. So, our challenge here in an ongoing operation is to maintain and improve a level of service to remain competitive.

There are really two competitive groups in marketing: our competitors in the industry, and then our true competitors—peoples' houses. Because that's what prospects are really considering. They're not fighting, "Oh, do I love this CCRC or the one across town?" They're fighting, "Our daughter was married in our backyard. My dogs are all buried under the oak tree. How can I leave this home?" Even though it's probably impractical. Emotionally, the prospects are not tied into the senior CCRC market; emotionally, they're tied into their 151 Smith Way. That's what matters to them. Their sense of identity. And that competitor you can't beat. You just have to continue to show how your product is a viable alternative to their house. Not better. Nobody is going to have a better experience in their mind in a retirement community versus in their house. Because in their house, they're young, they have children who are young, they're driving their kids to school and their husband to the train. In reality, in a retirement community, they're old. People do things for them. Their friends are dying. There are people on walkers. Nobody wants to admit that they're old enough to qualify for a retirement community. So, you have to show them—you have to be the first one on their doorstep with flowers after the big storm has knocked the tree over into their house (which we have done) and deliver meals to them because their kitchen was totally wrecked by the storm. Or, when we hear that they have had minor surgery, we invite them to come and stay, at marketing's expense, in our assisted-living wing, to show them how, if they're laid up, they're going to be better off in a place where people wait on you hand and foot than in their house, where they have to hire a cleaning lady and someone to come and bring meals, and so on.

We take a percentage of the sales and the resales. We just take a flat percentage, and then a piece of that commission goes into a marketing fund. We know how much to spend every year. Initially, it came out of the developer's pocket, because what you need to spend on initial sales is far greater than on resales, just because of the volume.

Sales Strategy

John Raiser suggests that part of the challenge is that we are trying to provide residents with a support system that nobody wants to admit they need.

That is where marketing and sales has to be very sensitive not to push features that we know are there, like grab bars or pull cords.

Everybody acknowledges in the back of their minds, "Oh, it's a nice feature," but most seniors do not want to talk about it. And this is where we have found that commercial real estate agents that are very successful in selling single-family homes and condominiums have been true failures in marketing senior communities. Many communities started by developers will hire one well-known real estate agency after another. They advertise life-style; they advertise all types of things, but they are not successful because they are not addressing the scary issues that nobody wants to talk about. Also, most sales take years to conclude, and residential real estate brokers get paid when they close a sale. They generally are not inclined to follow a sale for several years.

The CCRC salesperson is looked on as a consultant or a confidant. Here a rapport develops. The long-term manager of the project must be sold to the prospective client: "We know your reputation. We know you're not a typical developer that will build and sell out and go and build another project. You will be here to take care of me when I need that walker to get around in, and I can rely on you." That reputation has a lot to do with the decision. Sometimes, the decision can be made by the residents themselves, who have always been independent, who often rationalize that "I don't want my children to take care of me," or, if they don't have children, "I don't want the society to take care of me. I'll make my own decisions." The other group brings children into the picture, and the children say, "We want the very best for Mom and Dad, and we want them to have all the support that's available." And after looking at all the various facilities, they make a choice. We have another group of children that say (even though it is not articulated), "We want Mom and Dad to be here, because we don't want to or are not able to take care of them ourselves." Some of them live far away, some travel a lot, and they don't want the responsibility of taking care of the elderly, as opposed to the old European concept of the elderly always transferring the real estate and part of the unwritten code was that you take care of the elderly as they age in the same house and in exchange you get free housing that you will eventually inherit. In our society, the government does not want family assets to go from one generation to the next, so they impose heavy death taxes. These make it difficult to follow the European model. So, it's a matter of sorting out who is making the decision and what the motives are for the decision.

Selling to perception and selling reality—you really do need to think about both. I think that's very relevant. A guy from United Airlines was talking about how it needs to revise its staff point of view from the customer perspective. On-time arrival and getting your baggage are the price of admission, whereas some of the folks at United still think: "Hey, it's great. We actually had an on-time departure and an on-time arrival. And look—all the bags arrived!" They don't understand that that's no longer a variable. It's immutable, and when you don't do that, you have violated the deepest trust of your customer. And I think with marketing and sales, we have to look at things from that point of view, too. There are certain things you absolutely have to have that the customer expects. You have to have a certain level of health care service. You have to have decent enough food. You have to have a basic spectrum of services. And then what you may do on top of that makes you distinctive or different—your food is particularly good, or your units are especially large, or you have certain features that no one else has—valet parking, or whatever. Just like when I'm flying United, I'm buying a plane that leaves on time, a plane that gets there on time, and a plane that delivers my luggage with me. So, I'm buying that whole package of health care, food, and services. But what gets me excited is not health care, food, and services; it's sort of like—I need those things, it's like buying underwear. You've got to do it, but it's very hard to get excited about something that you're just going to wear out and need to buy again.

What we need to think about are the other things that spin the business that people get excited about. The gourmet kitchens in the units are a good example. Nobody needs them, nobody uses them. But they're very important as a marketing tool. Swimming pool. Very few people use it—but you've got to have it. People ask all about it in the marketing phase, and then a few people actually decide to use it. One of our biggest challenges at our other facility, the one we didn't build, is that people have those little Pullman kitchens with one burner and a microwave, no oven, and a mini-fridge. Although it is quite adequate for their actual needs, numerous people either reject the kitchen as not big enough or spend the $15,000 to upgrade to full-size appliances in their kitchen because they think they're going to need a full kitchen when they move to a retirement community. And then, they don't use it. A lot of people say, once they move in, "Oh, that was so stupid; why did I do that?" But before they moved in, it was psychologically crucial to them to be able to move into some place that they had control of.

The whole marketing and sales idea is about giving the customer control. You want to have a panoply of things that are available, so that people feel they still have control of their destiny. That's why people don't like to hear about activities programs. Even though, when they get here, they actually enjoy them, they don't want to think that someone's going to be marching them off to the symphony or to crafts class or stuff that they wouldn't normally have done when they lived in their house. So, a lot of what you're selling in your marketing situation, and then in your sales, are features. You know, in sales, they're talking a lot about real estate features of the property. They don't spend a lot of time talking about long-term health care because no one wants to think about that, even though they need to know it's there. It's kind of this dichotomy.

The other problem with marketing is the notion of truthfulness. If I see one more community marketed as a luxury retirement community, I'm going to scream, because your version of luxury may be whipped cream on the pudding, and another person's version of luxury may be only fresh clotted cream on out-of-season raspberries. That term is used flagrantly, and it's really lost its meaning. People are always saying, "the premier retirement community," "the finest retirement community," "elegant, luxurious, country club living." And there's truly no honest basis of comparison in the customer's head. They go and they see it. The advertising is all inflated. There is no control over the advertising. It's one of the least regulated industries. I don't think you could get away with saying the things about retirement communities that they do now if this were detergent, where you have to prove that it's "better, whiter, cleaner." You have to demonstrate versus the competition. Nobody does that here. They just slyly slam the competition in terms of their financial structure. The equity places say, "Why give them all your money, and not get it back?" The deposit places say, "Why tie up all your assets in real estate? Why not enjoy it now?" And so everyone's got an angle, and I don't think the customer understands the true difference. I think the customer ends up making the decision primarily on how does the place feel, how does it look, and is it going to reflect well on me that I have chosen to live there? So, the customer looks at peer cohorts. What are the other residents like? If there are too many wheelchairs lined up, too many walkers, the customer is not coming because he or she doesn't want to be seen as joining the old folks group.

That's why peer marketing is the best. It's the best advertising. But, peers don't want to appear to be making money off their friends, so they won't give you referrals. What they'll do is, if their friend is interested, they'll march the friend down to the salesperson and say, "Why don't you show my friend Margaret what you have available?" I think people talk a lot about decision influencers, but the influencers rarely make the decision. People make this decision on their own for themselves. Their influencers can quash the decision, but they never make the decision for them. Their children say, "Mom, that's a stupid idea," or "Mom, that's a good idea." But that's as far as it goes. The mother makes this decision because this is one of the last vestiges of control in her life. So, even though you have to be mindful of keeping a good market image for the children, marketing to the children is a waste of money and time, from my experience. The majority of children really can't make their mother do something against her wishes.

Social Functions

Our experience shows that giving people opportunities to visit the property in a nonthreatening manner is what really does the trick. For years, we've had garden club groups, benefit functions, and charity boards using our meeting rooms. We have hosted a number of events that you would never consider marketing events, and we really make sure the place looks good. We see these events as a way to get people in the door, in a way that people never think they are being marketed to. Because what they got was to see the premises. They were never sure who at the parties were residents and who were guests, and that was always very good, too. We always try to make sure and mix those up so that the group is very vibrant and happy to be here. When we do an event, it's all hands on deck, so that we actually have our director of human resources, our executive director, the director of marketing, as many salespeople as we have on staff, the developer, everybody making sure the event is a success. So guests don't know who lives here, who works here, and who's just visiting. Then, afterwards, we'd have these come together meetings where we'd report and sort of figure out, "All right, who, of all the people we spoke to, very indirectly, are potential prospects, even 10 years down the road? What did we learn? How could we use that?" Then try to cultivate them from there.

The nice thing about having a social function here is that there will be name tags or you'll be working with the group, and someone always comes up to you and expresses an interest. You'll be talking about something else, and they'll interrupt and say, "You know, I'd love to see more around here. Could you show me?" You make a point of learning their name or finding someone you know who knows who they are and just writing it down. You just never let them leave without at least learning who they are. And our experience at both communities has been very much the same. We did an open house last week and we said on the invitation: "Please come and view unsold units at your leisure. There will be no sales presentation." And we got a very good turnout. I'm convinced that's because people had a chance to come and sort of poke in the closets and look around without feeling that they were going to be trapped before they left. People are comfortable with that format because they think they're anonymous, which they like.

Marketing and the Enterprise Team

So, that's marketing and sales. The one other comment I would make is that the integration of marketing and sales into the enterprise team is most essential. It's obvious, but when sales-people are left to their own devices, they're expected to sell, and oftentimes they will sell by hook and by crook. And you're doing them and yourselves and the community a great disservice if you don't have them involved in all the aspects of the planning and all the problems that emerge from the planning so that they're up to date, so that they aren't the last person to hear about construction delays, so that they're not busy selling a feature that nobody actually wants. And then you can revise the plans and figure it out. We learned so much during our pre-marketing phase about features that people didn't care for. We thought people would get very excited about the wet bars in each unit. People were less excited than we thought, whereas bidets were something that we did not include in every unit and everybody asked for, which surprised us. Bidets in retirement communities in this country are just not standard. But they turned out to be a feature people wanted. We had a hard time retrofitting, but have put them in.

The developer and the operations people were involved in marketing from the start. It was always expected that anyone working on the project was also doing marketing; so that our architect, our construction manager, they were at marketing events, and they were meeting with the guests, and guests knew they could come and talk to them about, you know, "Is our mural going to go up on time?" "How do we look on the schedule?" You got people very, very involved in the process, and it made the work much more relevant to the professionals doing it who, oftentimes, never see a resident until opening day. I think it really worked for marketing because people thought, "Hey, this is real. There's that big, beefy guy with the hard hat that I normally see on-site. He's here with a coat and tie telling me how my unit's going to look, and he knew about my change order, and he knew about my paint color, and he knew exactly what was going on with my unit."

The other thing we felt was important in marketing and, in retrospect, might not have been, was the degree of customization. We felt that when people are paying the kind of prices we were requiring at *The Stratford*, that they would want almost completely free rein. With the exception of plumbing and electrical, they were able to move walls and do all kinds of things, which cost a lot of money, much more money than it cost to do the construction. "Oh, you want a butler's pantry? You want your shower to be positioned in a certain way? Certainly." I think we could have left it down to a few cabinets, carpeting, a lot of features that we didn't have to move mountains to fix. Now, on the up side, we learned a couple of the customizations that people did do were brilliant, and we ended up using them in other parts of the building. People thought of moving walls because they wanted a certain pattern and flow in their space. So we ended up having the flexibility to do that because we saw their plans. Complete customization was something we incorrectly thought was an important first-time feature. In resales, people don't have much of a choice, so it doesn't matter to them, and we should have taken that point of view from the initial sales perspective.

■ Sales Attitude

The Cypress director of sales tells us she was hired first as the move-in coordinator about a year before construction started.

So I started calling all these folks and trying to set up appointments and make arrangements to get together, to talk about changes that they wanted to make. In the apartments, we tried to limit changes, because when you're building 109 apartments and you're trying to get it done in 1 year, it makes it very difficult to also worry about lots of changes. We built fifty-five cottages in Phase I and that really turned into a custom home project. When these folks met with us, that meant this was real. It's one thing to sign a contract and know that you're going to do something like this, but also know that it's in the future. Then you have to meet with us, and it means it's really happening. And we've got to make our decisions.

    The salespeople would say to me, "Oh, I can't wait for you to meet Mr. Smith! He's just so nice." Well, when Mr. Smith met with me, his defenses were up. Some of those people that I was expecting to be real easy to work with were difficult. You get a completely different personality when it's becoming a reality to them. And so I met with them for a year, we built their homes, and I developed a real strong relationship with most of these people. It's a real hard decision. I don't care if you're moving to the best community in the country, it is a very difficult decision for these people. They feel that they're giving up something, their independence. I find that men have a harder time. It's sort of like giving up driving to a man when you're moving out of your home and into a continuing care community. That little step of giving up some of their independence. Then once they move in, it's a completely different story. They're thrilled to be here, and they're very thankful that they're here. And sometimes they have a health crisis, and they're saying, "Oh, my gosh! What if we had waited?" So once they've made the move, they're okay. But it's just getting them over that psychological hurdle.

I believe that they really did not become comfortable until after they had moved in. For one reason, they're trying to sell their homes at the same time that they're thinking about moving here. I say to people all the time that I don't care how many times you've moved in your lifetime, moving to a continuing care community is tough. And when you're older, if you're 75 or older, everything's hard. They're calling and they're saying, "Oh my gosh, they're over here today and they're checking for termites. What happens if they find termites?" "Well, if they find termites, they'll take care of it." They just need hand holding. And it really isn't until after they move in that I see them take that nice easy breath.

Qualifying

We have a confidential membership application that they're required to complete, even if they're only going on the waiting list. And so that helps us to see what they can afford. We look to see that their monthly income is around 2.5 to 3 times the monthly fee. That helps them determine what type of unit they can afford. If their monthly income is adequate, I don't worry too much about their assets. But if their monthly income is adequate, probably they're going to have the assets. I find that most people sell their homes and buy a unit here that is of equal value to the home that they sold. Sometimes they'll go up, but usually they buy pretty much at the same price level.

Occasionally, people do not qualify financially. That's really hard for me, because I become very involved with my clients. I develop a relationship with them, so that they'll depend on me to help them out in making a decision. And I try to qualify them early on in the relationship. But just yesterday, I had a woman who came in, and she had said on the phone that her husband died a few months ago, and I had been working with them as a couple. And they had lost a lot of money. He had not invested wisely. So she told me that she wanted to come over and take a look at a one-bedroom apartment. And she was really good. I mean, this is unusual, but she had filled out a little sheet so that I could see exactly what her expenses were monthly, and what her income was monthly, and I helped her with her assets. I didn't just come out and say to her, "You cannot afford the Cypress." It's going to be close. But she was also making comments on her own. "Well, I'm just not sure if this is for me. I don't know if I want to leave my home yet." So it may work out so that I don't have to say anything.

When qualifying, we just want the assurance that they can afford an inflation increase every year, and that they could afford the extra cost if one of them is in the Health Center.

Promoting the Product

The thing that becomes so evident is how responsible you are. This is serious stuff. This is not running a real estate agency. These are more than clients. They are your ethical and fiduciary responsibility.

We've been open for 5 years, and now we have homes that are selling at an increase in value that's enough to cover the 10% membership fee, and also the 7% real estate commission. That's 17% in 5 years, and some people are making a little over that. I explain that our monthly fees basically cover the operations of the community, to include all the services that we offer, and that they increase about 2.5% a year. We had one year where they didn't increase at all.

When I meet with folks, I look at myself as an educator. I'm educating these people as to what a continuing care community is, and I try to make it real clear that the folks who live here are very independent. For the people who come from Hilton Head, I'd say, "Look, you can continue your volunteer work. You can keep your friends. Really, you're only changing your address." And so that's helpful, I think, to them. We can get younger people. Our average age is really about 75 or 76. That's pretty young. We've got an unusual number of couples, also. I think that's because we've got a hundred acres here, and it is spread out. People think about walking over to the clubhouse from their apartment. We don't have covered walkways, so it's not like an institution in any way. When you can get that across to them, it doesn't hurt quite so much to make that decision. I'm pretty detailed, so I don't get people coming back to me and saying, "Why didn't you tell me this?" Or, " I wish I had known that." Instead, they say, "You happen to have a home that we like available. We'll go ahead and buy it." I'm sure in the back of their mind, they're thinking, "Oh isn't it great? They've got a nursing facility." But that's not upper-most in their mind. It's getting into a community that they know is debt-free and has all the positive aspects that we have. More than having a health crisis of any kind. A lot of these folks have enough money that it's not a concern to them, really, that we include 90 days at no extra charge in the Health Center. It's not a concern to them; they think they could get somebody to come over as an assistant in their home if it was needed. It's the life-style that they're buying here, as much as anything.

As much as I talk about the nursing facility—there's a peace of mind that comes with living in a community like this, because there is a nursing home on-site—I really think that people have a hard time admitting that this is why they'd be moving to a continuing care community. In their minds, they're thinking, "I'm tired of the yard work, tired of worrying about whether the sprinkler system is going to blow up, or I'm going to have to replace the roof." Things like that. It's easier for them to say to themselves or to somebody else, "I just like the life-style. I just want a free and easy life-style. I don't want to worry about all the little house things. I want to be able to close my door and go away for 3 weeks, and know that someone will walk through my home once a week, and take care of everything."

I always think it's interesting to talk to people who are involved with the life care communities because we include 90 days in the Health Center at no extra charge for our members, and many times I get people who are considering either a nursing home insurance policy or moving to *The Cypress*. So I tell them, it's all well and good if you have a nursing home insurance policy. That's great. It gets expensive as your age increases, but the big question is: Where are you going to go? If you have to go to a nursing home, what nursing home are you going to use? The they say, "I guess I really should move to *The Cypress*." Then I explain to them that 20% of our residents will need to use the nursing facility on a permanent basis. When I say permanent, I'm thinking in terms of a year or more. The rest of our residents will only need the nursing home 60 to 90 days in their lifetime. And that's why we include that as part of the monthly fee. So then I look at these people who are selling life care communities, and folks are paying $200,000 as an entrance fee which they lose. If they need to be in that nursing home for 4 or 5 years, that could be financially devastating.

A Collaboration

We keep ourselves open to suggestion, and I think that's really important. Because the residents own this community, they need to feel that we listen to them, and we need to listen to them. They have so much to offer! These folks are very intelligent. They've all been in business, and they know the ropes. We have a few who have their fax machines, and many of them have computers. Some have copiers, the works, an office in their home. Maybe 15%. It's not a huge percentage. They may do some consulting.

For those interested in governance, I explain that the property owners' board of directors is not truly a governing board. They can make a good number of decisions on anything that would be considered a condominium expense: landscaping, pest control, insurance, all the things that you might pay if you lived in a condominium. Yes, those items they have a little more control over, and they certainly have a hand in looking to the future. We've got so many bright people here. You've got people who can make wonderful suggestions for the activities director, and every aspect of the community is covered. The younger clients that we appeal to—when I say younger, I'm thinking in terms of 67—are a little bit more demanding. They want to be more involved—much more involved. I think when you're older, let's say, 72 or 73, just those few years, I think you're more needs driven.

A Responsibility to Members

I have a responsibility to the members. And yes, I'm paid well, and I'm glad of that, but my responsibility is definitely to the members. If it looks as though you're going to need to live in the Health Center permanently, then you can list your condominium and get it sold. As soon as it closes, you're no longer responsible for the monthly fee. However, you retain your membership status, and so you continue to pay member rates in the Health Center. If I have a listing agreement, and I have told these folks that I'm going to get their home sold for them, that's what I do. And my relationship is with the members. I don't care if I sell that one-bedroom apartment or that $700,000 home. That's what keeps me here, because I've been here for so long, and I have such strong feeling for the people who live here, and have sold most of them on the community. There are times when you think about leaving and doing something else. You think maybe there'd be something a little more challenging. I could never leave the people here. It's just, you're entrenched. I think anybody who's been here for a couple of years will say that.

The Cypress: **Cottage interior**

The Cypress: Bay Club cottage interior

5.0 Residents

This is where we consider what must be achieved on a day-to-day basis for each resident. To achieve their quality-of-life standards, *The Cypress* and *The Stratford* ensure that the receptionist is alert, the concierge anticipates events and needs, the dining room staff knows each resident's preferences for seating and service, and every staff member is taught to recognize changes in behavior or abilities that may be precursors. The housekeepers and maintenance staff accept the responsibility of knowing each resident and maintaining a comforting presence. The heart of *The Cypress* and *The Stratford* is the dining room, where both communities focus a great deal of attention on a first-class dining service program. Many residents and guests feel meals rival their area's finest restaurants. The directors of dining services, executive chefs, sous chefs, and kitchen and service staff are exceptional. The maintenance staffs are crucial, too. They are able to fix plumbing problems, repair electrical appliances, and mend broken furniture. They may build shelves or make other improvements in a resident's unit. On request, they check residents' automobile oil and water, check or recharge batteries. They fill in the blanks when residents ask for help.

■ An Exceptional Contributor

An exceptional contributor to life at *The Cypress* shared his experience with us. He begins with the view that what old used to be years ago isn't that old any more.

It is younger now. Middle age 20 years ago was different than middle age now. I mean, people in their early 60s and 70s are still very active. We have people here in their 80s that play golf every day and still play tennis. I think you're going to get more of that type of person, because people are taking better care of themselves.

I think it's a great concept. At any age, this would be great. We have three holes of golf here. You can just go out there and play. They have a little tournament out here every year and they play, you know, six holes or something. And it's great, because they can walk it. If it was a regular golf course, they couldn't walk it, but here they can walk. And if they get tired, they're not more than two holes from the clubhouse. They had a nice party here the other night. A croquet party, and the women were all dressed in these white dresses and it turned out real nice. They have a lot of nice parties here—4th of July cookouts and dances. There's always something to do. I think when people were interested in moving here, they filled out questionnaires and they put in things that these people were interested in.

What Residents Need

At a facility the size of *The Cypress* with this amount of people, you never know what's going to come up. It could be anything from a serious problem, an electrical problem, or just someone's personal problem. You do get a lot of personal requests—it could be anything from just helping someone open a bottle of pills or some type of food item, or helping them with their pets, or transportation problems. I remember not too long after we opened up, a couple had a golf outing and that evening they had a dinner dance. She had forgotten the gown she was going to wear that evening for this dance. They had already gotten down there and they were playing golf when they realized they had forgotten it. So they called up here and I drove the dress down there to them and returned the next day. It's meeting personal needs like that which is what we do. In another case, a woman thought she was going to have to have surgery and be in the hospital for few weeks. She lived here alone and she had a small dog that was basically the focal point of her life. She was worried to death about what was going to happen to this dog and she asked me if I would move into her house here and sleep in her bed so the dog could sleep with me. And we probably would have done it, but fortunately she didn't have to have the surgery. It's things like that that you would never even think of. If people are out for a bike ride and their tires are low, they don't have a tire pump, so we do that. Their batteries go dead because they don't drive their cars very often, so we jump-start them.

When people move in here, they have a lot of personal assistance and a lot of help because moving is quite a traumatic experience, and especially at this age. A lot of them have given up homes that they have lived in and raised their children in for years, and this is moving somewhere new and not really knowing what they are getting into. We all make it easier for them, the personnel here. We help them a great deal with personal items, with hanging pictures and making their homes here a smaller version of what they left behind. We just give a lot of personal attention. The best way that I can describe it, and the feeling that I get . . . I came from a small town in the Midwest where you kind of knew everyone and you get that feeling here. Because the clubhouse is the focal point of the campus, you get to know people on a personal, one-to-one level, and it's almost like a small-town atmosphere. You get to know their backgrounds, and they get to know something about you, and you're on a first-name basis, and it feels like that Mayberry type of atmosphere.

Learning the Job

I've been here a little over 5 years now. I started here about 2 weeks before they opened, so I really got to know everyone as they moved in. We didn't have too many major problems, but in the beginning, there's always growing pains you go through. And I think we handled those right away and people were happy with that, and I think that kind of made their life here happier and more enjoyable because they really didn't have any worries. It's basically like taking care of 300 homes. Anything that can go wrong can go wrong in a home. Before moving here, that was their responsibility and worry to take care of, and now they don't have to worry about anything. The concept here would be great at any age, even someone my age. It'd be great to live here because you always have friends to call up, to play golf with, to go to dinner with. There's always something to do. You make new friends. A lot of the single women here have bonded quite well and do things together on their own outside of *The Cypress*. *The Cypress* has a lot of activities and trips for them, but a lot of them have just formed their own little groups and go off to dinner together. It's great, especially for some of the members that have lost their husbands or wives. And, as you well know, it's a big relief for their children. They don't have to worry about them so much. Anyway, in my department, we basically do just about anything you can think of. If there's something wrong, we take care of it.

There aren't a lot of big remodeling requests because Jim and Mark foresaw a lot of those problems and addressed them initially and really worked with the people on a custom program and made those big changes before they even moved in. But a lot of the requests are for things like they want another telephone installed or maybe another television outlet put somewhere, or maybe some additional lighting. Some of them have eye problems and just don't see like they used to and they just need brighter lights, in the bathrooms and in the closets, especially. So additional lighting, things like that, that's basically it. Small items. And it's just usually things to enhance their units.

A Small-Town Atmosphere

This is a small-town atmosphere. You run into residents all the time. You ask them how they're doing and they'll tell you. They develop a bond with certain members of the staff here, and they say, "Oh, I want Mike to come take care of that." They may feel more comfortable with certain people, not that anyone couldn't do it; it's just that they feel comfortable with having familiar faces. A lot people trust me to go into their homes if they're not home. A lot of them will leave for the summer and go to the mountains or other areas that are a little cooler. I check on their homes on a regular basis, if they want me to, and I'll water their plants, or feed their animals, or anything. I've had people call me who have been out of town during a hurricane warning who wanted me to take their animals. And we'll do that. We'll do whatever it takes. That's our job and that's why we're here.

Giving Assistance

Some of the people that need some assistance will choose not to go to the Health Center but will either get a nurse's aide or a live-in aide to help them out. When people can't walk from the Villas to the Clubhouse, we'll pick them up, either in a car or we use a lot of golf carts around here. We bring them over for dinner. We have valet parking for them, so they really don't have to walk very far. Even to the Health Center and back, which is 100 yards, we'll pick them up and take them home. So they really don't have to struggle. Everything has been covered fairly well. Some people have a problem with their balance, so we'll go through their apartment and we'll sit down and talk to them and walk them through their apartments and see where the grab bars should be put. They might not need them when they first move in, but a few years down the road they find that they do need a grab bar to help them a little bit.

We Do It All

Tomorrow, for instance, we have to take an individual to Charleston, an individual to Savannah, and there's a group trip to Beaufort. People have asked us if we could drive them up the East Coast; they needed to get up there, but they didn't want to drive. We've done all that. We cover this with our staff some-how. We usually can work around it. We cover for each other. We have a transportation department and sometimes, like tomorrow, with three of them being gone, we'll use some of the maintenance people to cover. And we'll do the local doctors' visits and things like church. We have a bus to take people to church and we also use the cars, depending on how many people go. When we take people to the airport, we'll get the luggage out and get them to the check-in counter. We don't just drop them at the curb. We stay with them every step of the way.

In our maintenance and transportation departments, there are five to six employees and usually two or three work at a time. Our staff people have to be available 24 hours a day. We'll often stay until 8:30 at night to help out with the dinner transportation. Some people won't feel like coming to dinner, so they'll order their dinner and we deliver it to their door. If they need groceries, we'll take them to the grocery store. If they need a prescription, we'll go pick it up for them. Just about anything. We have quite a few pets, especially in the cottages. That to me would be a big selling point to move here, because a lot of people have had a pet all of their lives, and, as you know, pets really can help people extend their lives. If they have to go to the hospital for any type of emergency, we take care of their pets. We feed them and walk them and do anything they need. We'll take them to the vet, we'll take them to go get their hair cut, or anything. We have one specially trained hearing dog. His name is Alex, a golden retriever.

A lot of residents still drive their own cars. When we see a problem, someone talks to them, perhaps their children, and says, "Maybe it's time to think about getting rid of the car." It's tough sometimes for people to give up their car, but they really don't need a car here. Anywhere they want to go, we can take them. A few of the men go on a routine basis to the VA hospitals in Charleston and Savannah. We'll stay with them; usually it's an all-day thing. I think when you go to the VA hospital you get a number and you wait. We'll stay with them; it doesn't matter how long it takes.

Emergencies

We have had two hurricane evacuations and we really help our residents out a great deal. We went to Macon, Georgia, to a hotel we've contracted with. I think last time we had close to 100 rooms. We take medicine, pets, everything. We don't leave anyone behind. I am one of the last people to leave because some people don't leave when they're supposed to and you just can't leave them here because they all need help doing something, even if it's just getting luggage in the car or getting some information.

On the entrance door to every Villa, we have a little flipper, and every night the security man goes around and flips those up. As soon as the resident opens the door, it falls down. During the day, the housekeepers check on those and make a list of the ones that haven't dropped. If someone were to have an accident and be in there a while, we would know about it because we would know he or she hadn't left the Villa. If I'm working in someone's home and I think that I notice some type of change in the resident, I'll contact our Resident Service Director and suggest that she stop by and see them and see how things are going. Someone's condition can change quickly.

We have smoke detectors, and in every bathroom and in the master bedroom, we have an emergency switch on the wall. If they have an accident or need help in any way, they just pull that and it's wired into a computer in the Health Center at the nurses' station. It'll show their account number and health profile, so that the person responding knows what the problem may be. Their smoke detectors will go off if they forget things on the stove. I went to a call once and the smoke detector had gone off and there was stuff all over the walls and ceiling and I couldn't figure out what it was. They had boiled eggs and left it, and all the water boiled out and those eggs exploded.

If someone were to fall down, and I was in his home, I'm not allowed to try and pick him up. We have to call a nurse to come out right away and check him out. A lot of people fall down and there's nothing wrong with them, but you don't know for sure. And they can get kind of angry at times. It's harder not to pick them up then it is to pick them up, because they're embarrassed. But a nurse always has to come over and check them out, because they could be injured. Someone could break a hip and not even know it. That hasn't happened, but it can happen, and there's usually a reason they fell. Sometimes they have to go to the hospital and have some tests done. We have a good nursing staff. We use radios, so we can be in touch with anyone, any time, anywhere around the campus. Our transportation can get anywhere within a few minutes.

John Raiser notes that at *The Stratford*, every aspect of accessibility and emergency situations was considered.

Such things as emergency pull cords and two-way communication throughout the building are absolutely essential. When people choose a residence, they want to ignore these features until they need them, so we disguise them as architectural features—wall moldings as hand rails, that sort of thing. Things such as motion detectors in each residence have proven to be valuable in allowing independence and providing surveillance at the same time. If a resident is not feeling well, she's certainly entitled to her privacy—to stay at home, stay in bed, or just putter around the apartment. But if the motion detector does not detect motion in that apartment within a preset time—12 hours, let us say—we get an alarm bell and someone checks in on her, phones up, and says, "Mrs. Jones, how are you doing? Are you feeling okay?" If there is no answer, then a nurse goes in and checks.

■ Moving In

This is planned from the moment a purchase and sales agreement is concluded. At *The Stratford* it is customary to have a fresh flower arrangement and a welcome basket in the condominium on the move-in date for all new residents. The concierge and managers make a point of personally welcoming each new resident in the first days after the move. Managers of each department make separate appointments with them to offer explanations of how the department can help them and how to arrange for services. The activities director provides them with a calendar of events for the month, listing services such as transportation to grocery shopping, exercise classes, the walking club, movie night, and so on. The director of assisted living calls and invites each new resident to visit the assisted-living wing. She explains the medical services offered on a weekly basis, as well as the provisions for routine health care or help during illness. The residents of *The Stratford* Sunshine Committee call on new residents to welcome them. The committee members invite the new residents for a cocktail and then escort them to their first night in the dining room. They are invited to sit at a large table, are introduced, and made to feel welcome by everyone at the table.

The staff is expected to identify each resident by formal name or title, never by first name. This helps the residents to feel at home and allows the staff to comfortably introduce them into the community. Each staff member is expected to treat each resident and guest with respect and concern, and to do his or her utmost to provide needed assistance.

Self-Governance

The residents' form of self-governance at most CCRCs is primarily through a resident council. The residents select council members and any and all residents are invited to participate in council meetings. The council shares their concerns with the executive director. They are responsible for communicating the results of their meetings to the residents. Additionally, at *The Stratford*, the residents have requested that quarterly meetings be announced and held in the casual setting of the library. These meetings are an open forum for discussions between the residents and management staff.

No Class Distinctions

One *Cypress* executive comments about the lack of "class" distinction despite the broad range of incomes.

We've got a neighborhood at *The Cypress*, called The Cypress Bay Club, which has different architecture and bigger homes. We just sold a waterfront home there for $750,000. We've got one-bed-room apartments for $170,000. So we've got people with very different income levels. The campus is big enough so that residents can find their own groups to be with. There's no stigma about where someone lives. The people who live in the small apartments and the people who live in large cottages sit at the dinner table with each other and they ride on the bus to a concert together. Obviously, couples tend to socialize with couples and singles with singles. An 85-year-old and a 75-year-old don't necessarily have the same interests, just like a 40-year-old and a 50. That doesn't change as you go through life. But, there's no "we" and "they." I was worried about that before we opened, but there's no stigma associated with where someone came from or what they did in prior years They're all proud to be here.

Activities

Quality of life in a CCRC is based, in part, on assuring that residents have every possible opportunity to conduct their business and fill their day as they wish. At *The Stratford,* the activities coordinator requests input from residents for activities they would like offered, which are incorporated into the next month's activity calendar. The "Library News" will cite new books. Study opportunities are offered, such as guided genealogy research. Current events speakers give a lecture twice monthly, and art lecture series are offered two to three times yearly (6- to 11-week classes) for a small fee. The literary discussion group meets weekly. Stanford University's Continuing Education program offers one class per term for their normal tuition, with a senior discount. Lectures and classes are available at the community Wellness Center, a short stroll away. Ongoing events include morning coffees and teas, mall and grocery shopping, Thursday luncheons, walking club, basic stretching and exercise, announced and requested movies, investment club meetings, and reading discussions and meetings with medical professionals.

For those recovering from illness or surgery in the assisted-living wing, the activity director uses a questionnaire that asks whether patients would like to arrange a walk in the park, card or board games, books-on-tape, or movies. Guests of the assisted-living-wing patients may dine in their rooms or in the lounge with other patients, their family members, or personal guests. For those who require assisted living and have limited ambulation, free chauffeur drives through scenic areas are offered. Additionally, they may arrange for a walk to the park or assistance with errands for a small additional charge.

Outside Activities

The Stratford makes information available on a variety of ways to be involved in the community, and provides transportation whenever practical to allow residents to volunteer or participate. Also, independently, many residents are involved in various charities, clubs, the senior center, religious organizations, and community activities. A very pleasant meeting room is available at a minimal charge for use by resident-sponsored charity events. In the past, meetings have been held by such organizations as the American Lung Association, Peninsula ReCare, and the Mission Hospice Association. Numerous residents are involved with charitable organizations such as Samaritan House, the Wellness Center, various food banks, and the local library. Many residents have been involved in tutoring staff members who have limited knowledge of the English language.

Rewarding Staff

We have a happy and dedicated group of employees here at *The Cypress*. They feel that they are being treated fairly. I think right from the beginning, Mr. Coleman has done a great job and set up the program of wages and benefits. When people went with the hurricane evacuation, they received nice bonuses for that. It makes a difference. Employees get turkeys at Thanksgiving. Little things can go a long way. People here are treated very well and I think they're paid well. Every year, there's an employee appreciation fund to which the members contribute on a voluntary basis. They can put in whatever they want and that is distributed to employees based on number of hours worked in a year. So it doesn't matter if you've been here 5 years or 1 year, you'll get the same amount, and it's really very fair. People appreciate things like that. I think the one thing they really emphasize here in hiring people is personal attention to the members and treating them just like you'd like to be treated. Our job is to help them out in any way we can. We're not a business that has a product that we can sell. Our product here is our personal attention and our service to the members. And if you hire the right people and treat them well, that will be easy for them to do. The secret is finding the type of person who is willing to go out of his way to help people.

The Cypress: **Preston Health Center**

The Stratford: **Laurel Wing,
Assisted Living**

6.0 Health Care

At *The Cypress* and *The Stratford*, health care begins when applicants for residency are screened and found able to perform activities of daily living and to be alert and oriented so as to be eligible occupants of an independent living unit. At *The Cypress*, residents are assessed each year, or more often as needed, to determine their health needs. Findings are discussed with the resident, family members, and physicians when necessary interventions are appropriate. The health care plan promotes various activities to ensure well-being and provide preventive measures. These activities include walking, exercise programs, social gatherings, educational forums, and health-related safety talks. The food service staff accommodates special diets and works to plan menus that encourage good health and nutrition.

Our CCRC case studies highlight two versions of health care plans. In general, health care and promotion of wellness at *The Cypress* stresses individual attention and 90 days of residency in the Health Center for each *Cypress* member at no additional cost. After 90 days, the Health Center is available at a significantly reduced cost for as long as the member requires health care services. As part of the continuing care residence agreement, *The Stratford* provides assisted-living services in the resident's home or in the assisted-living unit. Skilled nursing and acute care are arranged at a licensed facility or hospital. Costs for assisted living and skilled nursing are included in the monthly fees. Acute care is provided by private and federal long-term insurance.

◼ Director of Nursing

The director of nursing at *The Cypress* is a special asset. She is a registered nurse with certification in case management and rehabilitation, as well as a retirement community industry marketing executive with a Master's Degree in management. Her experience in this area spans 15 years.

The Cypress is the most proactive company I have ever worked for. It is thinking about things long before people can even ask for them. It's pretty amazing. I think that's because the developers are so involved. They are right here. They hear what the service and health care managers are saying. This isn't always so in other communities. Working in marketing before I came here, I was able to see how facilities are developed or purchased and operated. From what I've seen, the goal of the person who has the cash too often determines how the business is run. Too many companies purchase or build a facility, and, from then on, you basically have to knock people's doors down to get them to look any further, to grow with the needs of residents, or new people coming in.

When the primary goal is to be economically successful and that's the top priority, the things that I might say aren't going to mean much to that owner. But if the goal starts out to be, "We want to provide the best service we possibly can to meet patients or residents' needs," then the things that I would say need to be done are going to be listened to in a totally different way. You can have all the wonderful "you shoulds" in the world, but it depends on the goals of the person who's holding the cash. I've seen attempts to meld existing facilities together when they weren't on the same campus. They didn't start out with the same ideal, and so it was much more difficult to make it all mesh, and have the residents as involved as you would like them to be. Trying to get the staff and everybody on the same sheet of music was almost impossible.

Health Care at The Cypress

Our health care capacity is for 77 residents. We have 44 skilled beds for people who need more than assisted living, 11 rooms with 22 beds for assisted living, and 11 private rooms for early to midstage Alzheimer's. Recently, we had an open house for our new assisted-living and Alzheimer's wings. During the open house, many people took the tour, not only people who currently live here, but also people who are planning to move into *The Cypress of Charlotte*, and people from the general health care community in surrounding areas. I was able to hear a lot of different perspectives during those tours. It's absolutely fantastic. Unlike any place else I've ever worked, I can tour people through and never once feel like I have to apologize for anything. In every place else I've worked, there are things that are apologized for on a tour or things that you feel you'd rather not show.

Home Ownership

The Cypress meets the CCRC ideal better than any place I've ever seen. There is a huge difference between a freestanding health care facility and a CCRC, because here you have the entire continuum of care. We start from the beginning and meet people's needs all the way through until the time they pass away.

I see lots of reasons why home ownership is important, as compared to an entry-fee community where a 70- to 75-year-old person is expected to say, "Okay. Now it's time to sell my home. Give up what I own. Go to a place and just basically pay rent or pay a fee." To me, that psychological step would be a very difficult one to make. Therefore, those communities end up with people that are very old, who don't have much of a choice anymore, who are almost forced to make the decision, and their families are sometimes making it for them. Here, they're not giving up anything; they're basically just purchasing a new home. And with that home come all kinds of amenities and services and a gorgeous place to live, so it's not necessarily like they're at the end of their life cycle and this is the last step. To me, that's a huge difference.

The CCRC organization and the level of communication lends itself to the residents being more involved in their own care. I hear most say that their life expectancy may not improve, but their self-confidence improves because they know they have the services that they may need. Not only do they have their own home, just like they used to have, they have a gorgeous setting to live in, all kinds of fun things to do, as well as health care services a phone call away. So, their level of confidence, not having to worry about those things, increases. I think older people tend to get a lot more isolated, as their friends move or pass on. Here, residents are encouraged to socialize and be more active. There are lots of opportunities for different kinds of socialization. That, coupled with the confidence of having health care services and transportation and basically anything they need, probably helps them feel more comfortable and, hopefully, that would then lead to a better life and a longer life expectancy.

One CCRC variant I would like to see is a lower-price community. I think what *The Cypress* offers is absolutely fantastic, but I think a lot of people are not able to afford this type of life-style. Some of the amenities that are offered here, some people have never had in their lives. So, I think if there was a more scaled-down version for low-to-middle-income retirees, that would be really nice.

Staffing

Staffing, of course, is our number one challenge in the Health Center. We are a 7-day-a-week, 24-hour service, always open, never closed. The challenge is training staff to understand what the expectations are and, even before that, helping them understand what this community is all about. A lot of people who apply here have only worked in a nursing home, where you get people who are very, very ill, who really don't have a choice in the matter. Here at *The Cypress*, we get all kinds of residents in the Health Center, from someone who had hip surgery and is recuperating and plans to go back home, to the people who are at the end of their life and need 24-hour care 7 days a week. So, it's a matter of helping staff understand where the Health Center fits in the CCRC picture, looking at each resident's situation, and seeing what that person needs. Does the person need heavy-duty, one-on-one constant care, or does he or she need some encouragement, some education? How to put on, for instance, surgical stockings that help keep the blood circulating. What is it, exactly, that each of these residents need? Instead of thinking that they're all typical nursing home patients, we treat them individually.

We also have an assisted-living wing. We're developing a home health care arm to *The Cypress*, so we will be licensed to service the resident at home. What we will offer depends on the acuity of the person, how many hours they require, and what they require. We will establish what we can do in the home and once this line has been crossed, it's time to look at assisted living or skilled care.

The Home Care and HMO Challenge

Are we challenged by home care and HMOs? Home care has been around now for quite a while and has a lot of problems with staffing and consistent care. I think home care has probably always been some competition for CCRCs, but the CCRCs offer lots of services and amenities and a full continuum of care. I think it depends on what the patients or the families want, their preferences and needs. If they're looking for the package that a CCRC has to offer, then, there is no competition. Home health care can cause tremendous stress on the entire family.

Managed care is here. Corporations are dominating and deciding what will be paid for. Most hospitals already have their own nursing home units, whatever they call them (there are several different terms for those). Managed care has decreased what they pay hospitals. They've decreased what they pay everybody. The margins that hospitals now make are less. So, they look to other avenues to make money, and say to themselves: "Look how many people we ship out to nursing homes every month. Let's keep them here." It's economically feasible. Patients' length of stay increases. All they have to do is license thirty beds as skilled and assign an administrator to run the wing. And, yet, there are many, many issues that arise that probably aren't looked at initially. The patient suffers in the end. When a nursing home company who has owned freestanding nursing homes starts buying CCRCs and trying to run them, or when a hospital, which has always done acute care, opens up a nursing home unit, very often the actual service and patient care are lacking.

The Human Condition

When residents enter the Health Center, we deal with all aspects of the human condition, medical, psychological, and emotional. There are often physical changes, both internally and externally, from skin to differences in eating habits, bowel habits, and hearing or vision problems. Psychologically, there may be changes in cognitive status and short- and long-term memory. Almost always, we see an emotional change prior to the actual physical or psychological change. Being aware of these possible conditions, and then looking for all the details behind them are what people in the nursing profession are trained to do.

What we discover depends on the staff members. Nursing people might not pick up on a condition as quickly as, for instance, an activities or a social worker might. It really depends on how much time they have spent with the person in question, and when they spent that time, and how observant they were of the issues. I don't think that nursing personnel need to be in every position where residents are being observed, but I think certain training needs to be in place and that the staff person in each position should be evaluated as to his or her observation skill.

Working with the Service Staff

We work directly with the service staff. They are very astute. We have a meeting every single morning and give status reports. In addition to a report from the Health Center, I give a report on any house calls that the nurses are making. The service director and social worker present information regarding anybody from independent living who may be experiencing any kinds of emotional, psychological, or physical changes. If somebody's been driving a car, and all of a sudden we're hearing reports that they're driving too slowly or they're not safe, we pick up on it right away.

We never argue in these meetings. I have never yet seen an argument. It's definitely more positive, more focused. The most frustrating part is the inconsistency that we're seeing in the individual. One day a resident may be cognitively with it and act the same as usual. The next day, someone might see that very same person doing something truly bizarre. When you've seen that person with your own eyes being okay, and then you hear something totally opposite, regardless of how long you've been in health care, it's hard to comprehend that. Yet, it happens. It's more of a "Really? You saw that?" kind of thing. The most difficult challenge we face as a team is trying to decide what's the most appropriate plan for the resident who is changing. Involving that resident in that plan is very important, but a lot of the time the resident is not aware that the changes are occurring, and doesn't want to know that the changes are occurring. There is a lot of discussion about how we deal with that. A resident losing his license or giving up his car or even having trouble parking the car is just a stressful thing to go through. Those are the kinds of things we deal with all the time. Rather than saying, "You'd better do this," I ask a lot of questions and ask, "What is your goal? What is it you're trying to accomplish?" From that, then I'll say, "You'd better do this."

Medical Services

The only physician on our Health Center staff is our Medical Director. Residents have to have a primary care physician. Many residents will say, "Well, I have a heart doctor. I've got a cardiologist." But if they go into the hospital, and they want to come back to our nursing home, they've got to have orders from a primary care doctor such as an internist or a family practitioner.

Residents usually come without a physician if they come from out of state. Our local medical center is Hilton Head Hospital. Five years ago, it was a not-for-profit. It has since gone through two evolutions and is now owned by one of the big companies. We've got a booklet that the hospital puts out with a picture and a description of every doctor and his specialty. I have my favorites because I want our residents to have somebody who cares about them and is available. So, if they ask me, I will tell them. Many of the doctors are not taking any more patients. A lot of women, particularly, have so many symptoms that they become a nuisance to the doctor and so they go to another one. He'll say, "I think you need to go and see so and so," and pretty soon, they've got fourteen bottles of pills from five different doctors. I'm sure you know that as people get elderly, they begin to concentrate on their physical condition. I think that may be what causes a lot of these physicians to be overloaded.

There is a young woman doctor here who came in about a year ago. I was very impressed. She has a background in geriatrics. I have been sending residents to her and everybody comes back and says, "Oh, thank you. She's wonderful." She cares. She stops and listens. She said to me, "I genuinely care. I want to hear what they have to say." A lot of times, the doctors don't have much patience with the elderly. The people say, "I've been going to him for 12 years, and now he doesn't have time for me. He brushes me off." So, often they'll call and say, "I need a doctor. Who do you recommend?" I will tell them who to go to. I know who's going to give them the time and who's good.

■ Nurse Consultant

Raiser Senior Services has added a new dimension to their staff, a nurse who serves as a medical risk manager.

They needed someone who could bring the medical perspective to their executive team, but maintain a business perspective on the whole project, not just health services. This perspective is, first of all, one of respect. First off, I think you absolutely must have a respect for the elderly. And like them. They are such a unique group of people, and there is so much energy there and so much that you can learn from them. If you don't feel that way, this is not the right business for you. I'm always fascinated when I sit down to meet a new resident, and developing that relationship with them and learning who they are. That's the best part of the job. Their lives are so rich with experience. Don't think of them as just old. People will tell me they're old and they're so young in their thoughts and in their actions. I remind them that it is age that they're referring to and not necessarily a state of mind, and it's a critical difference. Subtle. But it's critical. *The Stratford* executive director recognizes that in this industry, if you take care of people, it just pays so many dividends, versus not taking care of people. It's just crazy not to take care—senior wellness is so much cheaper than senior illness.

Evaluating a Take-Over Situation

My first assignment was to evaluate health care at *The Carlisle*, the project we acquired. *The Carlisle* is an equity CCRC located in the heart of San Francisco. I've spent most of my time trying to understand and get a clear picture of how the services are delivered at *The Carlisle*, and also at the same time look at it from a comparison point of view with the regulations that are put out by the state. Most of my efforts thus far have been to understand the population, and then to see how well the documentation complies with state regulations. This is very critical. People that are in the medical facilities, the nurses they hire and the management, must be in compliance with those regulations at all times. It not only protects the residents, but it also protects the owners to know that they are operating appropriately. *The Carlisle* is very different from *The Stratford* because *The Carlisle* doesn't have an assisted-living wing, and so their challenges are different.

Helping Executive Directors

In a take-over situation, you must recognize that the executive directors have so much to oversee. You just have to have a strong team, and I think it is important to have systems in place for monthly reviews with your managers, to know what they are doing, especially if they are not from the new management company. My role here is to really help the executive directors know that they're in compliance. If you could budget for that sort of oversight, it would help tremendously, because, in most cases, the executive directors do not have a medical background, and it is a worthwhile investment to have someone on your team who does. Ideally, your nursing manager could and should do that, but it's going to take an extremely strong manager to be able to know what the regulations are and follow through.

I can really see how difficult it is for executive directors to get the problem analysis information that I've been able to uncover because, in many cases, it's subtle. You'll find a clue here that someone has had a problem 4 or 5 years ago, and it's not disclosed in some of the assessments and records. So, it really does help to have someone that's familiar with the regulations and a medical background. If you're taking over, there's always the risk of medical staff in place not being open and comfortable with saying, "Here are my records. Take a look at this." So you should definitely get someone who is not tied to delivering patient care to oversee your risk and make sure that you're in compliance with the regulations and that the systems are working. One thing I haven't seen—and this may be my own personal sort of bias—I haven't seen any assessment of satisfaction with medical services, and I don't honestly know how critical that is. It is critical for me because I see satisfaction as the difference between residents' expectations for care and their perceptions of the care that they've actually received. Knowing how we measure up to their expectations provides insights into whether we are seeing residents' expectations appropriately. Is it something that we're conveying in our message and our philosophy?

Monitoring Staff Performance

There are a couple of ways to monitor staff performance. The first one would be documentation. I think that it's very advantageous to spend time up front looking at the medical documentation. Does it work? Does it reflect what we're actually doing? From an accounting point of view, use information to get trends on utilization of services and staffing and all of those things. I think that the documentation for the health services should be geared so that you reflect the state regulations, you have a clear picture of what you're doing, for whom and when and where, and how long it takes. And to make sure that this is tied into the administrative information so that you can see and project trends.

At *The Carlisle*, the care is delivered in the residents' units. The questions are: What care is undertaken in the residences? What responsibilities are assigned to nurse's aides? Does the nursing management staff fully monitor the care delivered? Are managers achieving time efficiency, keeping costs down? There's no question that their intentions are good and they are striving to provide really good care. The problem is they haven't had good management to instruct them in the boundaries of the relationships between staff and residents. I think that needs to be very clear. And I think that it takes a strong management team to help those people work well within their role and define it and expand it and let them feel very comfortable that they're doing the right thing. I see that as a great need. In most areas, there is room for interpretation, and that's why I think strong management is so essential, to make sure that those gray areas are interpreted in the best interests of the residents. For example, the policy for staff to resident relations is very vague. It says, in general, that you should respect the residents' privacy, safeguard their belongings, and not allow for a conflict of interest, such as receiving gifts from residents. Naturally, residents develop relationships with these caregivers and want to share with them, but I think that operators must be alert to when that's going over the line or inappropriate. Then there are issues of protecting those cognitively impaired individuals, and caring for them in emergency situations so that they're not in a position to harm themselves or other people, but can still function within a controlled and safe environment. That's always a difficult thing to regulate.

Care

The state requires regular assessments once a year, to make sure that staff have a handle on the residents' care and their needs, changes in their condition, and the need for other services that maybe shouldn't, or couldn't, be offered here. The resident staff in general is seeing individuals on a regular basis, an ongoing, informal assessment. It's not uncommon to have the activity director say, "Gee, I noticed so-and-so seems to be having some problems," and bringing that to the attention of the medical staff. It takes a strong management team and good communication. I think it makes good sense to invest in programs that reduce long-term risk. Specifically, exercise programs that maintain muscle strength, balance, and conditioning so that residents are able to avoid things such as falls. We know that nutrition and exercise and rest are critical in the senior population. Investing in activity programs is very beneficial from a health point of view. I love the resident activities, because that takes care of intellectual stimulation, which is so critical also. We find that as long as people are continuing to be challenged intellectually and learn, they maintain a zest for life that is missing in people that have sort of said, "I'm done, I'm done." When you accept people into the residence, you also have to consider what kind of services they're going to need. Ideally, we should look at them as a whole. This is their health state now. How can we maintain where they are? Can we improve their health and, thereby, improve their quality of life? Can we help them to be more proactive in managing their medical issues, if they have any? We need to get residents to accept responsibility for their health. It's a partnership.

There are specific conditions that send up alerts. To me, those are cerebral and neurovascular. I'm thinking of strokes and TIAs, transischemic attacks, or what laymen refer to as ministrokes. They're temporary and there's often no residual, but they can be a warning sign for an impending stroke, although some people never get one. These things are very disconcerting, and they can include things such as loss of speech, confusion, motor changes. Parkinson's is another one, because we know that it's such a progressive and debilitating disease. The frustrating thing with that is that the individual is completely intact, intellectually and mentally, but the body just won't do what he or she needs. People with Parkinson's have a very high need in the end stages for assistance with activities of daily living, mobility, changing positions, nutrition, and all of those things. I would encourage residents not to worry about care for heart disease and cancers. Those two conditions don't impose a big risk as far as the need for long-term support and care. With cancer, you have hospice care, as long as you make sure that the regulations in your state allow for the care to be delivered in a CCRC.

Getting Started

To understand all of this, to get assistance when starting a new enterprise, I would say go to the people who are currently in the business because they're going to be the ones who know. The insurance companies have their own actuarial studies for risk, but they don't necessarily reflect what the operators actually see. I wouldn't go to hospitals. They have a very different focus. Their focus is on acute care and decreasing the utilization of inpatient services. They would be an excellent resource for helping to fill your assisted-living wing with temporary residents on a private-pay basis. But, asking them to provide guidance, no. If you had access to some of the rehab centers where they deal with this population at risk for stroke and mobility, pain clinics, that would be fine. I wouldn't go to a hospital administrator and ask, "Here's what I'm doing, how do you think I should set my criteria?" I think I would go to the specific departments that deliver the care and talk with the medical directors and talk with the nurses there. Talk with the social workers and discharge planners. A home health agency would also be a good resource in learning what kinds of care they deliver in the home, the cost for doing so, and who they're able to keep in the home and who they're not.

The Cypress: **The Clubhouse library**

The Stratford: **Ground-floor library**

The Stratford: **Private dining room**

The Stratford: **Kitchen and dining bar**

7.0 Residents' Services

The Cypress and The Stratford established food service, house-keeping, moving-in assistance, maintenance services, and the services of a concierge prior to opening. Others services, such as chauffeurs, beauty salons, grocery shopping, and dog walking, were added as the needs arose. All of the services provided are available from one point of service. Staff are encouraged to engage in creative solutions to prevent added costs to the residents or facility operations. Executive leadership and action are the mandate. The determination of the scope of services and the execution of the service program requires experience and knowledge. *The Cypress of Hilton Head* and *The Cypress of Charlotte* are managed by Life Care Services Corporation and *The Stratford* by Raiser Senior Services. In the following, the assigned executives recount their experiences and provide the insights needed to be alert to what CCRC service is all about.

■ Responsibilities

The future of CCRCs is incredibly bright. If you look at any major city in the country, there will be retirement communities there. A large percentage of the population is just beginning to age. This is going to be a very solid business. *The Cypress* is my sixth career assignment, so I've had an opportunity to see quite a number of programs, including those that are not financially sound. Our company managed two retirement communities through a Chapter 11 reorganization, and I happened to be administrator of both of those communities, so I've had a chance to see quite a number of issues. My role is to manage *The Cypress Club*, which is the entity through which all the services are provided to members. My focus as executive director is on the services provided and making sure that they're provided in the highest-quality manner. Our monthly service fee includes all maintenance services, all housekeeping and laundry services, transportation, activities, and landscaping. It also includes 30 meal credits a month. We have about 160 employees.

A major area of responsibility is the Health Center, where we're licensed to provide skilled care. *The Cypress* members find comfort in knowing that facility is available to them. They certainly hope they never need it, but that Health Center is very important and critical to our marketing efforts. Security is a lot more than knowing the doors are locked. Security is peace of mind. The Health Center is their peace of mind, knowing that if they ever have to go there, it'll be a pleasant stay.

My day is largely spent dealing with a lot of different emotions that seniors have. Usually, they're on a very even keel, but sometimes they're not. We're working with seniors who have experienced life, held high positions, and have high expectations. When the service isn't at the expected level, it can become frustrating. When dealing with 430 seniors and all of the emotions that they bring to the table, it's difficult sometimes to balance everything. The important thing is just to keep it in perspective. We have to be empathetic. That's something that is very important—your ability to put yourself in someone's shoes and look at it from their standpoint.

Just Do It

Our philosophy is "Just Do It." We're not going to stand around and explain why we can't do it. We can't look at anything as a minor issue. These are 75-, 85-year-old people, and when they have a concern, it's not minor. Even if it's something insignificant, it's not to them. We take care of it. We follow through, and if we say we're going to do something, we do it. We continually remind ourselves of this in the weekly department head meetings and convey this to the residents' committees. We have five committees: Food and Beverage; Building and Grounds; Activities; Health and Safety; and Finance. Once a month, I sit down with the finance committee and fully disclose the monthly financial statements. The committees do not have any formal power, just the power of persuasion. That's a quote from them. Working with residents, we want to hear their concerns, come forth with the answers that apply, and explain why it is the way it is or maybe why it can't be the way somebody might suggest it be. They need to know that we care and are responsive.

Communication

It is essential to keep the flow of communication going through the organization. General conversation, talking to somebody and asking them about their day and any challenge they had. If they, in fact, explain something and how they took care of it, I might say, "That's great. I'm sure Mrs. Smith really appreciated that." Positive reinforcement with the employees is very important. If somebody needs help moving this or that, staff will stop what they're doing. If not, they will notify their supervisor that so-and-so needs help.

We have an in-house cable television channel and a monthly TV show. It's called the *Monthly Executive Director's Talk Show*. We do a variety of things with it. We show movies and we use it as a means of communication to *Cypress* members. It's not a professional program. We could spend more money on it, but we chose to just keep it informal. We interview the employee of the month, and talk about what's going on with *The Cypress*. We've had a lot of construction going on with the Health Center expansion, and that's been a topic of conversation every month because people are very interested in knowing about it. If there are things going on in the dining room, we announce it. A lot of retirement communities choose to have formal gatherings, where people are invited to the meetings. I've found that when you do your own TV show without an audience, it is more laid back. We publish a monthly TV schedule and our activities director sets the program. We have a different program every day of the week. We air the program twice a day, once at nine and once at two in the afternoon. The emphasis is on communication to the members as well as entertainment.

Resident Satisfaction

We recently compiled a resident satisfaction survey. One question was: "Would you recommend *The Cypress* to your friend or relative as a place to live?" Ninety-nine percent of the people at *The Cypress* said that they would.

In the delivery of services, seniors want to know that the people who are in a position of responsibility care what's going on and that they're going to be attentive to whatever situation needs attention. I've had to learn this time and time again. It doesn't matter how many years of experience I have, or that I've been with Life Care Services for 13 years. When I started here, basically, I started over. Yes, I've had some good experiences, and yes, I've built a good track record, but it didn't mean anything to the residents because they didn't know me. They didn't know I care. They didn't know how thorough I am. They just want to know that I'm going to follow through on something. The worse thing you can do is to not listen and act. It gets back to the little things, the minor things. The philosophy is, nothing is minor. And, if you say you're going to get back to somebody, you'd better do it because that's not going to bode well for that person's confidence in me. That is a philosophy we try to instill in all the managers, supervisors, and people in positions of decision-making ability. People appreciate it when you get back to them and say, "You know, you asked me the other day about this and I didn't have time—I've had a chance to look into that, and let me tell you a little bit about it."

We always reinforce with our managers in weekly meetings how we can do more for our staff members to make sure that they're treated with respect, feel they're valued, and feel like they're important. When somebody does a good job, we appreciate it and tell them. We started an Employee of the Month program. It's been real successful. We choose the Employee of the Month at a weekly department head meeting. We announce the Employee of the Month in a memo and we give the employee a $100 bonus. The employee is also interviewed on my TV show.

Questions to Ask

There are questions I would strongly urge any senior citizen contemplating moving to a retirement community to ask. Who is responsible for managing the facility and all the services? A facility that is in trouble financially should send up a red flag. What has been the monthly service fee increase? This is typically annually at most retirement communities. Has it been more frequent than annually? If a troubled community really starts feeling pinched, usually their resident agreement is structured such that it can provide an increase or make the adjustment with proper notice. You wouldn't want to move into a community that gives more than one increase a year. Other things that consumers might look for is financial reserves.

Usually, retirement communities, by statute, are required to have various levels of reserves for debt-service insurance and working capital. Does the community have any money in the bank, unrestricted, for whatever purpose? A rainy-day account? If they do, that's positive. If they don't, it could be questionable. Has it steadily been going down or up over the last year or 2 years? Does the community have a predictable source of funds to pay the bills? Those are things to look into. Hopefully, seniors will ask those questions. We recommend that they do.

■ Running the Business

I am deeply involved in the paperwork of the health care program. I'm more involved than I thought I would be, but it's been a great way for me to learn what goes on in the Health Center in terms of how much we spend a month on supplies that we can charge to residents. How can we cut back? Is there a better product we can use? One example would be our nutritional supplement shakes. We've recently changed because after hearing from a number of residents and their families that they just didn't taste that good, we all sat down and tasted them. They didn't taste good, so we looked for another product and made that change.

We are at a very interesting point right now in the Health Center, having just added thirty-three beds, including an Alzheimer's program and an assisted-living program. We have some big census goals right now. We have a large number of empty beds, so one long-term goal is managing those beds so that we somehow achieve the optimum balance of having beds available for *Cypress* members, but also being fiscally responsible and balancing on the other side of the equation with private-pay residents so that we have that revenue coming in. Last fall, we had forty-four beds in our Health Center, and when I left to go to Des Moines for some training, our census was forty-three. We had several *Cypress* members in the hospital, and we were scrambling trying to locate beds on the island for these *Cypress* members should they need them. Luckily, we didn't have to take that step, but we very easily could have. And it sent a very strong message to us. We are here primarily for *Cypress* members. There is a delicate balance. For a calendar quarter, there might not be a large number of *Cypress* members who need that Health Center. The next quarter it might triple. Last fall, we put into place a policy of not accepting any private-pay individuals. We were willing to let our census ride for a while, knowing for certain that we had beds available for *Cypress* members. Now with the new wing, we've got all of these extra beds. It's taken a while for word to kind of get out into the community that we can and will accept some private-pay individuals.

Lifecare Services has a preferred-vendor program where we've gone out and, based on the volume of business that we can provide a vendor, negotiated a really nice rate. We took advantage of that with this new Health Center when we purchased our bathing equipment and lifting equipment. Argo is a company with which Lifecare Services has established a preferred-vendor relationship whereby if we buy "x" number of dollars of lifting equipment, we get a 50% reduction and an added training package from Argo. The incentive is for us to keep our worker's compensation claims at a minimum, fewer strained backs from lifting inappropriately. There are a number of products in the preferred-vendor program.

Faces

A big part of all of our jobs revolves around the interrelationships here. In a Health Center that's even more pronounced when you have families and extended families of the resident who is living there. You come to know not only the individual living there, but his or her family. There are faces in front of you all day long. Even more important is customer service, everything from how a meal is served and presented in the dining room, and any conversation exchanged between a dietary person and the resident, to walking down the hall and being able to call every family member by name and know a little bit about what's going on with that family at that moment. It makes all the difference. My office is in the Health Center, though it is physically somewhat removed from the actual goings on. I would like to have my office right out there in the middle of what's going on just to keep even more of a finger on the pulse. I build time into my day when I'm not in my office, but walking through the Health Center.

The Industry

A lot of people seem to be jumping on the "aging-population" bandwagon to make a fast buck when in fact it's so much more than that. We have only four people this morning living in our Alzheimer's unit. It's a beautifully designed building, but I think the reason that it's there is far more important. My concern is that not enough people understand the importance of it. It's very easy to say that you have a special care unit on your campus, but when you really peel away all of the bells and whistles, what's really the substance of that program? That's something that I personally am interested in. Assisted living falls in that same category. It's one of those phrases that's easy to say, but what does it really mean? Home health is another niche for the future and one that we're dealing with here at the *Cypress*. We are in the process of starting a home health program. One of the reasons is that the quality of home health in this area is not what we would like it to be for *Cypress* members. Caregivers aren't showing up. Different people are showing up rather than those who are scheduled. Maybe not quite as nice appearing as they should be. So we concluded that we could do that as well as an outside agency and with familiar faces that members already know.

■ Director of Resident Services

My background is education and from education I went into counseling. I have a Master's Degree in counseling. When I was taking my Master's, which was 10 years ago, the person who was my advisor suggested that I look into the field of gerontology—specifically, communities that were being developed to accommodate elderly people.

I love my relationship with the people at *The Cypress*. The nicest thing that happened initially was that the lady who was the move-in coordinator changed jobs just as we opened. She had done most of the work with the people, planning their homes and making changes. I was helping her as we opened, because my job really hadn't developed. So, when she changed jobs, I took on the move-in coordinator's job. Now I am both move-in coordinator and director of resident services, but it was a magnificent fit because I got to know the people during the trauma and the thrill of the move-in. I got to know them when they were at their strongest, and they got to know me when they really needed that kind of help. As time has gone on, they feel very free to come and talk to me about just about everything. It runs from the humorous to the really very sad situations, but they will tell me what's going on in their lives. When they get sick, I follow them to the Health Center.

I have tried to create an open-door policy and sometimes they're lined up down the hall saying, "I'm next." They will talk to me, and my stock in trade is that I will talk to them. (I have a few gray hairs, too.) For instance, I have a lady who is going to be moving to our Dogwood Wing, which is our dementia wing. On the weekend, her husband fell and broke his arm, so he, too, is going to move over there for a while. That's a decision. I do a great deal with adult children of residents, who are in contact with me because they feel Mom really isn't doing that well. In one particular case, the resident is very resistant to any help. We met on Easter weekend with all her children. She agreed that she would allow some assistance in order to stay in her home. That lasted about 3 weeks and now she won't take any help. Well, what's the next step? What do we do? If we find that residents are not really able to manage independently, and resist moving to the Health Center, we send a letter. We give them the option of getting 24-hour help or moving to the Health Center or, ultimately, moving out because they will not give us the opportunity to work with them. Somewhere in the back of their minds, residents think that they are really moving to *The Cypress* for health care, but they don't want to talk about it and they don't want to think about it and they don't even want to walk over to that Health Center. So, when the time comes, say, in 5 years, they have to consider what they're going to do, and we have to present them with options. We are able to go back to their contract and say, you did agree and that is why you moved here; otherwise, you'd be without good choices. When push comes to shove, you are going to be cared for, at not only a reduced rate, but, hopefully, in a better environment than you would be in a local nursing home.

One of the best things about *The Cypress* is that when one spouse moves to the Health Center, the other doesn't have to get in the car and drive across town to visit. Both of them are right here on campus. We do so many different things. I have people who come over and ask me to read because they can't see. I may enlarge the print or show them how to use our reading machine or sit and read to them. I get a psychologist to come in and use my office. I'll put a Do Not Disturb sign on the door for privacy. And the humorous. Once a lady called to tell me her TV was broken and she couldn't turn it off. I went over and it was because the light was reflecting on the television screen. I kept saying, "There's nothing wrong. Watch this. When I turn the light out, the picture goes away." She said, "You don't know anything about it. I need a technician over here because I can't turn the TV off." You have to look at the humorous side or you become depressed.

The main thing is that the people on the staff need to be aware of the needs of both residents and staff and that it is not only a business. It's a business that really requires people who care and who are anxious to provide (sometimes even at their own expense in time and effort) a really welcoming homelike environment. There's got to be a substitute family. This is the only place I can work where I am young. Residents will say, "Oh, you're the same age as my child." So, essentially, this becomes a substitute family. There are times when I have to sit down and talk about the things that really aren't relative to an immediate problem. They just need somebody to be interested. To call them by name. And to know who they are. As we grow to be 400 plus, it's getting tougher and tougher to remember everybody's name. They absolutely love that we are interested in their health. This is a big, big concern. They love this Health

Center. They come out in large numbers for our health care symposium. We have wine and cheese for them and the doctor comes and speaks from 6:00 to 7:00 and then they get to ask questions. We've done it for 4 years, and they absolutely love it.

Some residents need to be protected because of their decreasing money management skills. They can get themselves into a lot of financial trouble. And they have very little opportunity to recover the money because of their age and their income. So, part of the responsibility we take on in the senior business is to make sure that we don't overleverage projects, and we look at the cash flow of the consumer. Normally, in real estate, you don't worry about the consumer's financial status, but in this case, we have to worry about him because we find that the consumer gets to a point where he cannot take care of himself. So, those developers that put senior projects together without making it their business to see that the seniors are taken care of and can actually service their debt are asking for trouble.

My Staff

I've got a wonderful staff of six people. I look for people who will reflect my attitude. I look for warm, caring people who know what they're doing, and I have had incredible luck. Every one of them is great. In fact, our former administrator told me it was the only department he'd never had a complaint about. I look for people who can do without me. I can walk away from here for 2 days, if I have to. They will do the scheduling and they will fill in where there's a gap. They really do a wonderful job. I look for maturity, and by maturity, I don't mean in years. I mean maturity in attitude and responsibility. We all feel we have the same goal, which is to make residents as comfortable as possible, both mentally and physically.

Extra Help

We sometimes have people very sick or dying, and I will put somebody with them for a whole day. Often, I have to find somebody for nights and I keep a file of outside people who I know are reliable, who usually are LPNs or CNAs. I quickly get somebody when I sense the need because the spouse often wears out and can't be effective the last 3 or 4 weeks. It's really an accommodation to our residents, and we now have a home health agency that greatly expands the services we can provide in the home.

We've had situations where we find things going on with outside agencies that *The Cypress* doesn't approve. They will contract with a family to have a 24-hour person, and then in the middle of the week, they'll send someone else. Elderly people aren't up to that kind of shifting around. I will go over and say, "No, this isn't working," and call the family. Many of the outside agencies will try to keep people in their home as long as possible. They are trying to keep residents at home for their own business reasons. The first thing they ask is: "Is she medically covered?" And they recruit constantly. There's a small pool of nurses in a community like this and a lot of them work for every agency and are really not committed. When a new agency pops up, they're trying for another dollar more an hour.

There is another group of home care specialists here, who are natives to this area, who have kind of built their own infrastructure, because if they go to work for an agency, they're going to get $6.50 an hour. If they work for themselves, they get $10.00 an hour, and they do a fine job. This group of women who have formed their own little network are certified, but like to work independently. They all know one another, and I can tap in very quickly and get good people. We have probably six people here who I can call and who will do a great job.

Automobiles

Remember the great feeling of independence the day you got your driver's license? "I'm out there now. I can go anywhere." That's how hard it is to get people to stop driving. You're taking away so much independence with taking the keys to the car. It's a huge issue. In this state, it's unbelievable the people that can go out and get their licenses renewed. I had one woman who has to have someone help her every day. She can hardly walk. One of the girls who works with me came back and said, "Her son is taking her to get her license." I said, "You've got to be joking." And he called me and said, "I'm doing this for her, but she's not going to drive. It's so that she'll keep her feeling of independence." And I thought, well, that's no problem because she'll never pass it. She did pass it! I couldn't believe it. I had a woman call the other day to give me the license plate number of a man. She said, "If I hadn't skidded to a halt, he'd have gone right through me backing out of his driveway." He's 91. He should not be driving. Some give it up willingly, but a lot of them give it up very unwillingly. In one case, we met with the children, and they took the car. She just said, "Take my car. I'll get another one." Her doctor sent her a fax and copied me saying she shouldn't be driving, and when I first approached her, I asked, "Well, did you get the fax?" "Yes." "Well, do you understand what that means?" "Yes." "Are you going to stop driving?" "No. Of course I'm not going to stop driving." And now, she's contacting dealers; she's going to buy another car.

So, you've got every kind of individual here. Every different type of person. The person who does everything according to the rules, and the person who—if it's what he or she did before—will continue to do it now.

We have transportation for residents. Every Monday, Tuesday, Thursday, and Friday, we have scheduled trips to the grocery store and to Main Street, which is our little village down the street. They can go at 10:00 or at 2:00 at no cost to them. They can go in and do their shopping and the driver will come and pick them up.

There is a lot of visual impairment in this population. We actually have a support group for the visually impaired. A lot of people can't drive simply because they can't see. And they give it up because, you know, there's not a fight there. It's emotionally upsetting, but losing your sight is even more upsetting, so, we don't have a problem with those people.

Expanding the CCRC Model

The way our society is set up, people eventually become unable to be independent. Then, cost becomes a big factor. I don't think that this kind of retirement community, or *The Stratford* in California, is for the average person. We have to think about the average person. Where am I going to go? I am now a very independent person, but I also face the fact that there will be a time when I'm no longer independent. We'll need different options somewhere within the CCRC concept. There's a book that was written in collaboration by Merrill Lynch and a company in Japan. The Japanese, for a long time, took care of their own, and now they are looking at this kind of community because of their own social issues. The daughters-in-law are not going to take care of Mom anymore as they have in the past. A lot of the people in major corporations are talking about this same thing. Where are we going with it? The unfortunate thing is that when you get off this level, then you have the concerns of it being maybe not as attractive, and we go back to maybe the old county home concept. Certainly, we're all living longer. We know right behind us is that baby-boomer generation. They're all used to living well, but whether they've put enough money away is the question.

■ A Quality Experience

The Stratford follows all State of California, OSHA, and ADA regulations to the best of its ability. The state conducts an on-site visit to every CCRC annually, and *The Stratford* was recently recognized for "zero deficiencies" for the third year in a row. This is quite an accomplishment given the number of areas that are examined. The executive director is a licensed administrator. *The Stratford* is required to send fingerprints of employees to the state within 20 days of employment, and to conduct physicals and a tuberculosis test within 7 days. A detailed disaster plan is also in place.

Remembering What You Said

Helen Raiser, co-developer, comments:

What is the challenge involved in maintaining this quality experience for residents of *The Stratford*? Keeping your promises. What we do find is that anything that we mention at meetings prior to people moving in, they remember, and we have to be very careful that we can deliver what we have promised. For instance, in the Laurel Wing, we said that we would have a nurse on duty around the clock. We didn't say an RN. We now have an RN around the clock. We just feel better knowing that there is an RN there. And another thing we apparently said was that we would take people to the airport when they're going on a trip, and pick them up. Now, we didn't say without cost, but one of our owners thought that it was without cost, and so, to this day, we still take that one couple without charging them. Everyone else pays. We just must be very careful because everything's remembered. One of the things that we have heard a number of times that we mentioned was valet parking. I think in the original meetings we had with the homeowners we mentioned valet parking, and yet we have not provided someone to stand out front and be ready to park cars. What we have said is: Anyone who doesn't want to go to the garage should just leave the car out front, and the concierge or someone will park that car.

We see the solution as absolute clarity and consistency. For instance, and just a small for instance, for the last four and a half years, I've been voluntarily providing fresh-flower arrangements for residents' dinner parties. This is just something that's happened. I'm not sure that they thought about it, but if I had flowers, it was a pleasure to do it. And I just decided this year that I can't keep this up because there are a lot of parties. If there's something that the entire community is involved in, I'm glad to meet with whoever is hosting and do something, and I will pass along the wholesale cost of flowers, not labor. But to keep doing flowers for every party, I just couldn't. Apparently, it wasn't conveyed very well. This Sunday, there was a party that took place, and the dining room manager mentioned that there were several choices—you can buy your flowers from a florist for about $25 or bring your own. Apparently, it was agreed that they would bring their own. Then Friday, the couple hosting the outside guests called down and said, "We want free flower arrangements." The wait staff said, "I'm terribly sorry but we can't supply those. We haven't been to the flower market. We don't have the flowers." And it became a very big brouhaha. The home-owners came down and were very difficult. And, as it turned out, I had some flowers in the garden, and I came in especially and did them. But so many of these things are just expected, and perhaps it's because we set it up in a way that everything was given. So, we thought, well, we have to make that clear with a memo. I wasn't quite sure how we were going to say it, but the staff came through. "Let's just give out the memo when someone books a party. There's no need to bring that information to everyone, because many people will never have a party, so, when they book a party, we'll just make it very clear, these are the options." And it's worked very well. Again, clarity and consistency of communi-cations.

Everything Varies

There is a wonderful woman at *The Stratford*, and she's in her 90s. And she really works at trying to stay well. She's been a writer in her day. She's just one of our very special people. And not every-one is out there going to the Wellness Center. There's a small group trying to work on keeping well and, again, what are your seniors? They're just a group of people who are aging, so you get the gamut, varying a lot, depending on their age and their health. The day moves much slower for them. I notice when I am out and about at 9:00, a lot of the newspapers are still at the front door, so life just moves at a slower pace. We would like to have the home-owners more involved outside of *The Stratford*. Volunteering, per-haps, at the Volunteer Center, and in the community. I think that's one area where we've fallen down. We can't seem to get people too interested in doing things outside the community. It may be that they feel they've done that or they just don't have the energy, or I don't know what. We would have thought that if we take care of the cooking and cleaning, they would have the time and inclination to volunteer. But, with few exceptions, they don't.

Over time, most of them have been in the assisted-living wing at one time or another. They're very enthusiastic about the health care, and so are people who come in from the outside. We get very complimentary letters about the care. Again, I think it's our food. It's our presentation of the food, the fact that there's always a little bouquet on their tray. There's a very caring staff. The rooms are beautiful—all those things keep them happy. When a death takes place, surprisingly, they are very accepting. One would think that there would be sort of a pall over the whole place when this happened. It doesn't happen, and I think it's because, at their age, our staff takes it much harder than the homeowners. The staff members, I find, because they're younger, haven't been in touch with death in the same way. They are very depressed. And our homeowners just carry on. They'll attend the service, and if there's a reception upstairs, they'll all be up there to have a drink, and I don't hear that person mentioned in a way that you would think. It's just part of living. The family will invite our residents. We do not allow any memorial services to take place at *The Stratford*. We don't allow any plaques to be hung "in memory of." But we do host receptions after the service.

Another consideration with residents is that single women end up feeling lonely, and couples end up feeling obliged to take care of the single women, because there but for the grace of God go I. Single men, who tend to be widowers, end up feeling somewhat besieged. So, you really have to make sure you provide opportunities for people to mix in a nongender-specific way and in a noncourtship kind of way. Big cocktail parties are good, things where if you go alone, you're fine, and if you go together, you're fine. Things that don't work are things like dances, where the women feel obliged to have a partner, where they want to be escorted by a man, where they feel bereft of a companion, or where the few men get picked up right away, and everyone else is left feeling like a wallflower.

Patience

Communication is encouraged between residents and staff. All managers have an open-door policy for any complaints, suggestions, and feedback. Ideally, you'll have groups of friends move in, or people who are like-minded enough to become friends. In the beginning, that's because everyone wants to get along. Sort of like high school; in the beginning, everyone is sort of wary and looks at each other, and then, after a few years, people sort of, you know, glom on to each other and form their own opinions. There is definitely a bias against those who are more infirm. There's a bias against dementia. People don't want to have meals with or sit with or be seen with the least mentally able residents. That's a big issue. And even those who are least mentally able discriminate against those who they perceive to be less able than they. So, it goes right down the line. There are certainly groups of people who socialize together, belong to the same clubs together, who tend to gravitate toward one another. But we have not found that to be completely debilitating or polarizing.

Homeowners and the Administrative Policies

Generally, residents are very supportive. There are certainly a few families that always make a point of telling you so. I hear from them at Christmas or after their parent has weathered a health crisis. Some you just don't hear from at all. And, certainly, the same with the homeowners. I do keep a box with all their notes—these are great letter writers, great note writers, and certainly they've learned how to say thank you by a note, so we hear from many of them. We don't have that much contact with the family, and perhaps this is an independent group of people who decided to make the move so they wouldn't be a burden to their families.

I think the one thing that divides people is if certain people are supportive of administrative policies and other people disapprove of them. That's where you end up getting real polarization. It's better if all the residents are against administration or all generally happy, but when you start getting divisions, it gets very ugly for the residents themselves, because they feel it gets to be sort of an extreme political party kind of point of view. There are always going to be a few troublemakers in the group. There are always going to be in every facility a few residents whose main purpose in life becomes being what they perceive as the self-appointed Ralph Nader of the community. They're the ones that are in the administrator's office. They're the ones speaking up at the resident meetings about issues. They're the ones often trying to become president of the residents' council. Oftentimes, the people who are happiest could care less about the residents' association and want little to do with it, so your association can sometimes end up being quite a polarizing force and quite a destructive force. People think that the most extreme voice on the association represents all the homeowners. The association has to be worked with; it can't be ignored. But it is a mistake to give in to the association on every issue, either. I think we were much too solicitous in the beginning. We were so eager for harmony, and frankly, we were marketing. We didn't want anyone to say anything bad. We gave people a sense that because they didn't like something, we would fix it, even when it wasn't in the community's best interest. And now I'm taking a much harder line. If we can fix it, and it doesn't cause anyone any problem, we fix it right away. But if it, indeed, is going to have deeper repercussions, we can't be irresponsible and give people what they think they want because, ultimately, they don't thank you for it and it's not really what they want.

The more you can have the reasonable members of your association on your side, the better. And that means you need to take the time to be reasonable with them, and cultivate them and understand where you're going to disagree. That's why it's so important to have that CCRC license. If you have the ultimate liability for the facility, you have the ultimate responsibility for the facility, and you can't let the association's short-term perspective—"I need this now because I'm not going to be here in 7 years when that reserve fund is put into place"—dictate what happens for the long-term health of the facility. The next guy who comes in needs to have the same caliber of reserves and replacement, the same chair covering quality as you did when you came in when the building was new. Or, the value of the unit's going to depreciate. And if the value of the unit depreciates, everybody loses, including your estate. But people don't think about it that way. They think about: What can I get here and now? What did you promise me? Not future generations. Not that you can blame someone in their 90s for living in the present. Future thinking is our job, not theirs.

Housekeeping

Housekeeping requires a special identity. It's a uniform that staff members could wear proudly out on the street, even. I think that they deserve to feel comfortable and confident. It's important that it's not in any way a demeaning uniform. I think they're happy about that. And our driver and our maintenance people in a nice blue polo shirt and khakis; they look very professional. You just forget what a difference it makes until you sometimes see them in their street clothes and realize we would just have total disarray if we didn't have them in uniform. We started out with uniforms for the front desk, and I picked out blazers and skirts and they were to wear a white blouse, but that just didn't work. It's too difficult to keep that up. People would come and go, and we were left with a lot of expensive blazers. It was just too expensive, so now we do let the front desk people wear what they want, within certain guidelines. No jeans or T-shirts. Professional dress, nothing sleeveless or suggestive. It's too important to create a strong first impression when people come in that front door.

The Stratford:
Under construction

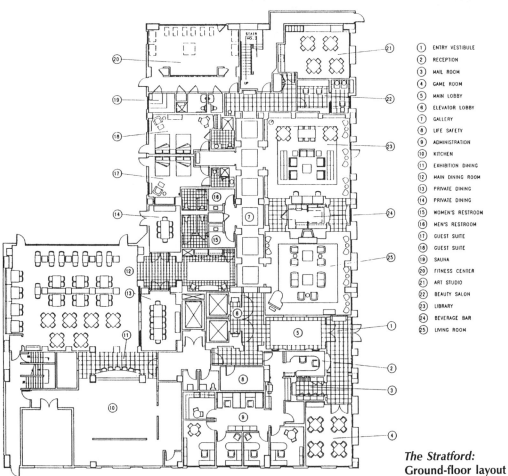

①	ENTRY VESTIBULE
②	RECEPTION
③	MAIL ROOM
④	GAME ROOM
⑤	MAIN LOBBY
⑥	ELEVATOR LOBBY
⑦	GALLERY
⑧	LIFE SAFETY
⑨	ADMINISTRATION
⑩	KITCHEN
⑪	EXHIBITION DINING
⑫	MAIN DINING ROOM
⑬	PRIVATE DINING
⑭	PRIVATE DINING
⑮	WOMEN'S RESTROOM
⑯	MEN'S RESTROOM
⑰	GUEST SUITE
⑱	GUEST SUITE
⑲	SAUNA
⑳	FITNESS CENTER
㉑	ART STUDIO
㉒	BEAUTY SALON
㉓	LIBRARY
㉔	BEVERAGE BAR
㉕	LIVING ROOM

The Stratford:
Ground-floor layout

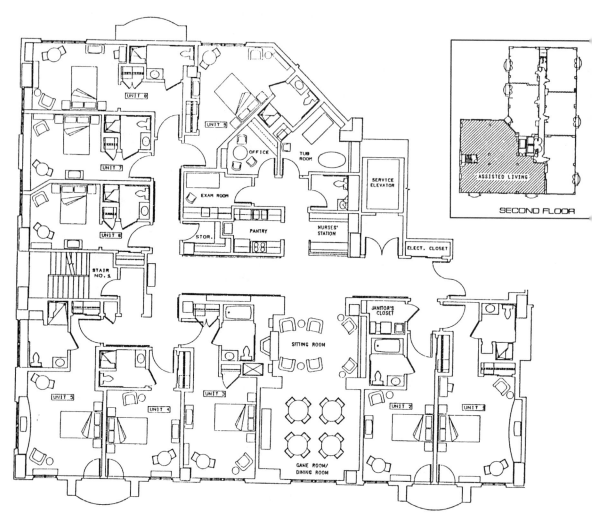

The Stratford: Laurel Wing, Assisted Living, floor plan

THE OSPREY SOUTH (406 and 410)

2444 square feet

The Cypress: **Villa apartments**

THE PARK

1515 square feet

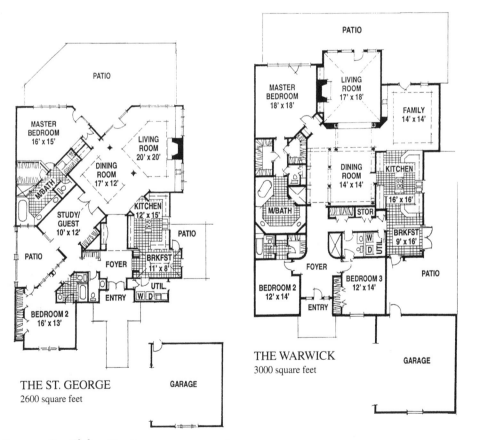

THE ST. GEORGE
2600 square feet

THE WARWICK
3000 square feet

The Cypress: **Bay Club cottages**

8.0 Design and Build

The Cypress and *The Stratford* share the same standard of building image, performance, and value. All recent safety features exist. Both are excellent examples of "life safety." Buildings are constructed of incombustible materials. All materials and carpets, upholstery, and wallpaper have incombustible ratings. All common areas and living units have monitored fire systems and immediate response systems. The common areas are designed to accommodate wheelchairs and walkers with room for safe clearance. Residences are designed to meet an assisted living standard, as well as meeting all requirements of the Americans with Disabilities Act (ADA). As a high-rise structure in an earthquake zone, *The Stratford* was built with the most advanced structural system possible. Corridors, elevator vestibules, and stairwells are a safe haven in the event of fire. Even nonambulatory residents would be able to find safety until the fire department was able to control the fire.

Exemplary design and engineering standards are important achievements. Accommodating the design as a principal contributor to quality of life is just as essential. To achieve this, every insight developed in the preceding sections must be employed. Contractors and architects must see themselves in every role and understand all the subtleties involved. They must never make a design decision without a clear image of the implications of that decision on resident life and the ability of the CCRC staff to fulfill its responsibilities. This requires a professional preparation that is uncommon in the construction industry.

■ Design/Build

How does John Raiser present the capabilities needed for a CCRC development? He draws from his Greek heritage in this fashion.

The ancient Greeks believed that their fates were determined by the whims of gods sitting on Mount Olympus. We try to remember this in the midst of a CCRC development project, when the gods of financial analysis, municipal approvals, and market dynamics are gazing down from the clouds, lightning bolts at the ready. Decisions made at the development stage of a CCRC enterprise are critical to its success for decades to come. The goal is to create an asset where there might otherwise be just a building. We coordinate design drawings, identify financing, negotiate with municipalities, and supervise construction drawings as an elaborate and intricate interplay of ideas, objectives, and outcomes. By coordinating all of the development elements in tandem, instead of the traditional succession, the CCRC design/build executive is able to save time and encourage collaboration much earlier in the development process. In turn, this saves money and ideally positions the project for the construction phase.

As the design/build contractor for *The Stratford*, we functioned a lot like Hephaestus, the master builder for the Greek gods. We provided single-source accountability from architectural programming to financing and to permit approvals and budgeting. Then we put together the executive organization that made the project happen. We used a sizable network of strategic alliances to build an organization of professionals to match our needs: architects, engineers, subcontractors, and consultants. We were always the project coordinator, the central point of communication. We were always on time and nearly always on budget. We brought to *The Stratford* enterprise a distinguished track record of service and maintenance. We understood the predictable competition of residences, cost controls, and reasonable investor returns, and the importance of appeasing those deities without undue sacrifice.

The Design/Build Strategy

The preferred way of working in a CCRC enterprise is design/build, where the developer, the operator, or whoever takes the long-term responsibility, takes the architect and the contractor into his or her confidence and says, "Let's all work together." This is what I try to do. Obviously, we try to do it as economically as we can. Here are the numbers, this is what our clientele can afford, and we cannot build something they cannot afford or we are all spinning our wheels. Therefore, here is the budget, and how do we bring all the forces together to build a building that serves a purpose at the right price and is going to maintain itself in the long term? It is a different kind of construction approach. It is a construction company and an architectural company and a development company that puts the mathematics first, but keeps the commitment of quality and service to the community very close in front of them at all times. In the low-bid process, service to the community does not exist. If a contractor has service to the community and service to the client in front of him, he will never be the low bidder because the next guy that doesn't have those standards is going to beat him every time, and he will be out of business very quickly.

Convincing People to Design/Build

That's the age-old question of how you convince people to design/build. I define the bid process as an invitation to litigation because, invariably, when there are different goals and different attitudes, litigation comes first. So, I suggest that you don't look at the initial cost of the building, but look at the team you are building. How many lawsuits has the contractor had in the last 5 years? And investigate the lawsuits. Investigate the clients that the low bidder has built for and try to assess their selection process. This is somewhat similar to what we do in medicine when we need help. We would almost never ask the doctors how much they charge and pick them based on the low bidder. We will pick somebody that we can trust with knowing his or her profession. In forming the design/build team I will tell people, "I trust you as a human being. I trust your professional ability." The contractor and the architect should be selected simultaneously for a philosophical meeting of the minds to provide the clients with the proper product. In the design/build industry, we have not developed case law of litigation, which frustrates attorneys. They cannot really deal with recommending a process that has not been clarified by the courts, and it is a Catch-22 syndrome. We have not had too many attorneys recommending design/build because the thinking of the legal profession is that the courts set a precedent method of operation through failures. And where there has not been that series of failures, they throw up their hands and they don't want to have anything to do with it.

The Flawed Bid Process

The design/build strategy is fundamentally a response to what it takes to be a bidding contractor. We're finding that if a contractor is willing to be a bidding contractor, then the only way he can be successful is by being the low bidder. By being the low bidder, he must compete against other low bidders, and every bidder is in that pool trying to beat the lowest bidder. However, we forget that all the contractors will hire the local plumbers and the local electricians and the local carpentry specialists, so, how can they be low bidder? Either by not making a profit, if they pay the same for their materials, or by not buying top-end materials. So, the choice that the contractor has is either not make a profit (and you take the chance that he will go broke on your job and leave it unfinished) or buying inferior materials, or using cheap, inferior workmen. So bidding is a race for the most inferior. And this causes a tug of war between the owner, who pays the bills, and the architect, who is trying to enforce some semblance of order. The low bidder succeeds getting the job by beating the other contractors by trying to cut corners. The electrician has the same predicament, as he hires workmen and gets proposals for his material. He competes with other electricians who are also trying to get the job and are going through the same process. The low-bid process ensures that we'll get somebody that has found either a gimmick or a trick to cheapen the plan, totally ignoring the fact that the structure needs to be maintained long-term.

The architect has another very difficult predicament. Developers want them to build a monument for a very low budget. And architects, if they are good architects, are seldom good business people, at least they are not in the forefront of economic analysis. Having gone through architectural school myself, I know that my classmates were very talented students who relied on their artistic inclination but did not want to play with numbers all day long and avoided the College of Business as much as they could. Therefore, they don't have the deep instinct for dealing with numbers. A client makes a fundamental error in asking the architect for budgets or relying on architects' estimates for his long-term economic analysis. These budgets and projections should come from the contractor who is much better equipped to make these projections.

■ The Executive Architect

The Raiser Organization's executive architect notes that architects can bring some very interesting thought processes to the whole CCRC development process because they're trained to think creatively. They're trained not to shy away from the unknown, and good developers think the same way. They look at projects and they look at proposals and they don't necessarily follow a scheme that's already been tried. They're all such creative thinkers, they go forward and find a hybrid between different solutions that work. So, the thinking process of an architect is very helpful in the entire enterprise. All the way through, from development to operations, including marketing, believe it or not.

In any CCRC development project, there are risks. There's a certain amount of guesswork and there's a certain amount of luck that's mixed in with a lot of very hard work and due diligence. You have to be responsive and creative in many different ways as the process evolves. For instance, the conceptualization of a site. You have to be creative in thinking about the site. How can you use it? How can it respond to the needs and the potential for the CCRC product? As you work your way through, developing the program specifics, how do you respond to the program, how do the structural concepts integrate themselves, and how does the architectural image work to satisfy the needs and expectations of the clients?

Your thinking must go all the way down to the marketing aspects. In a CCRC enterprise ,the design/build team must be totally aware of the level of income of prospective residents. What are their resources? What kind of facility could they support? What would their demands be? You're going to get some numbers that tell you there are so many people that live here, have this sort of income or that sort of balance sheet. But the gap between a market survey or market study and building the product is the developer's perception, what his gut tells him. So, there is a gap where analytical thinking stops and where the creative thinking starts. That is the risk. Those who are good at it and have a certain amount of luck in timing do well, and those who don't have a very good perception are troubled through the entire life of the CCRC.

The High-Rise CCRC

When you look at the different CCRC prototypes, you have the urban, which is a high-rise model, and then you have the suburban, which can either be in a midrise fashion or a low-rise campus style. If you start to think about the future, and you start to think about the organization of our communities and how growth is managed or the lack of good management, you can't help but wonder how those two models are going to evolve. How valid is a campus-style setting, for instance? You look at *The Stratford* and you look at the Santa Clara Valley, and you see these communities continuing to spread in suburban style, and you have to wonder if the campus-style setting is really limited in terms of the future.

The reality is that as you grow older, your mobility becomes more and more limited. I think we realized that in a campus-style setting, getting around the community becomes much more difficult as you get 85 to 90 years old In a vertical model like *The Stratford* in an urban setting, transportation is quite easy, which facilitates getting around. Being close to a regional center or a downtown is valuable. Now, the campus settings are initially very appealing. Beautiful scenery, but all the buildings are two-story, one-story. They're all spread out over the site, which is delightful, but you end up with these lengths between the dining areas, the community areas, and all the residences. You have to come up with a transportation system to get people around. So, there are real limitations. I keep thinking back about Palo Solari and his concepts for urbanization. I think we all recognize and realize that his concepts, sooner or later, are going to be embraced, and that, more than likely, is the future of our urban growth. So, it really supports the urban concept of CCRCs.

I think there is a real benefit to the urban setting. One of the things that I think that we tend to do is we take the term "aged" or "aging people" and all of a sudden it becomes a class of people, and, yet, they are individuals. They have different limitations but it is wrong to isolate them out in the country away from a larger community. Their health and well-being really have to do with their interaction with a lot of other people. Older and younger. In an urban setting, there's more opportunity for that sort of thing.

The CCRC Design Image

There are tremendous opportunities and the demographics are going to force us to build more communities; there's no question about it. The question is: Who's going to do it well? And how is it going to be done well? How do we anticipate what it's going to look like in 20 years? To approach the design image at the beginning, I think we're limited, to a certain extent, because of the clientele. We're dealing with people who have 50 or 60 years' experience owning buildings, homes, and living in homes. What are you going to provide that's going to be marketable that people are going to feel comfortable moving into? You have to start by thinking about, well, who are the users and what are their history and their experience. Because, if you were to approach it maybe too innovatively, and take a Frank Gehry approach, for instance— "I want to develop this retirement community and I want Frank Gehry as my architect." The question is how far can you push the envelope with people who have a certain previous position toward architecture? You might get a few that are very extreme, who would love the fact that you're terribly innovative. More likely than not, you're going to get a whole bunch of people who don't understand what you're trying to do, don't appreciate it, and, therefore, it'll be a marketing failure. So, there's a distinct line. It may be disappointing that the interior architecture looks so much the same, but, again, it's based on where people come from. What do their own homes look like? Are they basically living room, dining room, kitchen, baths, and bedrooms? Okay, well let's vary the ceiling heights, let's vary the finishes, let's vary the draperies, let's vary a whole number of things but, basically, end up with the components that they're used to.

Obviously, that's going to change, you know. What you and I would perceive as a good living setting 20 or 30 years from now is probably going to be much different. The way present communities are operated is very static. You basically move into one condominium, and you eat in one dining room and you pretty much remain in one setting. I think what's going to happen is that as time goes by, people are not going to be satisfied with that anymore. I think that they're going to want more variety. I mean, we have variety when we're younger. There's no reason why we shouldn't have variety when we're older, too. It's what keeps you alive and keeps you invigorated about the possibilities. So, I think what may evolve is more of a "Club Med" concept for retirement communities, where you can buy a condominium and make arrangements with a number of facilities in various locales around the world, whether it's St. Petersburg or Sydney, or the Fiji Islands, or San Francisco. I think there will be more opportunity to spend 6 months in Fiji and 3 months in the Caribbean. Maybe it would get into a timeshare. I don't know how that would work, but I think that people would find more excitement if they could move around and experience other things, rather than staying static and living in one community until they pass away. If you look at Club Med, as a corporation, they're tremendously successful. They've tapped into something that works. I think that the retirement community really should look at Club Med and ask, "Is there anything parallel?" "Is there anything like that that makes sense for us?" And investigate that a little bit more.

Our minds and our souls really don't want to stop, basically, until our parts stop, and to think that somebody, when he gets to be 65 or 70, will feel that, "Well, I'm ready to stop now, for the next 20 years," is delusional. I think that technology can help support a mobile life-style. The use of communication and transportation and information should reinforce the fact that we don't have to sit in one apartment in one locale.

The Design/Build Responsibility

Part of the methodology of design/build is designing to the budget. What drives design/build efficiency is dollars. The traditional system is flawed in that a designer never has all the information he should have, simply because it's impossible to share with him all the finite information. You wouldn't have time to design the building and work on the pro forma and work on all the other aspects. So, there's a limited amount of design that's going on in a vacuum. What happens, traditionally, is that you find out, once you've designed it, once you've drawn it, you bid it out, and you find out that's it probably more expensive than you really can afford. So you have to go back again, and try and redesign to the dollars again, whereas, in a design/build method, you're designing to the dollars as you go along because you have more complete information. Even then, you have the flexibility during the construction process to make changes that benefit the architecture and respond to the dollars, and you can make decisions based on both, whereas, in a traditional system, you ask the architect to come in to take a look at this, because you think that all of a sudden there is a better way.

A good example would be from our work on *The Stratford*. We were under construction. The dining room was designed by the architects of record. They designed it like one in a previous community where there was a complete separation between the kitchen and the dining room itself. The concrete was poured, the floors were up and some of the framing was started, and plumbing was going in. We were having lunch one day at a restaurant, and we started to ask ourselves: What is that dining room going to be like with a complete separation of kitchen and dining room? Isn't it going to be awfully quiet, and aren't you going to hear the forks on the plates, and all the sounds of people eating? We thought, isn't it going to be a little bit sterile? And we realized that with an open display kitchen, like the one in the restaurant, there's more excitement, there's more activity, more fun. We realized we should consider making a change. We went back to construction at that time, after lunch, and decided to knock out walls and redesign the kitchen to open up into the dining room. The design/build process allowed us to do that very quickly without having to go back to the architects and all the other participants and somehow manage the process of trying to make a change. We were able to make a change at a reasonable cost, to the benefit of the architecture and the final product. That's the desirability of the design/build process.

The Future

Our challenge is going to be how to make the equity CCRC concept work for middle-income retirees, and maybe even lower-than-middle-income retirees, who may only have $200,000 to retire on for 20 years. It's easier to make it work for the high end; spend a lot of money and have high monthly fees. But if that only works for 1% of the population, then it sort of stops short of trying to solve the bigger issues. Building technologies. New ways to do things less expensively and still meet the requirements. Numbers of the community, the size of the community, the overall actuarials, and the economics. How can we make this more affordable? Does it mean we have to get larger and spread out the costs over a larger pool? And then, also, the numbers of facilities. Can we make this work? Can we manage some of the less profitable facilities? Can we partially subsidize them with some of the more profitable communities?

We see a possible solution. We're building affordable housing now, as well. Affordable housing, over the last 8 years, has been funded solely from low-income housing tax credits, a government program that was enacted after the '86 Tax Act, which has been terribly successful. It allows for government to aid in the development of affordable housing for people of limited income. There's a tremendous potential for a program like that to be applied to senior communities, and maybe we'll see something like that happen in the next 20 years because of the demographics.

The Worst Architectural Details

What's wrong with current low-cost senior communities? Well, I think it has to do with a couple of things. One would be the building imagery. Some of the architecture is horrible, and some of the facilities, some of the buildings, are grim. I've seen acoustical ceilings, you know, T-bar ceilings, in corridors that run on for 75 or 100 feet. Not very attractive. You have to go to a motel to see stuff like that, and yet, you see it used in senior communities all the time. And then there are the planning aspects. I walked into a community a year ago, and as you walk through the front door, the reception desk is to your right, and immediately ahead of you in full view is a whole line of residents who are sitting against a back wall in a communal room or a parlor, and half of them are in wheelchairs with blankets over their legs. So, the question is, how elegant is this setting? And then, the apartments themselves are poorly planned and designed. Sometimes the units get to be so small that the rooms are just compartments. And yet, it's 1997. That's not a function of low cost. It's a function of bad design and planning.

It all gets back to the same thing, which is that all these projects are built by teams of people, and the project is only successful if the individual strengths of the team are good, if they're effective, and they care enough about what they're doing. It's a real challenge to make it work from concept through the entire turnkey process. No matter how much money you have to work with, there is no guarantee that you're going to get a good product. I think you could give some people $500 to build a fish camp and they'd do a terrific job. It would be terrifically detailed, and it would be terrifically executed, and it would be well conceptualized. It's often irrespective of money. It really has to do with vision. It's having a team of people with complimentary skills, who are dedicated and that are diligent.

How do you put a design/build team together? There's no easy answer to that. That's a tough one. I think networking is probably the most important thing, because when you interact with other people, you get to know people, and you find people that are complementary and who have similar expectations and levels of demands. I think the flexibility of thought and the responsiveness to different conditions are as important as is the team's ability to interpret effectively any set of circumstances.

■ The Cypress

We interviewed several different architects and chose Thompson, Hancock and Witte of Atlanta. They had not done much retirement community work, but had good experience in country clubs, hotels, and multifamily. They have a midsized firm with ten to twelve architects and a total staff of twenty-five to thirty. There are firms that specialize in this product in the Philadelphia area. We interviewed them, but we just weren't as comfortable. We do know how to work with architects and we knew what we wanted in terms of plans, so we didn't feel like we needed somebody who'd done that many of these communities. We were doing something new, a country club CCRC. We're using THW in Charlotte also, so, obviously, we are happy with them. The fact that they did *The Cypress* has gotten them several jobs and a large part of their business is now CCRCs. We're happy to entertain their clients, and they have been helpful to us in may ways. What I like the best about what they did is the line of sight. You walk into the lobby and you can see into the community hall, the library, the living room, out on the patio, into the dining room, and you can see the private dining room. If you take three steps forward, you can see all the way down the activities hall. There is a feeling of life in the clubhouse. Even if there is just a handful of people around in this big building, you feel like things are happening. We've obviously learned some lessons about floor plans; how to balance a mix of units, what sells at what price. We've got a broad range of products. We can take care of an 85-year old widow in a one-bedroom at $160,000 with a net worth of $400,000 and also appeal to a couple with a net worth of $10 million in a $550,000 cottage.

Notes

1. N. Van Amberg. (1993). Cypress wins "Oscar." *Real Estate/Homes* (November): 7.
2. E. Craig. (1993). The U.S.A.'s 20 best. *New Choices* (November): 66–67.
3. P. Feinberg. (1992). Retirement planning: Investing for the good life. *Barron's.* (August 31): 5–6.
4. Senior highs. *Builder* (1993). (October): 64–66.
5. Large-scale residential award for excellence. *Urban Land Magazine* (1993). (December): 15–16.
6. S. Dorn. (1993). The Cypress of Hilton Head Island. *Hospitality Design* (November): 44–49.
7. J. Micklewait and A. Wooldridge. (1996). *The Witch Doctors.* New York: Times Books.
8. P. Gordon. (1993). *Developing Retirement Communities*, 2nd ed. New York: John Wiley & Sons.

PART II

THE STANDARD OF PERFORMANCE

The standard of performance—shown in its entirety in the Appendix—establishes a scope of work in which all CCRC enterprise participants are involved and all are asked to contribute their insights and recommendations. The standard of performance is a means for accumulating ideas and sharpening perceptions, for combining speculation and rigorous analysis. When we consider what must be accomplished within a retirement community enterprise, the standard of performance sets the agenda. When reviewing accomplished work, it is the criteria for assessing how successfully each critical success factor was addressed. People must recognize from the very beginning that the standard of performance does not supplant their expertise; rather, it is a complement to the best practices and professional standards of all participants.

The standard of performance is particularly promising because it puts all enterprise participants to work within the same information structure, making them one deliberative body. One of the challenges facing the CCRC executive is that participants in a retirement community enterprise want to be more than a source of information; they want to be part of project deliberations. Adherence to the standard of performance provides this opportunity. Within applications of the standard there is no hesitancy in sharing insights and recommendations as these come to mind. At any time and at any place in a deliberation, an individual can call attention to any question item in the standard of performance, forthrightly saying that she knows something other people do not know or that she is capable of achieving something that is impossible for others to achieve.

An Open Process

The standard of performance is the core of the CCRC executive strategy. The two hundred question items presented in the Appendix are designed to precisely order CCRC enterprise deliberations into mutually exclusive information categories. Each question item is uniquely identified by an index number, title, and topic. With this protocol, the standard of performance is readily established as a computer-based applications system.

It is essential to remember that although the standard of performance is presented in a numerical sequence, this index does not indicate a sequential application of the question items. All the question items in the standard of performance remain open from the beginning of the enterprise to the very end. Rather than thinking in terms of a starting point and an ending point, think in terms of obtaining the maximum from every enterprise associate. Although an open process, the standard of performance is not the least bit chaotic; as depicted in Figure 2, there is a special place for every insight and analysis.

■ A Way to Become Smarter

During the course of a retirement community enterprise, we meet daily to discuss what has been accomplished, what is the next step, and then select one course of action, personnel assignment, design feature, or funding allocation over another. None of this is simple and nothing is gained by attempts to simplify this process. The premise of the standard of performance is that these deliberations can be structured in a precise, thorough, and comprehensive fashion and still make room for the aggressive promotion of ideas and points of view. To this end, we present here a clear and simple information development format with a special place for every insight, research finding, and record of deliberations.

The points that follow outline a number of benefits. Guided by the thinking of Christopher Bartlett and Sumantra Ghoshal,[1] we want to design a standard of performance application that:

- Gets the total organization involved
- Puts knowledge in the hands of people who use it
- Builds an enterprise based on purpose, process, and people
- Works out differences in the way enterprise associates work
- Empowers all project participants
- Fosters collaboration

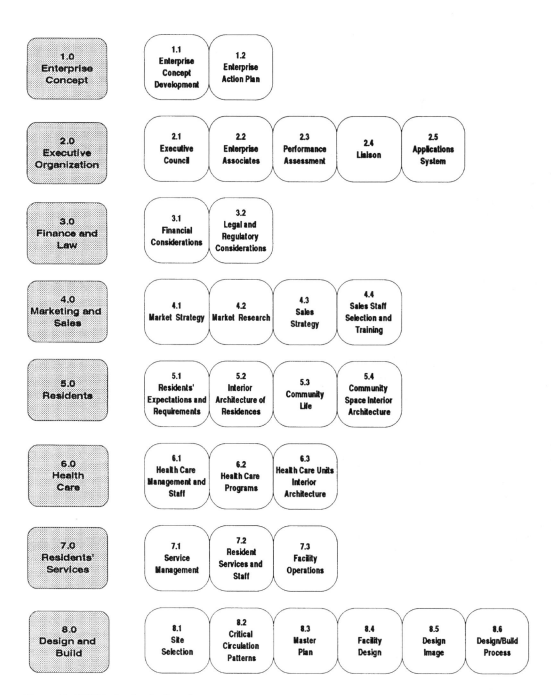

Figure 2. CCRC standard of performance menu

We see the standard of performance as a means to:

- Capture people's attention and interest
- Create momentum
- Recognize individual accomplishments
- Achieve a commitment to developing new expertise
- Foster individual initiative
- Provide a safety net for risks takers
- Prevent surprises

Train People for New Responsibilities

The standard of performance is a training experience for people assuming new responsibilities. It presents to them the entire CCRC enterprise, leaving nothing out. This comprehensive view produces the sense of confidence that is always the basis for excellent on-the-job performance.

Creating Ties Between People

Enterprise success is dependent on trust. Shared information, which results from standard of performance applications, is the basis of mutual trust. First, open books symbolize trust. Second, it is evident that the goal is to obtain optimum solutions for every problem and challenge. When you fail to share information, you tell people that your conclusions and recommendations are not open to review and critique.

■ Commentary

The following presentation of the CCRC standard of performance fosters the view that as organizations attempt to solve problems never faced before, they must learn by design rather than by chance.[2] It is always the case that when a situation is filled with good ideas, the problem is one of implementation.[3] In this context, consider the advantage gained when enterprise participants know what other people are working on and what they are attempting to achieve, and are encouraged to contribute their own unique perspective. This counters the usual practice of assigning individual tasks. We do not want work to become formalized or inflexible or to see thinking stop when a report or task is finished. We want unimpeded communication between all enterprise participants, people who see that every individual is an essential and valuable resource. For this reason, the items in the standard of performance are written as questions. When asked a question, an individual begins to contribute immediately, putting what he or she knows to work. When project participants see the questions in the standard of performance and know they are open for discussion, their knowledge and insight become a resource.

1.0 Enterprise Concept

The question items in this section of the standard of performance establish a reference point for all enterprise deliberations. These question items provide an opportunity for debate and argument. No retirement community enterprise is free of uncertainty and controversy, particularly when emphasis is placed on achieving both profit and service excellence. Certain question items direct the development of enterprise concept options and alternatives and evaluation criteria. Other questions help us develop an enterprise overview and perspectives on resources and assets. These undertakings can become a liability if we do not assess the merit of recent technological advances as these apply to facility design and construction, fully understand health care delivery systems, respond to evolving social and political views, and listen to the elderly as they speak to their future.

■ 1.1 Enterprise Concept Development

Areas to Address

1.1.1 CANDIDATE CONCEPTS. Taking into account the existing situation, anticipated events, desired enterprise outcomes, and image of the future, what are the candidate retirement community concepts?

1.1.2 CONCEPT EVALUATION CRITERIA. What criteria should be used to evaluate candidate concepts?

1.1.3 EVALUATION RESULTS. What are the evaluation results and concluding recommendations for candidate concepts?

1.1.4 ENTERPRISE CONCEPT. What is the mutually agreed upon enterprise concept?

The search here is as much for opposing points of view as for achieving mutual agreement and understanding of enterprise concepts. Concepts never achieve noteworthy results without addressing and resolving aspects of the retirement community enterprise that are complex, troublesome, unique, or subtle. Certainly, concepts that are a response to what everyone believes is the obvious, those that are not subjected to rigorous analysis, and those that create a sense of certainty that is only rhetorical lead to a problem enterprise.

In response to question item 1.1.1 Candidate Concepts, each proposal must state the business or market intent, and must be in the form of options and alternatives. It must originate not only from individuals, but must also reflect the best practices and benchmarks of the retirement community industry. The success of this deliberation is assured when you establish evaluation criteria and apply these to candidate options and alternatives.

■ 1.2 Enterprise Action Plan

Areas to Address

1.2.1 ACTION PLAN. What is the proposed enterprise action plan?

1.2.2 ENTERPRISE SCHEDULE. What are the enterprise milestone events and schedule?

1.2.3 REQUIRED RESOURCES AND ASSETS. What resources and assets are needed to fulfill the promise of the enterprise concept and action plan?

1.2.4 REQUIRED RESEARCH. What research is required to augment the enterprise strategy?

At this point in the application of the standard of performance, we ask: What is the best way to put our experience and expertise to work? As the information developed here is shared again and again with investors, lenders, underwriters, government regulators, and the public, it is written as much to persuade as it is to inform. The lead question items, 1.2.1 Action Plan and 1.2.2 Enterprise Schedule, result in a statement that describes what you actually are going to do and what results you anticipate in the coming months and years. With regard to item 1.2.3 Required Resources and Assets, no action plan can have validity without a statement of required resources and assets with evidence that these exist within the enterprise. Address here your professional, partnership, and alliance assets. Likewise, no action plan has validity without a statement of the research required. In 1.2.4 Required Research, we consider the research needed to confirm our enterprise concept and devise the best scope of work for this undertaking. As you begin your research, you must consider every possible point of view that will be used to critique your enterprise. Guidelines for designing this undertaking in terms of market, human factors, design, and legal research are presented in Part III: Strategic Research.

2.0 Executive Organization

The formation of the executive organization is the most critical undertaking in a retirement community enterprise. Without established leadership, desired performance may soon give way to marginal performance and all the dangers associated with the superficial monitoring of progress. The questions items in this section of the standard of performance address the selection criteria for the executive council and how this group should be organized to fulfill its mandate. Question items lead to the building of a disciplined management philosophy, measures of progress, establishment of liaison functions, and the design and management of the computer-based applications system.

▩ 2.1 The Executive Council

Areas to Address

2.1.1 EXECUTIVE COUNCIL APPOINTMENT CRITERIA. What are the criteria for appointment to the executive council?

2.1.2 EXECUTIVE COUNCIL CANDIDATES. Who are the candidates for placement on the executive council?

2.1.3 EXECUTIVE COUNCIL APPOINTMENTS. Applying the selection criteria to candidates, which individuals are recommended for appointment to the executive council?

2.1.4 EXECUTIVE COUNCIL MANDATE. What are the primary responsibilities of the executive council?

2.1.5 INDIVIDUAL RESPONSIBILITIES. What are the responsibilities of individual executive council members?

This is the first step toward establishing effective executive leadership and action in a retirement community enterprise. Executive council membership is not a matter of right, status, or influence. It is a matter of critical knowledge and the ability to lead. We need to form a team of individuals with these qualifications, with an enduring regard for others, and a total commitment to the enterprise as an ethical charge, a community and business responsibility. In terms of items 2.1.1 Executive Council Selection Criteria, 2.1.2 Executive Council Candidates, and 2.1.3 Executive Council Appointments, the executive council is built one person at a time, by carefully developing and applying selection criteria. The result should be an executive council with six or seven people. This number is a critical mass of skills while fostering maximum communication and commitment to an enterprise.[4]

The basis for responding to items 2.1.4 Executive Council Mandate and 2.1.5 Individual Responsibilities can best be found in the work of Jon Katzenbach and Douglas Smith.[5] This work presents two principles for the development and work of the executive council: "Organizational leaders can foster team performance best by building a strong performance ethic rather than by establishing a team-promoting environment," and "Discipline—both within the team and across the organization—creates the conditions for team performance." Following this guideline, Katzenbach and Smith promote a view that must be a standard for the executive council: "In any situation requiring the real-time combination of multiple skills, experiences, and judgments, a team inevitably gets better results than a collection of individuals operating within confined job roles and responsibilities." In his more recent work, Jon Katzenback[6] makes the distinction that teamwork is broad-based cooperation and supportive behavior; a team is a small, tightly focused performance unit. The creation of such a "team" is the primary objective of the standard of performance.

■ 2.2 Enterprise Associates

Areas to Address

2.2.1 OWNERS, INVESTORS, AND LENDERS. Who represents the owners, investors, and lenders during executive organization deliberations?

2.2.2 MARKETING AND SALES MANAGER. Who represents the marketing and sales perspectives during executive organization deliberations?

2.2.3 DEVELOPER'S REPRESENTATIVE. Who represents the developer's interests and concerns during executive organization deliberations?

2.2.4 ARCHITECTS. Who represents the architectural design interests and concerns during executive organization deliberations?

2.2.5 DESIGN/BUILD MANAGEMENT. Who represents the design/ build management team during executive organization deliberations?

2.2.6 SERVICE PROVIDERS. Who represents the service providers' interests and concerns during executive organization deliberations?

2.2.7 HEALTH CARE REPRESENTATIVE. Who represents the interests and concerns of those managing and maintaining the health care program during executive organization deliberations?

2.2.8 FOOD SERVICE REPRESENTATIVE. Who speaks for the interests and concerns of those who provide food services?

2.2.9 LEGAL COUNSEL. Who provides legal counsel to the executive organization?

2.2.10 FINANCIAL ADVISORS. Who provides financial advice to the executive organization?

2.2.11 INSURANCE PROVIDERS. Who represents the interests and concerns of the insurance providers?

2.2.12 RESIDENTS' SPOKESPERSONS. Who represents the interests and concerns of residents during executive organization deliberations?

These question items provide the identities of all the men and women representing the knowledge and experience needed to form an effective CCRC executive organization. These question items recognize that the human element is the foundation of business success. Regardless of the sophistication of our management processes, it is the enthusiasm of the people involved in making and selling things that creates the competitive potential of a company.[7]

■ 2.3 Performance Assessment

Areas to Address

2.3.1 OVERSIGHT. As the cornerstone of the enterprise, how is the work of the executive organization evaluated?

2.3.2 PEER REVIEW. What experts are responsible for assessing proposed and in-progress work?

2.3.3 BOARD OF DIRECTORS. Recognizing that liaison and oversight are the primary responsibilities of the enterprise

With regard to 2.3.1 Oversight, the executive council and enterprise associates must continually monitor and review the information that develops during application of the standard of performance. This habit of critique provides an exacting evaluation process. We want to use the standard of performance for self-assessment. It pertains directly to the task at hand, clearly showing our accomplishments and deliberations and where problems remain. Item 2.3.2 Peer Review presents another opportunity to promote the success of the enterprise through the use of performance assessment. The benefits derived are so valuable that these appointments must be made at the earliest possible time. With regard to items 2.3.3 Board of Directors and 2.3.4 Residents' Enterprise Review Board, Nancy Axelrod, president of the National Center for Nonprofit Boards, states that a knowledgeable and engaged board of directors is an asset to every enterprise. To attain the very best of benefits, she suggests that it is important to invest time in educating the board, providing board members with the information they need to monitor performance, and the opportunity to participate in policy formulation at an early stage.[8]

■ 2.4 Liaison

The public's scrutiny of retirement community developments is becoming increasingly more responsible. The preceding question items prepare us for this collaborative undertaking. The strategy for turning governmental entities and the public into enterprise partners must be carefully crafted. Question item 2.4.4 Preparation suggests that before any contact or meeting, we must discover what people want to hear, what their concerns and apprehensions are, and how they perceive their responsibilities. Enterprise spokespersons must undertake the research needed to be fully informed as to the interests, questions, and attitudes they will face. In fact, during the first minutes of every meeting, you want people to recognize the depth of your understanding of their situation. Likewise, government entities, local politicians, and neighborhood interest groups can only make the contact positive for the enterprise if they are as fully informed about enterprise scope and direction as every member of the executive organization. Michael Porter speaks to the question of overcoming impediments to development in terms of entrenched attitudes and prejudices. The executive organization must assume a lead role when confronting the intolerable burden of outdated approaches.[9]

2.5 Applications System

Areas to Address

2.5.1 APPLICATIONS SYSTEM REQUIREMENTS. Responding to enterprise objectives and executive and associates responsibilities, what are the applications system requirements?

2.5.2 APPLICATIONS SYSTEM DESIGN. Responding to specified applications system requirements, what are the best software suites and network features for the enterprise?

2.5.3 APPLICATIONS SYSTEM COMPLIANCE. Considering that the applications system is mandated for enterprise deliberations, what is the means for familiarizing all enterprise participants with its structure and utility features?

The applications system must be in constant use. Its use is not a matter of choice, it is mandated. Information technology professionals suggest that an effective knowledge system requires executive support and oversight. Our view is that we can forget about "support" and "oversight," and for that matter, "acceptance" and "persuasion." We must make the applications system the primary tool for enterprise deliberations. It is the most effective and efficient vehicle for blending all the experience and expertise that participants bring to the retirement community enterprise. When enterprise participants share an applications system and network, every individual can freely communicate with every member of the executive organization and still maintain order in the total process.

3.0 Finance and Law

The financial work-ups called for here range from enterprise costs to financing requirements to anticipated return on investments. The legal research is a matter of due diligence that guards the enterprise in terms of regulatory mandates and the investors, lenders, and enterprise participants in terms of rights and legal safeguards. This fiduciary responsibility extends to consideration of the rights and legal safeguards of residents and their families.

■ 3.1 Financial Considerations

Areas to Address

3.1.1 ENTERPRISE BUSINESS PLAN. What enterprise business plan is proposed to achieve sustainable profits and respond to financial opportunities, anticipated pitfalls, and ethical considerations?

3.1.2 PROFIT/NONPROFIT CONSIDERATIONS. What information is needed to identify and evaluate profit/nonprofit options?

3.1.3 FINANCIAL STRUCTURE. What are the financial requirements for the various development phases of the retirement community enterprise?

3.1.4 OPERATING COSTS. What are the anticipated operating costs for the enterprise, prior to occupancy, at occupancy, and over time?

3.1.5 MANAGING ENTERPRISE COSTS. What is the oversight process for milestone approvals and scheduled allocation of funds for each phase of the enterprise?

3.1.6 POTENTIAL INVESTORS AND LENDERS. Who are the potential investors and lenders?

3.1.7 SOLICITATION OF SUPPORT. What steps must be taken to attract investors and lenders?

3.1.8 EQUITY REQUIREMENTS. What are the equity requirements for each phase of the enterprise?

3.1.9 REPORT TO UNDERWRITERS. What question items in the standard of performance must be addressed when preparing the report to underwriters?

3.1.10 PRESALE REQUIREMENTS. What are the presale and nonrefundable deposit requirements for the various enterprise phases?

3.1.11 ON-SITE SOURCES OF INCOME. What are the revenue categories and anticipated on-site revenues for the enterprise?

3.1.12 OFF-SITE SOURCES OF INCOME. What are the revenue categories and anticipated revenues associated with off-site activities?

3.1.13 LOCAL ECONOMIC BENEFITS. As the enterprise means tax or negotiated revenues, jobs, and increased economic activity in the local community, what is the best way to present the associated financial benefits?

3.1.14 FINANCIAL FEASIBILITY PRESENTATION. As each of the preceding question items are candidates for inclusion in the enterprise feasibility study, what is the best possible financial feasibility presentation? What detailed information is required in this presentation?

These question items guide the study of the financial requirements for the various phases of the retirement community enterprise. The results become the basis for the financial feasibility presentation. The question items address the information needed to guide deliberations associated with reports to underwriters, equity requirements, presale requirements, on-site and off-site sources of income, return from units by type, and managing enterprise costs.

Financial feasibility, sources of financing, and cost management influence deliberations throughout the application of the CCRC executive strategy. In reality, financial analysis has more to do with judgment than with spreadsheets. Whether in the context of a for-profit or nonprofit enterprise, financial resources must be available; this happens only when investors, lenders, and underwriters find a promising venture and sound executive leadership. Consequently, study of this critical success factor ranges from financial feasibility studies, to the anticipation of schedules of payment and associated cash flow, to the anticipated revenue stream. This emphasis relates to the fact that financial matters are exposed to the most thorough scrutiny by investors, lenders, and regulatory agencies. It is their standard of performance to which we must be responsive.

These question items stress the need to develop a business design that is responsive to financial opportunities and alert to possible pitfalls. The fundamentals have been identified: When looking for financing, make sure that you understand the regulatory process and market demographics; present a comprehensive marketing plan; and understand the ideal facility layout that at a modest price produces a setting that meets the market preferences.[10] This is only a sketch, not a reference point for a business design. The fundamental reference point is sustainable income and profit. This holds true for investors and lenders and is even more true for the elderly who have placed their trust in what you represent as the best of situations for them. The primary consideration is that the retirement community enterprise is not a real estate play and amateurs will miss the complexities of design and care.[11]

The basic elements of a financial feasibility study[12] are listed in what follows. These schedules are the language of success:

Base Schedules

- *Summary of Significant Assumptions:* such as anticipated occupancy levels, annual revenue and expense adjustment rates, reinvestment rates, and financing terms.

- *Projected Construction and Development Costs:* assumptions are based on the total construction loan and interest rate relative to payments of interest on multiple draws as needed during construction.

- *Development Period Source and Applications of Funds:* this schedule reflects the flow of monies during the construction period and the required equity contribution by the sponsor to fund any development costs which occur prior to project financing.

- *Projected Source and Application of Funds:* a summary schedule showing the total sources and application of funds for initial construction loan, corporate equity, and reservation deposits for the condominium units.

- *Projected Unit Mix and Occupancy Ratio:* a schedule related to average density in the independent units and assisted-living units.

- *Projected Fee Schedule:* the average monthly rate for the first person in all independent units with a charge for the second person and specified services associated with fees.

- *Projected Staffing Budget*: staffing requirements and wage data.

- *Projected Departmental Operating Budget:* based on the experience of existing operations throughout the nation.

- *Projected Cash Flow—Years 1 and 2:* start-up schedules calculate the projected cash flow during the months in which the project fills to 100% occupancy.

- *Projected 10 Year Cash Flow:* a schedule showing cash revenues and expenditures projected for the first 10 years, calculated according to occupancy and inflation assumptions.

Supporting Schedules

- *Food Service Utilization Projection:* the schedule reflects, for instance, an independent dietary program that provides one meal per day and three meals per day for any resident of the assisted-living units.
- *Projected Covered Parking Income*
- *Project Guest Room Income*
- *Projected Commercial Lease Income*
- *Furnishings, Fixtures, and Equipment Budget*
- *Projected Residential Occupancies*
- *Fee Summary—Assisted Living:* this and the following two schedules reflect the project revenues to be generated by the assisted-living units in the Health Center, and by the first and second persons occupying the condominium units.
- *Projected Revenues—First Person*
- *Projected Revenues—Second Person*
- *Analysis of Projected Operating Budget Components:* this schedule reflects how expenses are allocated during the fill-up period.
- *Analysis of Weighted Average Fees and Charges:* a working schedule that summarizes the average monthly and entry fees for various uses throughout the computer model.
- *Long-Term Care Insurance Costs:* a base from which future insurance costs will be allocated. The cost of this amenity is indirectly funded through the independent resident's monthly service fee.
- *Projected Residential Unit Reservations and Entry Fee Collections:* the schedule may assume an estimated number of months to presell 65% of the total units. Prospective residents may be asked to make a 10% deposit at the time of reservation and an additional 15% deposit once the construction commences. The remaining 75% of the unit price will be paid once the resident occupies the unit.
- *Interest Earned on Entry Fees*
- *Projected Transfer Fees on Unit Resales:* estimating a total unit turnover in 15 years.
- *Projected Health Care Utilization:* this is the estimated portion of the CCRC population that resides in either assisted-living units or nursing beds.
- *Projected Health Care Revenues and Expenses Projection:* for instance, a schedule provided primarily for the benefit of the California State Department of Social Services of Life Care Contracts. The schedule illustrates that the sum of revenues generated from long-term care insurance and the reduced resident fees paid for either nursing or assisted living are sufficient to fund the expenses incurred in the provision of those services.

Accounting Schedules

- *Projected Statement of Revenue, Expense, and Changes in Fund Balance*
- *Projected Balance Sheet*
- *Projected Statement of Cash Flow*

Department of Social Services Schedules

- *Statement of Net Cash per Capita Cost:* This schedule takes all operating expenses and divides the total by the combined mean number of residents. The net cash expenses per capita are then used to determine the Statutory Reserve Requirement.
- *Statement of Projected Life Care Cost:* This schedule takes the Net Cash per Capita and projects the total expenses over the projected life of the residents. A conservative average life expectancy is 13 years.
- *Statement of Projected Life Care Revenue:* This schedule takes the yearly revenues generated from the resident monthly service fees and projects them over the anticipated life of the residents.
- *Statement of Statutory Reserve Requirements:* This schedule calculates the difference between Projected Life Care Cost and Projected Life Care Revenue and incorporates the amount into the Statutory Reserve Requirement.

In addition to this schedule of information, a feasibility study must also address the assumptions that pertain to the required length of time to meet presale requirements. The estimates could be something like: Time to Sell 65%—5 months; Time to Sell 85%—15 months; and Time to Sell 100%—25 months.

■ 3.2 Legal and Regulatory Considerations

Areas to Address

- 3.2.1 LEGAL RESEARCH. What must be undertaken to diligently address the rights of investors, lenders, enterprise participants, health care and service providers, and residents?
- 3.2.2 LEGAL AGREEMENTS. What contracts must be produced to address transfer of property rights and service agreements?
- 3.2.3 REGULATORY AGENCIES. What federal, state, and local regulatory and licensing bodies are responsible for enterprise approval?

3.2.4 MEETING REGULATORY REQUIREMENTS. How are regulatory and licensing requirements met? What reporting requirements are mandated by state agencies?

3.2.5 RESIDENTS' RIGHTS. How should contracts and manuals be formulated so as to clearly present the legal rights of residents?

These question items address legal due diligence, from the initial consideration of legal mandates to the final transfer of property rights and approval of service agreements. Items in this section are associated with meeting federal, state, and local regulatory requirements. As you address these questions, it is essential to retain experienced legal counsel.

Conversations at national conferences suggest that "something wicked this way cometh." At every conference, there is a hallway full of people discussing vulnerability to legal entrepreneurs, state authorities who misinterpret their own regulations, the most recent negligence suits, and union and resident activism. To a degree, what we put in writing in such documents as contracts, sales manuals, homeowners' manuals, health and financial screening forms, and residents' association guidelines, works as a safeguard. When we see hefty settlements derived from the consequences of inadequate care and the bringing of class-action suits, no legal service seems too costly.[13] Edward Cherof suggests a legal review strategy that should be put in place when unions target you for an aggressive organizing campaign: Review personal policies, practices, and procedures; review key personnel policies; assess fairness and consistency in administration of personnel policies; assess overall satisfaction with benefits and pay; and review employee evaluation programs and techniques.[14] When you work to protect your residents and your reputation in the community, consider the need to guard against malpractice suits with preemployment screening. When an employee you select turns out to have a record of abusive behavior, the blame will be at your door.[15] In total, it is our ability to anticipate and resolve the problems that confront every enterprise that determines where liabilities and suits occur or are avoided.

4.0 Marketing and Sales

In a retirement community enterprise, we are marketing a place, a service, and an image. We are selling not only to individuals, but also to a community of interests. First, our marketing and sales strategy and the associated details are incorporated into the enterprise feasibility study. Then, we go on to promote the promise of our enterprise to all communities of interest and regulatory

agencies. These presentations must demonstrate a thorough and sophisticated market study, and a strategy representative of the best practices of marketing professionals. In this instance, 4.1 Market Strategy and 4.2 Market Research are functionally one undertaking.

■ 4.1 Market Strategy

Areas to Address

4.1.1 MARKET POTENTIAL. The assessment of market potential is the initial step in the development of a market strategy; thus, what do the results of market research (question items 4.2.1 through 4.2.5) identify as opportunities and challenges?

4.1.2 MARKETING STRATEGY DEVELOPMENT. Which identified market strategies have promise for the enterprise? What are the pros and cons of each? What are the costs associated with each? What program of activities best meets the needs of the enterprise?

4.1.3 MARKETING PROGRAM SCHEDULE. What are the first steps in the marketing program? What is the timeline for all subsequent activities? What are the costs associated with each activity?

4.1.4 MARKETING AUDIT PLAN. What is the audit plan for assessing the effectiveness of the market strategy and associated activities?

4.1.5 PROMOTIONS. Which media have been selected to promote the retirement community enterprise? Which hold the greatest potential and why is this so? What are the projected costs for promotional activities?

4.1.6 WORKING WITH THE COMMUNITY. Recognizing that the local community can foster a positive view of the development, what steps should be taken to familiarize people with the retirement community opportunity?

4.1.7 LIMITED MARKET RESPONSE. When interest in the retirement community is below expectations, what additional efforts should be undertaken?

4.1.8 CONTRIBUTING TO THE FEASIBILITY STUDY. As each of the preceding question items is a candidate for inclusion in the enterprise feasibility study, what is the best possible description of our marketing and sales strategy? What detailed information is required?

In a marketplace where significant changes are taking place and where competition is increasingly relentless, we must rethink our marketing strategies. In particular, we must be more alert to life-style and cultural diversity and associated circumstances and context. The elderly are too diverse a population to be considered in the simple terms that are commonly found in marketing deliberations and brochures.

Market strategy must be based on judgment as much as on data and information. To the degree of confidence provided by sources of information, we must anticipate new market forces and opportunities. Market strategy must be directed to intangibles. When asked about her competitors, one person we interviewed simply said, "People's homes." In her mind, it isn't existing and proposed retirement communities that she must struggle with, it is memories, family life, old friends, and the comfort of being in one's own neighborhood. Market strategy can also address tangibles when we predict, with a stated degree of probability, changes in retirement community demands in the coming decades. Advances in the theories of social science and gerontology, and in communications and medical care and technology, will have a significant impact on the future of the retirement community industry, and must be accounted for in the market strategy.

■ 4.2 Market Research

Areas to Address

4.2.1 DEMOGRAPHICS. What are the demographics of the market region for the general and elderly populations? What is the current and anticipated future demand for retirement communities?

4.2.2 COMPETITORS. What are the existing competing developments? Where are others proposed?

4.2.3 COMPETING CONCEPTS. What do competing developments offer in terms of admission standards, services, quality of life, and financial arrangements?

4.2.4 MARKET CHARACTERISTICS. What descriptive categories best identify and distinguish potential residents?

4.2.5 MARKET DYNAMICS. Where are fundamental changes in the market developing?

On one hand, this research is a requirement, and, on the other, an investment in the future. As a basic enterprise requirement, market research is designed to assure investors, lenders, underwriters, and regulatory agencies that the need for the retirement community exists. It is also a necessary source of information when developing marketing and sales strategies. As an investment in the future, market research helps identify opportunities and reveal innovations that may increase our business potential.

Market research is the effort to understand the significance of demographic data and competitive facility surveys. Demographic analysis, 4.2.1 Demographics, provides data and information needed to estimate the existence of a population of a sufficient size to support the proposed enterprise. These descriptive statistics classify and enumerate existing and projected population characteristics. The degree of penetration of the market by age and income is stated as the percentage of the market that must be captured if the enterprise is to succeed. Consideration is also given to the impact of existing and proposed developments and resale reserves on the market. In 4.2.2 Competitors and 4.2.3 Competing Concepts, we compile information about competing senior living operations and anticipated new developments. What services do they provide? What are the financial arrangements? How large are the waiting lists? The competitive survey usually identifies and describes retirement communities similar to the proposed enterprise within a reasonable radius of the proposed site and then considers exceptional examples within the region. Comparisons cite ranges of costs, services provided, relative size, and location.

Question item 4.2.4 Market Characteristics takes us beyond demographics. There can be no confidence in a market strategy that is not based on a valid and reliable definition of market characteristics. It cautions us to consider the heterogeneity of the elderly. The essential starting point is the identification of the specific individuals and groups of individuals we need to question in order to assure that our market research is directed to those who matter and can provide the information we need to support marketing deliberations and activities. For 4.2.5 Market Dynamics, to the degree of confidence supported by research methodology, we must anticipate new market forces and opportunities. In terms of market dynamics, consider how quickly things can change. A recent Duke University report found a steady shrinkage in the percentage of people aged 65 and over who are classified as disabled, most likely because of some combination of better nutrition and hygiene and medical advances. The Duke researchers found that 1.7 million people were in nursing homes and other such institutions in 1994, some 400,000 fewer than would have been expected if disability rates had remained at 1982 levels.[16]

■ 4.3 Sales Strategy

Areas to Address

4.3 1 INITIAL PRESENTATION. How should the retirement community opportunity be presented to prospective residents?

4.3.2 SELLING TO FAMILY MEMBERS AND FRIENDS. How should the retirement community opportunity be presented to the families and friends of prospective residents?

4.3.3 CLIENT RELATIONS. What steps should be taken to establish in prospective residents a sense of trust in the sales staff?

4.3.4 FOLLOW-UP STEPS. After the initial presentation to prospective residents, what is the strategy for maintaining contact and encouraging reconsideration of the retirement community opportunity?

4.3.5 COMPETING SALES STRATEGIES. Within the market area, what are the sales strategies of competing retirement communities?

4.3.6 INFORMATION BROCHURE. What should be included in the retirement community marketing brochure regarding distinguishing facility features, the master plan, qualification standards, resident services, financial arrangements, quality of life, and health care services?

4.3.7 CLIENT COMPLAINTS. What complaints are common regarding the sales experience? What is the process for dealing with complaints and ensuring that problems are remedied?

4.3.8 LOST CLIENTS. What do we know about prospective clients who did not respond to the retirement community opportunity?

These question items must be placed in the context of such things as identifying and meeting with communities of interest, monitoring the market, and direct personal contacts with potential clients. Although labels can be used in demographic analysis to identify enumerated categories, there is a need for an in-depth characterization of the essential differences between market groups. For instance, if we focus on the next market phenomenon, those born between 1925 and 1942, we find inferences that this group values intangibles more than "things," that their goal is to experience and enjoy life, that money is only a means to an end, that they seek options and demand values, and that they hunger for information. The "I'll move in only if I have to" feeling that we presently confront now has the underlying emotion of "I did it my way," producing a market that stresses individuality, emphasizes comfort over luxury, wants nursing services that are more homelike and life-style-driven, and puts a premium on financial options and considerable value.[17] Considering the heterogeneity of these people, building one-on-one relations with prospective residents is a key strategy.

■ 4.4 Sales Staff Selection and Training

Areas to Address

4.4.1 SALES STAFF MANDATE. What are the primary responsibilities of the sales staff?

4.4.2 SALES STAFF SELECTION CRITERIA. What are the skill and licensing criteria for appointing individuals to sales management and staff positions?

4.4.3 SALES STAFF CANDIDATES. Who are the candidates for sales management and staff positions?

4.4.4 SELECTION OF SALES STAFF. Applying the selection criteria to candidates, which individuals should be appointed to sales staff and management positions?

4.4.5 SALES STAFF ORGANIZATION. How should the sales staff be organized to fulfill its mandate?

4.4.6 WORKING WITH THE ELDERLY. What knowledge and skills are required to promote an interest in the enterprise among prospective residents?

4.4.7 WORKING WITH FAMILIES AND FRIENDS. What knowledge and skills are required to promote an interest in the enterprise among family and friends of prospective residents?

4.4.8 ROLE OF RETIREMENT COMMUNITY STAFF. Recognizing that every person with whom a prospective client comes in

---

Robert Simons[18] offers a useful perspective about selecting and training sales staff. "A fundamental problem facing managers is how to exercise adequate control in organizations that demand flexibility, innovation, and creativity. Competitive businesses with demanding and informed customers must rely on employee initiative to seek out opportunities and respond to customers' needs. But pursuing some opportunities can expose businesses to excessive risk or invite behaviors that can damage a company's integrity." This succinct statement describes our challenge. We certainly want sales staff members who are innovative and responsive, yet at the same time, we want them to have values that never jeopardize the retirement community enterprise. Simmons goes on to suggest some guidelines for selecting and training sales staff. We should emphasize the values and mission of the retirement community enterprise. We should encourage them to do what is right, emphasizing the relationships between sales staff and residents. If you want sales staff candidates and trainees to achieve what is expected of them, then you must present them with unequivocal standards and ask them to continue to learn every day on the job.

5.0 Residents

The information developed here must be precise, thorough, comprehensive, and as error-free as possible. The goal is to obtain a characterization of residents' expectations and requirements that provides the framework within which we create and justify facility design and service and health care recommendations. We seek here a reference point for determining how much more we need to know before our market research is complete; that is, have we anticipated all possible resident groups and within-group distinctions that indicate special needs and wants? Each prospective resident will have his or her own living pattern, determined by life-style, activity limitations and capabilities associated with age and health, and by individual and family circumstances.

■ 5.1 Residents' Expectations and Requirements

Areas to Address

5.1.1 DISTINGUISHING CHARACTERISTICS. What characteristics and factors can be used to distinguish residents?

5.1.2 DAILY ACTIVITIES. What are the daily activities of residents? What is known about the extent, time of occurrence, and duration of activities?

5.1.3 INDIVIDUAL PERCEPTIONS. How are residents likely to perceive themselves, other residents, and staff in terms of their individual rights and anticipated perquisites?

5.1.4 LIFE-STYLES. What are the social customs, relationship norms, and cultural traditions of residents?

This is the core of design and service-related deliberations and requires that we identify every need, concern, and preference. These question items serve to keep the retirement community enterprise on target; it is impossible to succeed without this information. Every facility and service must be responsive to a wide range of daily activities. When budgets are formulated, these must be justified in terms of the activities being supported and how critical these are for quality of life. The answers to these question items range from the general to the specific.

In particular, we need to discover the extent and variety of expectations: Where do residents want to experiment with new life-styles, and where do they want the comfort of the traditional? When we fail to assess the sociocultural content of retirement community life, recognize residents' preferences for one facility scheme or feature over another, and fail to give full weight to the traditions and customs that permeate daily life, we always end up distorting the reality of life as the elderly perceive it. For this reason, every question item has two aspects—facts about residents' expectations and requirements and interpretation of these facts as they apply to our deliberations. There is a second qualification that is helpful to keep in mind—the difference between how the residents perceive themselves and how they are perceived by others. An additional caution: Gerontology references such as the *Handbook of Aging and Social Sciences*[20] and the *Handbook of the Psychology of Aging*[21] only provide background information. It is our interviews with individuals and group study sessions that provide the specifics. What we do anticipate is that the distinctions between lifestyles may be difficult to understand or so complex or subtle that they are difficult to respond to, and yet that is the challenge that must be accepted.

5.2 Interior Architecture of Residences

Areas to Address

5.2.1 RESIDENTIAL DESIGN OBJECTIVES. Which expectations and requirements of residents should be emphasized in interior design deliberations for private residences?

5.2.2 RESIDENTIAL UNIT AND SPACE PLAN OPTIONS. What residential unit and space plan options best correspond to residents' expectations and requirements? How are these justified in terms of benefits and costs?

5.2.3 RESIDENCE FURNISHING, FIXTURES, AND EQUIPMENT. In regard to safety, security, and convenience, what furnishing, fixtures, and equipment options, fixed or mobile, do residential units require?

5.2.4 RESIDENCE COMMUNICATION, SURVEILLANCE, AND COMPUTER EQUIPMENT. What are the communication, surveillance, and computer equipment requirements of residences?

5.2.5 RESIDENCE ENVIRONMENTAL CRITERIA. What provisions should be made for the effect on residents of temperature, humidity, air quality, air movement, illumination, noise, distractions, annoyances, hazards, and climatic conditions?

5.2.6 SURFACE TREATMENTS. Where do surfaces require special attention in terms of durability, maintainability, and safety?

5.2.7 INFORMATION REQUIREMENTS. What general and emergency information is required in residences?

5.2.8 INFORMATION PRESENTATIONS. Considering the possible sensory limitations of the residents, how should general and emergency information be presented?

5.2.9 RESIDENTIAL DESIGN CHALLENGES. In summary, what are the residential design challenges associated with resi-

Every design concept, scheme, form, and feature must be responsive to the expectations and requirements of residents and staff. In these question items, we provide a means to evaluate the relative significance of proposed facility designs. We are concerned here with the tendency of designers to reduce the complexity of how the elderly want to live so as to fit them into what has been designed. The dictum latent in these question items is that a concern with the facility design in all its complexity must be matched by a concern with the needs of the elderly residents in all their complexity.

The challenge here is to discover what is significant, not just what is possible. When developers, architects, and care and service providers fail, it is usually because some aspect of residents' needs and concerns did not occur to them or was misunderstood. Individual expectations and requirements force us to confront diverse and often conflicting preferences for interior architectural features. When we consider the recommendations that develop here, we must recognize the potential of interior architectural spaces for helping elderly individuals experience a personal sense of satisfaction and accomplishment. Conversely, inappropriate interior features can interfere with actions, fail to support important activities, and be incompatible with the residents' preferred way of doing things. In regards to question item 5.2.4 Residence Communication, Surveillance, and Computer Equipment, we find that companies such as NYNEX suggest that technology, including new information and telecommunications technologies, is becoming an indispensable partner, along with design, in facilitating the independent function of older adults.[21]

■ 5.3 Community Life

Areas to Address

5.3.1 COMMUNITY SPACE REQUIREMENTS. What community spaces are required?

5.3.2 COMMUNITY SPACE ACTIVITIES. What is known about the extent, time of occurrence, and duration of community activities?

5.3.3 COMMUNITY SPACE PERCEPTIONS. How are residents likely to perceive community space in terms of their individual rights and perquisites?

5.3.4 COMMUNITY LIFE-STYLES. What are the social customs, relationship norms, and cultural traditions common to community space?

5.3.5 COMMUNITY RECREATION AND LEISURE PREFERENCES. What are the community recreation and leisure preferences of residents?

5.3.6 HOSPITALITY. What are the preferences of residents regarding hospitality services, food service, and spaces for guests and family members?

5.3.7 COMMUNITY FACILITY DESIGN CHALLENGES. In summary, what are the community facility design challenges associated with residents' abilities, activities, preferences, and health?

In reality, these questions are as challenging to answer as those in 5.1 Residents' Expectations and Requirements. We can be sure that it is impossible to dictate a way of life for a retirement community. We need to identify where attention must be given to specific life-styles. What are the various ways residents can enjoy their time with others? What situations are demanding or annoying? The requirements of those with physical, sensory, or cognitive limitations must be precisely defined. What daily tasks require special attention? The answers found will always compound the problem of establishing design objectives, yet the results will increase the value, performance, and image of the CCRC enterprise.

There is also a concern here with finding the basis for innovation. For instance, Dr. Gene Cohen,[22] president of The Gerontological Society of America, stresses the importance of looking at older people from the perspective of their contributions and their potential to contribute, not just their deficits and needs. This is mirrored by retirement community executive managers who search for ways and opportunities to involve their residents in the affairs of the local community.

■ 5.4 Community Space Interior Architecture

Areas to Address

5.4.1 COMMUNITY SPACE DESIGN OBJECTIVES. Which expectations and requirements of residents and staff should be emphasized in design deliberations for community space?

5.4.2 COMMUNITY SPACE DESIGN OPTIONS. What community space design options best correspond to residents' and staff expectations and requirements? How are these justified in terms of benefits and costs?

5.4.3 COMMUNITY SPACE FURNISHING, FIXTURES, AND EQUIPMENT. In regard to safety, security, and convenience, what furnishing, fixtures, and equipment options, fixed or mobile, do community spaces require?

5.4.4 COMMUNITY SPACE COMMUNICATION, SURVEILLANCE, AND COMPUTER EQUIPMENT. What are the communication, surveillance, and computer equipment requirements of community spaces?

5.4.5 COMMUNITY SPACE ENVIRONMENTAL CRITERIA. What provisions should be made for the effect of temperature, humidity, air quality, air movement, illumination, noise, distractions, annoyances, hazards, and climatic conditions in community spaces?

Design concepts, schemes, forms, and features must respond to the needs and preferences of residents and staff as they share communal spaces. As with every question item in the standard of performance, the answers to these questions require critique. Further, we are prepared to do this only if we have the experience to visualize residents unable to move easily through the community facilities because allowed space restricts movement; as failing to develop a sense of orientation and direction because the visual surround is confusing and information displays are inadequate; as experiencing fatigue and frustration because the interiors do not support specific activities; as attempting to adapt to light and sound levels that are intolerable; or as being exposed to an environment likely to produce accidents because of the failure to meet the safety needs of the elderly. Emergency situations must also be foreseen and thought given to the adequacy of facility design for such events.

6.0 Health Care

The premise that drives these question items is that residents receive better care in the retirement community than they can receive at home and, it is hoped, at less expense. The term "common enterprise" is the keynote for this. Nowhere is this term more important than in 6.1 Health Care Management and Staff, 6.2 Health Care Programs, and 6.3 Health Care Units Interior Architecture. We must seek answers that achieve a blending of people, programs, and spaces into a sustainable quality-of-life achievement, no matter how complex or demanding the needs of residents may be.

▓ 6.1 Health Care Management and Staff

Areas to Address

6.1.1 MANAGEMENT AND STAFF MANDATE. What are the primary responsibilities of health care managers and staff?

6.1.2 HEALTH CARE MANAGEMENT AND STAFF SELECTION CRITERIA. What are the criteria for appointing individuals to health care management and staff positions?

6.1.3 STAFF MANAGEMENT CANDIDATES. Who are the candidates for health care management and staff?

6.1.4 SELECTION OF HEALTH CARE MANAGEMENT AND STAFF. Applying the selection criteria to candidates, which individuals should be appointed to health care management and staff positions?

6.1.5 HEALTH CARE STAFF ORGANIZATION. How should health care management and staff be organized to fulfill their mandate?

6.1.6 MEDICAL COUNCIL. What is the medical council charter and how should it be organized to fulfill its mandate?

6.1.7 HEALTH CARE STAFF PERCEPTIONS. How are health care staff members likely to perceive themselves, other staff members, and residents in terms of their individual rights and perquisites?

6.1.8 HEALTH CARE STAFF LIFE-STYLES. What are the social customs, relationship norms, and cultural traditions of health care staff?

6.1.9 HEALTH CARE MANAGEMENT AND STAFF RESPONSIBILITIES. What are the responsibilities of individual health care managers and staff?

6.1.10 MANAGEMENT AND STAFF TRAINING. What continuing education programs should be offered to health care managers and staff?

6.1.11 LICENSED SERVICES. Who should be assigned the responsibility of managing licensed services? What are the job responsibilities and position requirements?

6.1.12 MANAGEMENT OF OFF-SITE SERVICES. Who should be assigned the responsibility of managing off-site services? What are the job responsibilities and position requirements?

6.1.13 PERFORMANCE MONITORING. What process should be followed when monitoring and evaluating management and staff performance in terms of residential life contributions and costs of operations?

Achieving and sustaining a common enterprise means that health care management and staff maintain a thorough awareness of advances in geriatrics and gerontology, best practices as these relate to methods, technologies, and care techniques, and the need to customize care. These are the qualities and capabilities to which these question items apply. As with every consideration in this section of the standard of performance, we emphasize solidarity. Managers and staff must be prepared to exchange leadership from one moment to the next and instantaneously replace it with a different order. The goal is to remove rank and replace it with commitment, flexibility, and innovation. It is better to have managers and staff probe and critique than to accept norms as given. The significance assigned to the answers obtained here must always be determined by the degree of involvement with residents' needs and wants.

In part, these question items, originate with the 1995 Health Care Pilot Criteria, Malcolm Baldrige National Quality Award.[23] Please note that the Health Care Pilot Criteria include much more than the material selected for attention here. The entire guideline manual should be obtained and read. Individual copies of this government document can be obtained free of charge from the National Institute of Standards and Technology, telephone number 301-975-2036.

Areas to Address

1. Health Care Staff Leadership

a. How senior executives and health care staff leaders provide effective coordination, leadership, and direction in building and improving delivery of health care, organizational performance, and capabilities. In this area, our research is designed to describe staff roles in: (1) creating, coordinating, and reinforcing mission, values, and expectations throughout the administrative and health care staff leadership systems; (2) creating and sustaining a focus on residents; and (3) setting directions and health care and performance excellence goals through strategic and business planning.

b. How senior executives and health care staff leaders evaluate and improve the effectiveness of the leadership system and the organization to pursue a focus on residents and health care and performance excellence goals.

c. How the organization effectively communicates, deploys, and reinforces its mission, values, expectations, and directions throughout the entire staff.

d. How the organization, departmental, and work unit performance are reviewed and how the reviews are used to improve the quality of health care and operational performance. Describe the types, frequency, and content of reviews, who conducts them, and how the results are aggregated for decision making.

e. How the organization leads as a citizen in its key communities.

2. Management of Information and Data

a. How information and data needed to drive improvement of overall performance as a health care provider are selected, integrated, and managed.

b. How competitive comparisons and benchmarking information and data are selected and used to help drive improvement of overall organization performance as a health care provider.

c. How information and data from all parts of the organization are integrated and analyzed to support reviews, organizational decision making and planning.

3. Human Resource Development and Management

a. How the organization translates overall requirements into human resource plans. The emphasis here is on (1) changes in work process design to improve flexibility, efficiency, coordination, and response time; (2) employee and health care staff development, education, and training, including needed credentials; (3) changes in compensation, recognition, and benefits; (4) expected or planned changes in the composition of the health care and/or employed staff; and (5) recruitment of new staff.

4. Process Management

a. How resident health care services are designed.

b. How resident health care service designs are reviewed to ensure safe, effective, and trouble-free care.

c. How residents' expectations are addressed and considered in the delivery of services. The emphasis is on (1) how health care service delivery is explained to set realistic resident expectations; (2) how likely health care outcomes are explained to establish realistic resident expectations; and (3) how residents' decision making and preferences are factored into the delivery of health care services.

d. How key resident care support services are determined and designed.

5. Focus on and Satisfaction of Residents

a. How the organization determines current and near-term requirements and expectations of residents.

b. How the organization addresses future requirements and expectations of residents.

c. How the organization provides information and easy access to enable residents to seek information and assistance.

d. How the organization ensures that formal and informal complaints and feedback received by all organizational units are resolved effectively and promptly.

e. How the organization evaluates and improves its resident relationship management.

f. How the organization determines resident satisfaction.

g. How residents' satisfaction relative to that for competitors and other organizations is determined.

■ 6.2 Health Care Programs

Areas to Address

6.2.1 HEALTH CARE PROGRAMS. What is the scope and content of mandated and support health care programs?

6.2.2 HEALTH CARE STAFF DISTINCTIONS. How may health care staff be distinguished in terms of program responsibilities? How many individuals are expected in each category?

6.2.3 HEALTH CARE ACTIVITIES. What are the daily and emergency activities of health care staff? What is known about the extent, time of occurrence, and duration of activities?

6.2.4 HEALTH CARE DESIGN CHALLENGES. In summary, what are the facility design challenges associated with health care programs?

These question items should be read as spanning the entire care continuum. We consider here the assumption of varying degrees of responsibility for the entry assessment program; the safety and well-being of residents; assisted living and skilled nursing care; acute care options; and associated licensing, financial, and insurance safeguards. Just as critical to the well-being of residents is the attention given to ethics and values, supervisory leadership skills, psychosocial aspects of mental health, care planning, effective partnerships between resident staff and associated medical staff, and leisure activities and community life opportunities.

In addition to establishing the basis for health care services, these question items provide an opportunity to ameliorate the concern of prospective residents that they will be subjected to imposing routines and limitations on their day. Like the answers obtained in every question item application, we are concerned with providing quality of life in the residents' terms, not ours. Richard Peck[24] would say the goal is not information per se. It is information sharing and an open system that can create "pictures," showing the manager and provider the needs and events that must be anticipated. We want to anticipate what might really happen in the health care setting if we establish a certain program—what's good and should be emphasized, and what might not be so good and should be discarded or improved.

■ 6.3 Health Care Units Interior Architecture

Areas to Address

6.3.1 HEALTH CARE UNIT DESIGN OBJECTIVES. Which expectations and requirements of health service and care staff and residents should be emphasized in interior architecture design deliberations?

6.3.2 HEALTH CARE UNIT DESIGN. What health care unit design options best correspond to staff and resident expectations and requirements? How are design features justified in terms of benefits and costs?

6.3.3 HEALTH CARE UNIT FURNISHING, FIXTURES, AND EQUIPMENT. With regard to safety, security, and convenience, what furnishing, fixtures, and equipment options, fixed or mobile, do health care units require?

6.3.4 HEALTH CARE UNIT COMMUNICATION, SURVEILLANCE, AND COMPUTER EQUIPMENT. What are the communication, surveillance, and computer equipment requirements of health care units?

6.3.5 HEALTH CARE UNIT ENVIRONMENTAL CRITERIA. What provisions should be made for the effect on staff and residents of temperature, humidity, air quality, air movement, illumination, noise, distractions, annoyances, hazards, and climatic conditions?

6.3.6 HEALTH CARE UNIT SURFACE TREATMENTS. Where do surfaces require special attention in terms of durability, maintainability, and safety?

6.3.7 HEALTH CARE UNIT INFORMATION REQUIREMENTS. What general and emergency information are required? How can these be made responsive to sensory limitations?

6.3.8 HEALTH CARE UNIT INFORMATION PRESENTATIONS. How can health care unit general and emergency information presentations be made responsive to sensory limitations?

Are we concerned here with the event that is so common to hospital design? As a dedication ceremony is being held in the front of the hospital, there is a work crew in the back of the building starting a remodeling project. To a degree, yes, particularly when you consider the life-span of a retirement community, which we hope will be decades of service and profit. As we consider the design of health care units, we always keep in mind the possible impact of new technologies and materials. Premature obsolescence carries with it cost and service penalties and implications for quality of life and marketability of the retirement community enterprise.

Entry into a health service setting is always an emotional experience. No matter how rationally prepared people are for this change in their lives, the experience is one of lost freedom. This is where the concept of common enterprise is most pertinent. Residents must see in the setting, the activities of staff, and resident activities, a validation of their competency and personal worth. Although much can be symbolized by interior architectural design and all the associated furnishings, fixtures, and equipment, it is the blending of all these factors that is the objective here. This is no place for design hubris. No single individual or architectural office can discover all the possibilities. Douglas Austin, F.A.I.A.,[25] proposes a highly interactive design process, where programming and design overlap. He starts his work by doing some basic research to familiarize his office with the client's situation. He learns as much as possible about the site, the residential programs he will be working with, and various other issues. The more sophisticated the enterprise, the more thorough he is. As soon as possible, he assembles those involved in the health care program for a process that is referred to as "designing out loud" or a "charrette." Some designers are intimidated by this, but Austin finds it invigorating. He is alert during this process that no one jumps to a quick or obvious solution as a result of the "group think" or group mentality, and fails to see a potentially better solution. If people can draw back a little bit, or go off by themselves and come up with individual solutions first, they will have a greater variety to consider when they come back to the table. People will buy into a solution, defend it a little more, and more possibilities will be explored.

7.0 Residents' Services

These question items are designed to assure that services and facility operations achieve the appropriate standards of quality of life for residents. Some question items pertain to recruitment, selection, and training of administration, service, and facility operations staff. Other items deal with the development of resident-focused services and facility management plans.

◼ 7.1 Service Management

Latent in these question items is the need for a service staff that is lively, accessible, and open to change. Few people have spoken as wisely as Abraham Maslow[26] about how to develop in others an ideal attitude toward work. If we want to succeed in creating the most favorable circumstances for the retirement community, we must begin with our perceptions of others. We create these circumstances when we assume everyone is to be trusted and informed as completely as possible of as many facts as possible. We can only produce the ideal service conditions for the retirement community when we assume in everyone good will and the impulse to achieve. Finally, as we guide those who work with us, we must assume that everyone prefers to feel important, needed, useful, successful, proud, respected, rather than unimportant, interchangeable, wasted, unused, expendable.

■ 7.2 Resident Services and Staff

Areas to Address

7.2.1 SERVICES. What resident services are expected and required and what is the justification for each? What must each service offer on a scheduled or as-needed basis?

7.2.2 TRANSPORTATION SERVICES. What are the daily and special transportation service requirements of residents?

7.2.3 SERVICE STAFF. Who provides direct service to residents? How may these individuals be grouped by service categories and responsibilities? How many individuals does each category include?

7.2.4 SERVICE STAFF ACTIVITIES. What are the anticipated activities of service staff? What is known about the extent, time of occurrence, and duration of anticipated activities?

7.2.5 SERVICE STAFF CUSTOMS. What are the significant work customs, life-styles, norms, and traditions of the service staff?

7.2.6 SERVICE STAFF SELECTION. What are the selection criteria for each staff category? How should prospective staff be screened with regard to undesirable traits and criminal activity history?

7.2.7 SERVICE STAFF TRAINING. For each staff category, what initial and continuing training is required?

7.2.8 SERVICE DESIGN CHALLENGES. In summary, what are the facility design challenges associated with service staff activities?

When we address these question items, we are doing more than creating an organization chart. The goal of these question items is the creation of exemplary relationships within the retirement community, between staff members and between staff and residents. The discussion of best practices is drawn from Bruno

Bettelheim's *The Home for the Heart*.[27] No one has spoken more wisely. We learn from his work that quality of life for residents is in the head, heart, and hands of every CCRC staff member.

Bettelheim's principles for staff selection tell us a great deal about how he perceives the care environment:

- The candidate must know as much as possible about the work of the institution and its philosophy.
- We must know about his background and outlook on life.
- We ask candidates to tell us what experiences of the past made them the person they see themselves as, and what in particular made them interested in working within a retirement community setting.
- We let candidates look around at their leisure.
- We let them decide if they did the right thing in applying for a position.
- With all candidates, we stress the demands and emotional difficulties of working within a retirement community.
- We want candidates to understand, accept, and appreciate that their work requires a great deal of patience and extra work.
- Even the most experienced candidates must demonstrate a deep respect for the residents, sensitivity to needs, and courtesy, even in trying situations.
- In conclusion, Bettelheim notes that it can easily take 6 months to a year before we can be sure how well a staff member is working out.

The salient feature of a CCRC is its physical and social indivisibility. It is home to the residents, but it must also be a place where staff would be willing to live. Bettelheim notes that if the community is not a desirable place for staff to live, how can it be a good place for residents to live? It must also be a situation where everyone from executives to support staff is willing to be available evenings, weekends, and holidays. Over time, traditions will evolve that will make staff members feel that they are part of the community. With this common commitment everyone contributes to the daily life of the community.

7.3 Facility Operations

Areas to Address

7.3.1 FACILITY OPERATIONS. What facility operations are required?

7.3.2 OPERATIONS STAFF. Who is responsible for facility operations? How may these individuals be grouped by responsibilities? How many individuals does each category include?

7.3.3 OPERATIONS STAFF ACTIVITY DESCRIPTIONS. What are the anticipated activities of the operations staff? What is known about the extent, time of occurrence, and duration of anticipated activities?

7.3.4 OPERATIONS STAFF CUSTOMS. What are the significant work customs, life-styles, norms, and traditions of the operations staff?

7.3.5 OPERATIONS STAFF SELECTION. What are the selection criteria that should be employed in each staff category?

7.3.6 OPERATIONS STAFF TRAINING. For each operations staff member category, what initial and continuing training is required?

7.3.7 FACILITY OPERATIONS DESIGN OBJECTIVES. In summary, responding to identified requirements of facility operations and staff, which should be emphasized in design deliberations?

7.3.8 FACILITY MANAGEMENT SCHEME. What are the required guidelines and manuals that describe to staff and residents the use of facility features?

These question items address what is necessary to establish and maintain the quality of every area, space, and facility. Facility operation standards must be of the highest. How do you know that a facility is well-maintained? It is as crisp and clean after 20 years of occupancy as it was on opening day, and operating costs have not depreciated property market value. The facility operations aspect of this critical success factor is also concerned with the increase in the value of a property over time, by not only maintaining, but improving spaces and facilities as a reflection of changing expectations and requirements.

8.0 Design and Build

Within the design/build strategy, we start paying attention to the details of architecture, engineering, and construction at the very beginning of the enterprise. The merit of the work of the executive council and enterprise associates is judged within the three-fold criteria of value, performance, and image. To prevail over the competition in the retirement community industry, we must promote in the minds of prospective residents the extraordinary achievement of the enterprise in these terms. This is also an area of deliberation where we must be known for husbanding investments, increasing returns, and guarding every cent in the construction budget. Scheduling is also a major consideration, as construction funding only begins when we are far enough along in an enterprise to start the presales effort and meet quotas. In terms of timing, these question items are addressed at the earliest possible time. We never wait for research findings before starting to develop design concepts, schemes, forms, and features and the options and alternatives that in some combination provide the best possible retirement community facility design and land development results. We put our professional expertise and experience to work immediately.

■ 8.1 Site Selection

Areas to Address

8.1.1   CANDIDATE SITES. What are the candidate sites for the retirement community?

8.1.2   SITE SELECTION CRITERIA. What are the retirement community site selection criteria?

8.1.3   CANDIDATE SITE EVALUATION. What are the results of the application of site selection criteria to candidate sites?

8.1.4   NEIGHBORHOOD GROUPS. Who lives and works in the neighborhood surrounding the site? How may these people be grouped by activities and concerns?

8.1.5   NEIGHBORHOOD IMPACT. What is the possible impact of facility activities on neighborhood life?

8.1.6   COMMUNITY GROUPS. Who lives and works in the local community? How may these people be grouped by activities and concerns?

8.1.7   COMMUNITY IMPACT. What is the likely impact of retirement community activities on community life and public and private services?

8.1.8   PROPERTY VALUE IMPACT. What is the possible impact of the retirement community on community property values?

8.1.9   VISUAL IMPACT. Anticipating the visual impact of the retirement community, what are the possible objectives?

8.1.10 ECOLOGICAL AND ENVIRONMENTAL IMPACT. What is the anticipated impact of the retirement community development in terms of ecological and environmental factors?

8.1.11 NEIGHBORHOOD AND COMMUNITY SUPPORT. In terms of community objections and resistance, what is the strategy for gaining neighborhood and community support?

The success of the retirement community enterprise is directly related to this deliberation. The primary consideration is the image created by the site in the minds of prospective residents. People who are moving to the retirement community want their friends and families to admire the decision. They want both the setting and the facilities to confirm their taste and the wisdom of their investment. We locate and evaluate candidate sites in terms of these question items. As potential sites are discovered, we study each in detail and assess candidates in terms of our site selection criteria. The challenge of obtaining neighborhood and community approval for the enterprise requires that every possible impact of each candidate site be discovered. One of the prime responsibilities of the executive council is to reduce the time spent on the approval process and obtain the associated cost savings. This can be achieved only if the critical differences between candidate sites are precisely defined. When the site is a given, the same question items apply. This is certainly one way to discover the potential of a predetermined site. In either case, market research findings must be incorporated into these deliberations.

■ 8.2 Critical Circulation Patterns

Areas to Address

8.2.1 MOVEMENT OF INDIVIDUALS. What is the anticipated number of people entering, leaving, and moving about within the retirement community, for what purposes, how frequently, and at what times?

8.2.2 EQUIPMENT AND MATERIAL TRANSPORT. What are the characteristics of the equipment and material that must be transported to and within the retirement community? How are these items transported, and what is the frequency and time of occurrence?

8.2.3 VEHICULAR TRAFFIC. From the perspective of neighborhood impact and safety and security, what aspects of vehicular traffic must be considered during facility design, site planning, and master plan development? What are the characteristics of the areas of concern?

These question items speak to the constraints that directly affect facility design and the enterprise master plan, and certainly augment the site selection process. When we find that the site accommodates a concept common to successful hotel design, the "front of the house" and the "back of the house" distinction, the gain in image and performance is notable.

These question items build on information gathered about the expectations and requirements of residents and staff and what is needed to make each day a success. With regard to quality of life and safety, we must envision the residents moving around the community, going from place to place throughout the day. We must consider such things as visual and noise sanctuaries, fields of view that make it possible for residents to see and be seen, and that secluded spot near a busy hallway or path that provides the experience of privacy. In terms of facility operations, normal events and emergency situations require attention. Descriptions of possible emergency situations, required equipment, means of handling, and advance preparation are additional information objectives.

8.3 Master Plan

Answers to these question items begin to evolve during work on 1.0 Enterprise Concept. Sketches are produced to provide visual reference points during preliminary discussion. Certainly, some would start by looking at existing ordinances and land characteristics to see how many buildings the site will accommodate. This is premature. What was originally a study soon becomes a solution, and fails to characterize what might be attractive to prospective residents. As noted earlier, a retirement community enterprise is far more than a real estate development.

This is the time to share the standard of performance with every person in the community who can build positive feelings about the enterprise. Political, business, neighborhood, environmental, and individual interests are all involved in such developments, and, whether we like it or not, we always start off in an adversarial position. If we can demonstrate from the beginning the willingness to respond to neighborhood and community concerns, we can greatly increase support and cooperation.

■ 8.4 Facility Design

Areas to Address

8.4.1 DESIGN CONCEPTS. Which expectations and requirements of residents, health care personnel, and service providers should be emphasized in design deliberations?

8.4.2 FACILITY DESIGN BENEFITS. In terms of residents' and staff expectations and requirements, what is the benefit and problem resolution potential of each suggested facility design concept?

8.4.3 PROPOSED FLOOR PLAN SCHEMES. Responding specifically to research regarding the expectations and requirements of residents and health care and service staff, what are the proposed facility floor plan schemes? What is the estimated square feet for each facility space?

8.4.4 ALTERATION EXPECTANCIES. How soon might it be necessary to modify or expand facilities? What events would most probably lead to this requirement? How do the proposed facility schemes account for this possibility? How do these schemes help reduce the distractions and annoyances associated with remodeling and expansion?

These question items synthesize the information and insights resulting from the entire standard of performance scope of work. The design/build team begins this work with reference to its experience and expertise, to be confirmed or modified as it becomes more fully informed as to what is expected and required by residents and staff, investors, lenders, and the executive council. We immediately want to visually characterize the design implications of every feature that is regarded as essential for enterprise success. Don't worry about being premature with specific design proposals. A drawing conveys more meaning with greater clarity than any rhetoric, and alternative arrangements can most readily be developed and evaluated with these depictions. The sooner we have some square foot numbers, the earlier we can consider the cost implications of design options and alternatives.

Design details associated with environmental quality may also be considered here. For example, in terms of heating, air conditioning, and ventilation, there is a need to reduce levels of allergy-causing pollens, dust, and chemical emissions, as well as to maintain comfortable levels of temperature and humidity. At this stage of design deliberations, we can evaluate advances in ventilation systems that can accomplish these needs more efficiently and less expensively than conventional systems. Consideration should also be given to the use of furniture, flooring materials, and wallpaper adhesives that do not contain or emit irritants or toxins.

■ 8.5 Design Image

Areas to Address

8.5.1 FORM AND STRUCTURE. What are the proposed facility form and structure design concepts?

8.5.2 EXTERIOR DESIGN IMAGES. What are the proposals for exterior facility design images, details, and accents?

8.5.3 INTERIOR DESIGN IMAGES. What are the proposals for interior spatial forms, design images, and surface colors, textures, and patterns?

8.5.4 DESIGN IMAGE JUSTIFICATION. What are the quality-of-life and community impact possibilities of each design image recommendation?

Who gets to be the designer? Everyone involved in the enterprise: the director of health care and the executive manager, the food service director and the concierge, the residents, and those in the local community who are aware of areas of sensitivity to which the enterprise must be responsive. Throughout the critique of proposed design images, all these individuals should be contributing every idea and possibility that they can justify as something worthy of attention. What is central is the attention to detail. The residents of a retirement community want to feel that the best possible effort has gone into the enterprise.

■ 8.6 Design/Build Process

Areas to Address

8.6.1 DESIGN/BUILD MANAGEMENT TEAM. Which executive council members and enterprise associates are members of the design/build management team?

8.6.2 DESIGN/BUILD MILESTONES. What are the design/build milestones? What is produced at each?

8.6.3 PROGRESS REPORTS. What is the means selected to inform all enterprise participants concerning the activities of the design/build management team and enterprise progress?

8.6.4 DESIGN EVALUATION CRITERIA. What are the criteria for evaluating proposed design concepts, schemes, forms, and features?

8.6.5 PROBLEM RESOLUTION. What is the procedure for resolving existing or anticipated design/build problems?

8.6.6 DOCUMENT CONTROL. What is the information system content and structure for enterprise document control following completion of the application of the standard of performance?

Application of the standard of performance is the first step in the design/build process and serves to assure that we obtain all the value possible from this method of design and construction. The question items in this section consider the responsibilities of design/build managers, management effectiveness and efficiency, the early detection of problems, resolution of conflicts, the value of peer-review processes, and document control. By recognizing the benefits of sharing information, question items extend information exchange considerations into every level of the participating organizations and contractors. Considering how work really gets done, Karen Stephenson[28] observes that very little of the working knowledge required for any enterprise lies in the rules, policies, and regulations. These are only procedures. Real working knowledge is in the heads of designers and builders and exists in the relationships between people. This working knowledge is not written down and is based on mutual trust. This is the benchmark for the design/build team.

Scopes of Work

Applications of the standard of performance have all the dynamics of a game of chess. Like chess pieces, the executive council members and their enterprise associates fulfill many different roles as they realize the potential of their own unique capabilities. This team effort has opening, middle, and end steps. Many strategies and methods are applied, yet the end game is always in mind. As in any game in which events follow events and information accumulates, enterprise participants must be prepared to alter strategy as new problems and opportunities arise. It is expected that members of the CCRC executive organization will aggressively formulate enterprise concepts, recommend service, and propose candidate designs. Unlike chess, however, our enterprise can accept no stalemates. CCRC enterprise requirements and expectations must be met in all their complexity.

New Enterprises

When we apply the standard of performance to a new enterprise, we work to provide justified and reasonably complete answers to the question items we have selected for attention. The required work ethic is that we consider the consequences of implementing every design, service, and health care concept. Do not consider the standard of performance to be a step-by-step program. This often produces generalities that lead to confusion. We are promoting, it is hoped, the flexibility needed to avoid rigidity and the uncritical application of the past to the future.

    Let's consider the case of an experienced developer, alert to profitable ventures, who considers the possibilities offered by a promising available site, a market opportunity, proposals from groups interested in establishing a CCRC enterprise in the community, or a real estate investment trust looking for investment opportunities. Aware of regional trends and local possibilities, the developer asks, "Is my speculation regarding a retirement community development sufficiently promising to attract partners to form a joint venture?" Although an experienced and well-regarded developer of quality properties, he has limited experience with retirement community developments. Recognizing that you don't jump into something so complex and risk-laden as a retirement community enterprise without looking for help, the owner asks, "What is the first step?"

During preliminary discussions, we present the standard of performance to the developer and explain what can be gained from a thorough assessment of his speculation regarding a retirement community. If we can convince him to think in terms of the eight critical success factors, we have already provided him with a safeguard. He knows what to listen for when he discusses his speculation with retirement community professionals and even more important, with those who think they have the ability, even though they do not have the experience, to lead such an enterprise. A review of the question items in the standard of performance defines the term "retirement community" in all its complexity. It immediately becomes apparent to the developer that the availability of experienced partners must be considered before he even begins to think about financing.

It becomes very natural to start thinking about the need for an executive council. Who will take responsibility for turning a speculation into a proposal that will withstand underwriting scrutiny? What parties are needed to form a joint venture? Who is a reliable first partner in the venture? Is it a developer of retirement communities who says, "Let me do it all for you"? Is it an architect who is exceptionally accomplished and experienced in retirement community design, who says she will undertake some preliminary work on speculation? It soon becomes evident that just putting together a group of individuals who have no concept of cooperation, collaboration, and shared responsibility for enterprise success is the worst possible decision.

We don't allow this situation to develop. Each individual who expresses interest in the enterprise is shown the standard of performance. We want everyone to realize that the enterprise is the essential focus, not roles, authority, or contracts. People will also see that they can contribute to every deliberation, are free to offer their ideas and recommendations, and have the opportunity to critique the work and accomplishments of others. This establishes a habit of open deliberation that precludes the development of the many problems associated with the misdirection of resources. Consider how quickly new enterprise participants can begin to contribute when they find the standard of performance foremost on every agenda as well as in every casual discussion.

■ Acquired Distressed Properties

Applications of the standard of performance can also be of value when working with financially distressed properties. The application possibilities are as follows:

Critical Success Factor	Application Possibilities
1.0 Enterprise Concept	Defining remedial concepts
2.0 Executive Organization	Establishing an executive action strategy
3.0 Finance and Law	Improving income and cash flow Evaluating existing contracts Evaluating regulatory compliance
4.0 Marketing and Sales	Establishing an effective market and sales strategy
5.0 Residents	Creating improved relations with current residents
6.0 Health Care	Assessing the existing health care system
7.0 Residents' Services	Creating new residential services
8.0 Design and Build	Remodeling an acquired property

Applications System Design

The standard of performance can be easily transformed into a computer-based applications system. This should be one of the first activities of the executive council, as it is the platform for all enterprise deliberations and research activities. Question items 2.4.1, 2.4.2, and 2.4.3 were placed within 2.0 Executive Organization to illustrate the importance of the applications system for enterprise success. In addition, these question items are neutral topics which provide an agreeable way for the executive council and enterprise associates to learn how to work together.

2.4.1 APPLICATIONS SYSTEM REQUIREMENTS. Responding to enterprise objectives and executive and professional associates responsibilities, what are the applications system requirements?

2.4.2 APPLICATIONS SYSTEM DESIGN. Responding to specified applications system requirements, what are the best software suites for the enterprise?

2.4.3 APPLICATIONS SYSTEM FAMILIARIZATION. Considering that the applications system is mandated for enterprise deliberations, what is the means for familiarizing all enterprise participants with its structure and utility features?

As a starting point for the design of the applications system, we draw from Stan Davis and Jim Botkin.[29] In their view, executive deliberations require a continuous stream of current and interlinked data and information formed as a model of the decision-making process that adjusts to changing circumstances and enables executives to act in a real-time system. Question items 2.4.1 Application System Requirements, 2.4.2 Applications System Design, and 2.4.3 Applications System Compliance guide the development of such an applications system. These question items ask us to show people how to put the CCRC applications system to use and to demonstrate exactly why we have mandated the system for all deliberations.

◼ Basic Index

The basic index for applications system entries consists of the question items in the standard of performance. The form of the data and information, derived from the research methods discussed in Part III: Strategic Research, is extended text, data tables, figures, line drawings, graphics, photographs, and reference to such sources as videocassettes and Internet sites.

◼ Source Index

Within the source index, entries are identified by the date of entry, the name of the contributor, the name of the organization, and references.

◼ Research Report Index

For purposes of efficiency and clarity, the executive organization should establish a standard research report format. To this end, we recommend a research report that addresses the following seven points and is indexed by letter and title:

A. Topic and Associated Concerns

The first part of the research report specifies the decision you are facing and the consequences associated with the action you might take. Never invest in research without this selective focus.

B. Recommendations

The objective here is to tell enterprise participants what is important. We state the exact nature of recommended actions and the justification for these recommendations.

C. Points of View

Every report must include the statements of the people questioned. A major characteristic of strategic research is that it encourages insight and stresses the identification of the dilemmas and conflicts that must be resolved. Allowing for the importance of insight helps people use their experience and knowledge and often leads them beyond what the facts indicate. Anecdotes are frequently omitted from research reports, which is a mistake. When we sanitize a strategic research report by stressing facts and numerical analyses over interpretations provided by participating individuals, we leave out what is most informative. Be particularly alert to conflicts in working relationships. These will always influence results. Attention must be given to the extent to which these conflicts relate to organizational pressures, differences in interpretation of information, role conflicts, group allegiances, differences in management styles, and lack of experience and training.

D. Situational Factors

At this point in the research report, the situation is reviewed as it pertains to research objectives. For instance, how did market and financial conditions influence findings? What was the significance of background factors such as regional history, culture, geography, and social and political dynamics?

E. Financial Implications

A review of the financial implications of research results is necessary. The reference points are enhanced value, construction costs, and details such as operating expenses, marketing expenses, and staff salaries.

F. Summary of Research Design

Summarize the scope of work for the strategic research, as well as the safeguards employed to assure reliable and valid results. Data, information, and recommendations are acceptable only when we present the steps taken to obtain information and confirm findings.

G. Supplemental Information

These can be data tables, graphic figures, photographs and videos, floor plans, master plans, or activity charts. Anything that is selected must provide a reference for, or clarification of, some complex feature of the retirement community undertaking. These reference points, when they consolidate a great deal of information, simplify the task of writing. You can write to the implications of findings, rather then spending time on verbal descriptions.

4.2
Market
Research

■ Platforms

There are three possible platforms for the applications system. It can be implemented with an office suite of software applications, which is sufficient for most executive strategy undertakings. The logic structure of the applications system also provides an algorithm that lends itself to relational database applications. As a third possibility, though the heuristics of the retirement community industry are somewhat unique, sufficient commonality exists between enterprise organizations and the general corporate environment to allow the use of many knowledge-base and expert systems as these now exist. However, this is more of a research concern; the development costs for a heuristics-based system are not justifiable and as such do not concern us here.

Office Suites Software

Office suites offer word processing, spreadsheet, database, e-mail, the Internet, importing and exporting data, and linking and embedding features of sufficient power to provide support for every CCRC executive strategy application. The cost is modest, memory is not a problem, and the learning curve is steep.

Relational Database

Robin Elaine Goodman, School of Civil and Environmental Engineering, Georgia Institute of Technology,[30] provides us with the algorithm for a relational database application. She recommends that the system be developed within three sections: base table structure, construction of data relationships, and user-interface formats. This system structure provides us with the greatest degree of flexibility and is totally compatible with all relational database systems.

To achieve the utility in this algorithm, the relational database comprises four base tables—question item, group, activity, and attributes—distinguished by data tables, data types, and associated examples. Information in the question item table specifically identifies the deliberation topic. Information belonging to the group table can be quite diverse. A group is any noun entity or entities that can be associated or related to a deliberation topic.

Activity data are verb statements. These establish *what* groups do with other groups. Information in the activity table establishes the association or relationship between groups. Explaining *how* or *when*, data in the attributes table characterize groups and activities.

In each application, the user selects data from the four base tables and constructs data relationships. These data relationships form descriptive strings of information akin to sentences, describing aspects of the topic question item. Further, an additional field is allocated for general text explanations, for example, notes, dates, and references, where any form of additional information can be attached. Thus, this process supports a distinctive capability—flexibility—in that the composition of data and data relationships can be uniquely built and retained.

The development of base tables and construction of data relationships are facilitated by appropriate user-interface formats, a standard requirement for the data-entry and query aspects of a relational database application. Every object on the screen has a function related to the data relationship algorithm. Three user-interface outputs are needed: prompt screens translated from the standard of performance question items, data-entry screens for the base tables, and data-entry screens for data relationship construction.

▦ Applications System Features

Let's say that, using an office suites software platform, you have entered the standard of performance into a file or made each of the eight sections of the standard of performance a file. Over a period of time, a number of people have responded to question items and are identified by name and organization. Now you wish to see, for instance, how the health care provider responded to the following item.

> 6.3.4 HEALTH CARE UNIT COMMUNICATION, SURVEILLANCE, AND COMPUTER EQUIPMENT. What are the communication, surveillance, and computer equipment requirements of health care units?

All that is required is a "Find" search by the name or organization of the health care provider. If you wish to review all the responses to this question item, you simply execute a keyword search by the question item numerical index—6.3.4. This is the reason why each question item is crafted as a mutually exclusive information category. Information of a certain type is always entered and found in one place only.

Taking this example a step further, perhaps you have used the standard of performance previously and are now beginning a similar enterprise. You can readily access all the information related to question item 6.3.4. Say that this entry includes a spreadsheet file, showing vendors, equipment type, and associated costs, allowing you to immediately determine the cost of previous installations. Now, just as conveniently, you can e-mail this file to the vendors and request price, availability, and new product specifications. Finally, as work progresses on the new enterprise, with an established network in place, all participants can monitor development by a date-of-entry search. What skill level is required? It is basic computer literacy. With basic proficiency, a new hire, trainee, or office clerk can undertake information entry, search, and retrieval tasks with confidence and efficiency. The caveat associated with computer applications is that every member of the executive council and all professional associates must be computer literate. It also means that all enterprise participants must use the same software.

Revising Question Items

In every application of the standard of performance, the constraint is to maintain a consistent numerical indexing system. This does not mean that the standard of performance cannot be customized to a specific enterprise or facility feature. For instance, this question item

> 6.3.2 HEALTH CARE UNIT DESIGN. What health care unit design options best correspond to staff and resident expectations and requirements? How are design features justified in terms of benefits and costs?

might change to

> 6.3.2 ASSISTED LIVING UNIT DESIGN. What assisted living unit design options best correspond to staff and resident expectations and requirements? How are design features justified in terms of benefits and costs?

Thus, while you have modified the question item 6.3.2 Health Care Unit Design to 6.3.2 Assisted Living Unit Design, the index number remains the same.

Perhaps you wish to make the following item more specific:

> 3.2.3 REGULATORY AGENCIES. What federal, state, and local regulatory and licensing bodies are responsible for enterprise approval?

Now it reads as

> 3.2.3 STATE OF CALIFORNIA REGULATORY REQUIREMENTS. Withinthe State of California, what regulatory and licensing bodies are responsible for enterprise approval?

If you have projects in other states and wish to do some comparisons, you might have a number of question items with the same numerical index, but with specific titles, such as

> 3.1.2 SOUTH CAROLINA REGULATORY REQUIREMENTS. Within the State of South Carolina, what regulatory and licensing bodies are responsible for enterprise approval?

This change does not alter the mutual exclusivity of the question item. A keyword search using "3.1.2" and "South Carolina" will yield all information pertaining to this state.

Notes

1. C. A. Bartlett and S. Ghoshal. (1994). Changing the role of top management: Beyond strategy to purpose. *Harvard Business Review* (November–December): 79–88. Idem. (1995). Changing the role of top management: Beyond systems to people. *Harvard Business Review* (May–June): 132–142. S. Ghoshal and C. A. Bartlett. (1994). Changing the role of top management: Beyond structure to processes. *Harvard Business Review* (January–February): 87–96.
2. J. Milojkovic. (1995). *Reinventing Organization Learning.* Videocassette, 58 min. Stanford: Stanford Video Media Group.
3. J. Pfeffer. (1992). *Managing with Power: Politics and Influence in Organizations.* Boston: Harvard Business School Press.
4. J. Quinn. (1985). Managing innovation: Controlled chaos. In *Managerial Excellence,* ed. Nan Stone. Boston: Harvard Business Revie, p. 114.
5. J. Katzenbach and D. K. Smith. (1993). *The Wisdom of Teams.* New York: HarperCollins, pp. 13–15.
6. J. Katzenback. (1997). *Teams at the Top.* Boston: Harvard Business School Press.

7. C. Luckman. (1996). "The Executive Architect." In *The Executive Architect: Transforming Designers into Leaders,* ed. J. Harrigan and Paul Neel. New York: John Wiley & Sons, pp. 19–20.

8. Nancy Axelrod. (1994). Who's in Charge? *The Nonprofit Times* (December): 32.

9. M. Porter. (1995). The competitive advantage of the inner city. *Harvard Business Review.* (May–June): 55–70.

10. R. Davidson (1996). Seniors' housing finance: Tight money, big growth. *Urban Land* (November): 33.

11. J. Moore, as quoted in J. Nordheimer. (1996). A mature housing market: Growing business of not-quite-nursing home care. *The New York Times,* April 10, pp. C1, C4.

12. Crown Research Corporation, Troutdale, Oregon, provided the financial and market analyses for *The Stratford.* Mark Miles gave permission for the authors to share the work of his corporation with our readers. Crown Research Corporation (1990). *Financial Feasibility Report: The Stratford.* Troutdale, OR: CRC.

13. D. Nichols. (1996). Florida class-action suit may be first of many. *Contemporary Long Term Care* (October): 11.

14. E. Cherof. (1996). What to do before the union knocks on your door. *Contemporary Long Term Care* (December): 58.

15. M. Infante. (1996) Preemployment screening: What the record won't show. *Contemporary Long Term Care* (November): 71.

16. G. Anders, (1997). Elderly enjoy better health than expected. *The Wall Street Journal.* March 18, pp. B1, B4.

17. S. Brooks, as quoted in D. Husi. (1996). Serving the "silent generation." *Urban Land.* (November): 34–35.

18. R. Simons. (1995). Control in an age of empowerment. *Harvard Business Review* (March–April): 80–89.

19. R. Binstock and L. George. (1996). *Handbook of Aging and the Social Sciences.* San Diego: Academic Press.

20. J. Birren and K. Schaie. (1996). *Handbook of the Psychology of Aging.* San Diego: Academic Press.

21. NYNEX. (1997). *Gerontechnology: New Tools for Independent Living.* Paper presented at the 43rd Meeting of the American Society on Aging, March 23–26, Nashville.

22. Dr. Gene Cohen as quoted in *Gerontology News,* March, 1997, pp. 1–3.

23. National Institute of Standards. (1995). *Malcolm Baldrige National Quality Award: Health Care Pilot Criteria.* Washington, D.C.: NIS.

24. R. Peck. (1997). Do you have the information? *Nursing Homes* (January): 4.

25. D. Austin. (1996). "Value, Performance, and Image." In *The Executive Architect: Transforming Designers into Leaders,* ed. J. Harrigan and Paul Neel. New York: John Wiley & Sons, pp. 320–321.

26. A. Maslow. (1965). *Eupsychian Management.* Homewood, IL: Dorsey Press.

27. B. Bettelheim. (1974). *A Home for the Heart.* New York: Alfred A. Knopf.

28. K. Stephenson. (1995). *Strategic Misalignment: Making Networks Work in Your Organization.* Videocassette, 55 min. Stanford: Stanford Video Media Group.

29. S. Davis and J. Botkin. (1994). The coming of knowledge-based business. *Harvard Business Review* (September–October): 165–170.

30. R. Goodman. (1995). *Client Assessment Knowledge System for Building Industry Application.* Department of Architecture. San Luis Obispo: California Polytechnic State University.

PART III

STRATEGIC RESEARCH

Strategic research is as much a way of thinking as a task to be accomplished. In the abstract, strategic research is all encompassing, addressing each critical success factor and every question item in the standard of performance. In application, it is about executive council members and enterprise associates working to develop the data, information, and knowledge needed to support specific deliberations. We use the word "strategic" as a reminder that research that is blind to purpose and need has limited value and can be very wasteful of time and funds. In strategic research, we think in terms of confirming the things we know, finding out all we can about what we need to know, and deciding what exploratory research we need to assure that we discover the things we are unaware of but that will dramatically affect our work.[1]

We invest in strategic research because insight and opinion that are not paired with appropriate research make us vulnerable to the dangers associated with faulty assumptions and incomplete speculations. Every page of this book considers some aspect of the fact that the CCRC enterprise is never a standard job nor a speculative undertaking. It is always a customized job targeting a specific market. In a retirement community enterprise, there are no simple choices among clear-cut alternatives. When the preferences of a specific market segment are identified, how stable are these? When a spectrum of residential and health care services is proposed, which will meet the current and future needs of residents? When the design/build process produces facility design concepts, schemes, forms, and features, which recommendations have the greatest potential for meeting quality-of-life expectations and cost/benefit requirements? In a CCRC enterprise, we will constantly be challenged to understand the world of the elderly, their preferences, concerns, and financial resources, and then make decisions about what should be built and provided and how the facility can be financed and sustained over the years. The discussions, guidelines, and exhibits that follow emphasize critical thinking and thorough analysis as much as methodology and techniques.

The Benefits of Personal Involvement

It is particularly important that members of the executive organization become personally involved in strategic research. Strategic research activity is a learning experience whose benefits should be as direct as possible. We must personally learn from people and learn about people. The objectives of research are best crafted by those who can recognize what aspects of research are particularly important and require the greatest amount of attention. When you are involved in research, as opposed to working with what others have developed, you always have more confidence in the results and recognize the limitations of your information. Certainly, the timing of research is best paced by those directly involved in the enterprise.

One consideration that is almost always overlooked during the assignment of research responsibilities is that we work in a public forum. Research results that bear on a retirement community enterprise will be subject to review and evaluation by others. Investors, lenders, jurisdictional agencies, and quite often, future residents of the retirement community will be the final judges of whether or not research findings have merit. If they find that the research design was faulty or the findings misinterpreted, it casts suspicion on the entire enterprise. This is one of the reasons that so much attention has been given here to research design and the thoughtful application of research methods.

If enterprise participants are directly involved in research, this also reduces the problem of translating research findings into application. Dr. Gene Cohen,[2] while president of the Gerontological Society of America, noted that a major challenge is to apply gerontological research to enterprise deliberations. This challenge applies to strategic research. How can we translate findings into applications for our retirement community enterprise? Those of us who often find it difficult to apply research findings should know that others have the same problem. Within the academic scene, intellectual networks rarely overlap, bridge building seldom exists.[3] In strategic research applications, this is never the case. We have no tolerance for discipline-bound thinking or ritual-based research.

Research Design

To derive full benefit from the CCRC executive strategy, we approach strategic research from four directions simultaneously—market, human factors, design, and legal research (Fig-

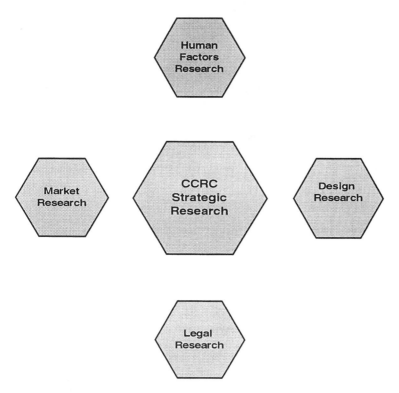

Figure 3. Strategic research

ure 3). This research is directly related to two basic elements, which are as follows:

- **Human Factors Perspective.** This theoretical construct is the core of strategic research, and indicates the need to maintain at all times an awareness of three aspects of the expectations and requirements of elderly people—individual differences, activity limitations and capabilities, and sociocultural dynamics.
- **Research Methods.** We rely on four research methods to answer standard of performance question items—progressive surveys, study sessions, interviews, and activity analyses.

■ Human Factors Perspective

Within the CCRC executive strategy, it is vital that we understand how the elderly differ in their expectations and requirements, create a specification of the activity limitations and capabilities of the elderly, and develop a valid description of the sociocultural factors that influence what the elderly need and want today and may need and want in the future. There is a distinction here that is important. A constantly changing view of the expectations and requirements of the elderly is acceptable for academics, who at one point can state that one thing is important, and after the next research endeavor, can state that something else is even more important. This is appropriate because science must always look for the exception. We are in a different situation. We have an enterprise to finance, buildings to design, and services to establish. We must make a judgment as to how we will view the elderly.

The human factors elements—individual differences, activity limitations and capabilities, and sociocultural dynamics—are significantly interrelated. When we speak to residents or prospective residents, we not only listen to what they say, we also consider the sociocultural dynamics and activity limitations and capabilities that influence their opinions and preferences. If you only listen to what people actually say without this associated information, it is very likely that you will misinterpret or distort what you are hearing. If you conduct a market study of the sociocultural dynamics that characterize the market without verifying the findings by listening to people or determining associated limits of ability, you will overlook important facility design and service requirements. Finally, if you consider the elderly only in terms of their apparent frailty without speaking to individuals or determining social and cultural influences that might be significant, you will always underestimate the individual strengths and resources of the elderly.

Individual Differences

One of the great challenges in a CCRC enterprise is accounting for individual differences in our designs and health care and residential services. Our facilities are bought and paid for by individuals, not the "elderly." When we maintain a perspective of individual differences, we will always be surprised by variety and uniqueness. When we begin our research with the following fundamental questions we are open to discovery. What is the best way to characterize the elderly? How should we talk to them? What should we talk about? What should we be listening for? How do we evaluate what they say in one circumstance when we find it contradicts what we have learned elsewhere? How do expectations and requirements change? What are the forces behind this change?

Activity Limitations and Capabilities

When we anticipate and identify the activities and daily tasks that will be of importance for each individual in each residence and facility unit, we facilitate individual behavior. We also minimize the need to correct later, with organization or with staff, problems that could have been avoided by more effective facility design and service features. Although the elderly are capable of demanding activities and can adapt to unsuitable environments, one must provide for the limits of endurance and frustration. Certainly, we must be fully aware that a person's specific strengths can be realized and maintained only through variety and flexibility in his or her environment.

Sociocultural Dynamics

The sociocultural perspective helps guard against unwarranted, misdirected, and premature application of design concepts and care and service schemes. The importance of this is easily recognized by calling to mind any number of designs and services that have failed to respond to sociocultural phenomena, resulting in alienation of residents, limited daily activities, lost opportunities for achieving quality of life, and impoverishment of retirement community life. Although your own experience may prepare you to deal with this complex aspect of retirement community life, care must be taken to assure that this experience does not distort the realities of existing social processes and cultural dynamics.

Sociocultural influences are a fundamental attribute of every individual. There is no question item in the standard of performance that cannot be answered more fully as a result of an assessment of the sociocultural dynamics of your retirement community enterprise. Our research must be conducted in such a way that one is ultimately able to see possible relationships between service and design concepts and the social structures the elderly use to organize their relationships and activities, the preferences for one design option over another, and the life-styles and traditions that permeate daily life. Some people maintain that the study of sociocultural dynamics is a high-risk, low-yield venture in terms of the time that must be committed to it and the fact that it is more suited to generating than verifying hunches or hypotheses.[4] We must do more than that. We need to create a definitive view of the sociocultural dynamics that influence the market and underlie the preferences of the elderly. We must also keep in mind that the search for sociocultural significance doesn't end. It continues to evolve as the sociocultural dynamics of the elderly continue to evolve.

■ Research Methods

It may seem that the recommended research methods—progressive surveys, study sessions, interviews, and activity analyses—are not sufficient for the task. However, when applying these methods, the concern is not for undertaking an exhaustive research program, but for directing simple applications wisely. These methods are modest in man-hour demands, but nevertheless assure that we discover what is essential for the success of our enterprise. The basic sequence for strategic research begins with progressive surveys, which we use to identify individuals qualified to answer specified standard of performance question items. We then ask verified sources to participate in a study session or interview. These three steps accomplish a great deal in a very short period of time. When we recognize that results warrant clarification, we undertake activity analyses to assess the situation in detail.

Progressive Surveys

The only way to be economical with the funds, time, and personnel allocated to strategic research is to identify those who are the most valuable sources of information for the deliberation at hand. Progressive surveys can be used to identify important individuals by asking knowledgeable sources to recommend who should be interviewed or asked to participate in study sessions. Research is often flawed because the people interviewed and participating in a study session are selected only because they are available, or selected randomly within some type of sampling plan. In strategic research for a retirement community enterprise, we select only those people who are identified in progressive surveys or specifically recommended by a highly informed source.

Study Sessions

The firsthand experience that results during study sessions (in current jargon, "focus groups") allows you to determine how much confidence you can place in your personal assumptions and speculations. Whatever your goal, it is important to realize that your success depends on how well you collaborate with those who are participating in study sessions and how well they share your responsibilities. A word of caution is needed here. Involving yourself directly in the activities of others may distract you from your principal information objectives. Care must be taken to assure that your standard of performance question items remain fixed and clear in your mind.

Interviews

Every individual is a valuable source of information when asked to talk about things that he or she knows well. It is best to interview in an unstructured way, since we are primarily interested in what people know and what they think is important enough to share with us, rather than in their responses to questions we pose. Even with this unstructured approach, results are usually comprehensive as people naturally address all the critical success factors.

Activity Analyses

Information gathered from study sessions and interviews is basic to strategic research. However, since this information comes directly from people—what they think and what they recommend—we need a counterpoint for these highly individualized views. Direct observation of the activities of the elderly within existing retirement communities is the best possible preparation. It is particularly valuable to observe the way in which interior designs mesh with actions and movements. These studies are especially useful for the task of evaluating proposed master plan and facility design options and alternatives related to circulation patterns, spatial configurations and arrangements, and space planning. To further understand activity analyses, take note of the ways product designers study activity limitations and capabilities to capture interest in new designs and assistive technologies when their products target those with hearing impairment, deafness, low vision, blindness, and physical, speech, and cognitive impairment.[5]

Market Research

Let's begin with the facts. First, you can never assume that, just because a CCRC is a "good product," people will want to live there. Second, even if the product is good, it will have both strengths and weaknesses when evaluated by prospective residents. Third, we have no choice but to design a CCRC to satisfy the needs of a market segment, not the general retirement community market. And, fourth, it is not the reality of a situation toward which we direct our marketing effort but the perception of that reality. To deal with these facts, we need a broad marketing strategy with many distinct features. The achievement of this is what market research is all about. [6]

When we work to create and execute the best possible market strategy, we need data and information descriptive of current, near-term, and projected market conditions. With this, we make it evident to investors, lenders, underwriters, and state regulators that there is a need for the proposed retirement community and demonstrate that a complete understanding of all market factors has been attained. For this work, the primary market research questions are as follows:

4.2.1 DEMOGRAPHICS. What are the demographics of the market region for the general and elderly populations? What is the current and anticipated future demand for retirement communities?

4.2.2 COMPETITORS. What are the existing competing developments? Where are others proposed?

4.2.3 COMPETING CONCEPTS. What do competing developments offer in terms of admission standards, services, quality of life, and financial arrangements?

4.2.4 MARKET CHARACTERISTICS. What descriptive categories best identify and distinguish potential residents?

4.2.5 MARKET DYNAMICS. Where are fundamental changes in the market developing?

In order to respond to these question items, a specific program of research is needed, with the appropriate safeguards to reduce error to a minimum. The research guideline questions are as follows:

- **Proposed Market Research Design.** What is the proposed market research design?
- **Evaluating Research Design.** How do we know the market research design will work?
- **Market Research Budget.** What are the costs associated with each market research activity? How are costs justified?
- **Research Performance.** How will the work of research participants be directed and monitored?
- **Trial Presentations.** How will marketing and sales programs designed to attract clients be tested?
- **New Findings.** When new facts and insights arise during marketing and sales activities, how will these be introduced into the deliberations of the executive organization?

■ Market Demographics

This is a descriptive statistical study of existing and projected population data. It is also a market penetration analysis estimating the degree of penetration of the market by age and income that must be achieved if the enterprise is to succeed. The guideline question item is

> 4.2.1 DEMOGRAPHICS. What are the demographics of the market region for the general and elderly populations? What is the current and anticipated future demand for retirement communities?

Market Penetration Ratios

Although the industry does not have rigid standards by which the competitive and demographic market can be analyzed for specific projects, there are guidelines that may be helpful in evaluating the relative health of competitive markets. The primary safeguards are market penetration calculations. Crown Research Corporation,[7] in its demographic analysis for *The Stratford*, used the following penetration ratios to estimate market potential.

Traditional Market Penetration. The methodology used to determine the traditional market penetration is to divide the number of proposed market rate units in the project by the total number of income- and age-qualified households in the primary service area, after removing from the list of eligible households those who have already opted to move into a retirement community. By using this methodology, qualified homeowner/households can be estimated with data generated by National Planning Data Corporation and the latest available U.S. Census information.

Dynamic Market Penetration. This calculation is designed to determine the number of dwelling units within primary service areas (which could be a 10-mile radius and a two-county area) that is likely to be available for occupancy and reoccupancy during a given period of time. Dynamic market penetration is expressed as the number of comparable market rate units that must be marketed and occupied during a specified period, divided by the net number of age- and income-eligible households within the service area.

Absolute Market Penetration. This calculation is a measurement of the total number of occupied and planned continuing care retirement dwelling units that offer services within the primary service area as a percentage of the number of households potentially eligible for occupancy of those units. In this calculation, we also limit the dwelling units and households by age and economic criteria. In the absence of unique circumstances, the industry tends to avoid entering the market when the absolute market penetration places the proposed project in the 15% to 18% range.

Interpretation of Penetration Ratios

The most common methodologies utilized to determine market penetration are the traditional market penetration formula and the absolute market penetration formula. Industry standards suggest that market penetration ratios of up to 7% are acceptable in some rental markets, and that market penetrations of up to 4% are acceptable in some continuing care markets, using the traditional computation formula. Although industry standards have not yet been established for the evaluation of dynamic market penetration ratios, a calculation that says that less than 4% in a two-county area, or less than 2% within a 10-mile radius, is required to move into market rate communities during the first 2 years in order for all existing and planned communities to achieve 95% occupancy.

Supplemental Sources

The demographic research undertaken to reach agreement as to the market potential of a financial scheme can be augmented with special data sources and services. It is particularly helpful to identify local databases from banks, realtors, and government planning departments. For instance, at *www.boston.com, keyword: banker,* you have access to Banker & Tradesman's recent home sales database.[8] This site also includes news and analyses featuring residential and commercial property, regulations, recent deals, and profiles. This is the type of source that probes what underlies government census data.

■ Competitors

Demographic analysis that goes beyond population statistics is certainly essential. The work undertaken by the Crown Research Corporation for the developers of *The Stratford* included information about competing senior living operations and anticipated new developments. What services do they provide? What are the financial arrangements? How large are the waiting lists? The guideline question items are

In the typical situation, compilations descriptive of competitors include the following:

Type of community	Description of setting
Description of neighborhood	Availability
Financial plan	Financial plan options
Ownership	Service management
Age qualification	Health qualification
Resident population	Number and types of living units
Residential services	Health services
Activities	Dining plan

Financial Plans

The federal government, through its information resources, has
attempted to identify the distinguishing financial characteristics
of the CCRC market.[9] The conclusion was that CCRCs assume
different levels of financial risk for the costs of residents' long-
term care services, such as skilled nursing care and assisted-
living services. These long-term care services are provided in
combination with residential services such as cleaning and
meals. Financial risks for residents' care are defined in lifetime
contracts between the CCRC and the individual resident. A
CCRC may offer more than one type of long-term care risk
arrangement from which residents may choose.

Some CCRCs are at full financial risk for the cost of long-term
care services. This means that the CCRC must pay all the costs of
required long-term care services except for those that may be reimbursed by third parties such as Medicare. These CCRCs typically
require that residents pay an entrance fee and a monthly fee,
which includes prepayment for long-term care costs, similar to an
insurance arrangement. Increases in monthly fees can occur as a
result of operating costs or inflation, but not as a consequence of
use of long-term care services. As a result, residents with these
contracts are not at risk for covered long-term care costs.

Some CCRCs are at partial financial risk for the cost of long-
term care services. These CCRCs must pay some, but not all, of
the costs of long-term care services beyond those reimbursed by
third parties such as Medicare. The financial risk of these CCRCs

is limited by a cap on the amount of long-term care services for which the CCRC will pay. For example, for each resident, a CCRC may pay a maximum of 30 or 60 days of skilled nursing care per year, whatever limit is specified in the resident's contract. Under these arrangements, CCRCs typically require that residents pay an entry fee and a monthly fee, which may be lower than the fees for arrangements under which CCRCs assume full financial risk for the costs of long-term care. Until the cap on long-term care services is reached, residents' monthly fees under the partial-risk agreement can increase based on changes in operating costs and inflation adjustments but not as a result of the use of long-term care services. If the contract cap is reached, however, the resident is at risk for the cost of all additional long-term care services not reimbursed by third parties. This kind of agreement is sometimes known as a modified, limited services contract.

Some CCRCs are not at risk for any of the cost of long-term care services. These CCRCs require residents to pay for services they use, either through a combination of an entry fee and a monthly fee or through a monthly fee alone. Monthly fees in either payment arrangement can increase based on operating costs, inflation adjustments, and the use of long-term care services. As a result, residents are at risk for all long-term care service costs not reimbursed by third parties.

■ Market Characteristics

This is an essential market research consideration. There can be no efficiency or confidence in a market strategy that is not based on a valid and encompassing definition of market characteristics. A common error in market research is to simplify market characteristics. People think they are being economical when they reduce market research to two primary indices—demographics and a survey of existing and proposed retirement communities in the market area. Actually, the cost/benefit ratio always favors extended research. The lead question item is

> 4.2.4 MARKET CHARACTERISTICS. What descriptive categories best identify and distinguish potential residents?

In answer to this question, we create a profile, or a reference that defines the variables descriptive of the elderly within the market segments identified by means of demographic analysis and the initial assumptions and speculations of the executive organization. The critical term for this undertaking is "customer fit." Hiroyuki Itami[10] uses this concept as a means to differentiate segment markets. He suggests that not everyone wants the same characteristics in a product. There is no "average customer," so we have to find a unique way to segment the market and narrow the focus to one or a few target groups. The idea is that not every elderly person is satisfied with the same retirement community opportunity. If that is so, then how do we distinguish between market segments? What are the critical market characteristics? How much attention should we give to preferences, feelings, attitudes, and values? Should we stay within the gerontological or geriatric model that emphasizes the ability and activity limitations and capabilities of the elderly or should we discard the obvious and consider the subtle? What we do know is that the market situation today and into the future requires the closest scrutiny.

Level of Detail

To what level of analysis do we want to be held accountable when distinguishing market characteristics? Here are some possibilities based on the three human factors categories:

Market Characteristics		
Individual Differences	*Activity Limitations and Capabilities*	*Sociocultural Dynamics*
Age	Health status	Ethnicity
Sex	Services needed	Cultural receptivity
Education	Medical history	Occupation
Quality of education	Cognitive abilities	Leadership capabilities
Intelligence	Perceptual and motor skills	World view
Special knowledge	Active recreations	Religious affiliation
Income resources	Driving ability	Political affiliation
Insurance resources	Willingness to grow	Political activities
Home location	Diet requirements	Need for privacy
Home features	Level of independence	Sense of community
Contractual risk	Self-enriching	Fun loving
Family situation	Long-range planner	Understanding nature
Proximity to relatives	Computer skilled	Sense of art appreciation
Proximity to friends	Ability to maintain cleanliness and order	Concern for security and safety

Progressive Survey

Many individuals can contribute to the development of market characteristics. Helpful individuals can be distinguished in terms of family, peer, interest, and activity affiliations, or may be representative of neighborhood, historic, cultural, religious, organization, and political groups. Individuals of particular value represent communities of interest committed to attaining quality of life for the elderly. Even more specific are individuals who represent local realtors, mortgage bankers, and savings-and-loan officials doing business with the elderly. Certainly, groups comprising managers of retirement communities, service staff, and health care providers are valuable sources.

The progressive survey is shared with individuals representative of these various groups. A personally administered survey produces the best results. When people are asked to merely answer some questions and mail them back, they are placed in a passive role. We want people to recognize that we are challenged by a significant problem and that they are being asked to help us work out a solution. Our effort to personally administer a survey demonstrates that we are not just collecting information, but are asking for insights and perspectives.

The following progressive survey has proven to be most efficient in identifying those who can best contribute to the development of a description of market characteristics:

Those Who Work with the Elderly

What type of undertaking is this?

We are distributing a workbook to thirty selected retirement community professionals, in which they will be asked to list the various sources of assistance for the elderly that exist in the community. This is the first step in a "progressive survey." After the workbooks are collected, we will edit the findings. In the next step, this listing will be sent to another group of retirement community professionals and various communities of interest. They will be asked to review the work of the first group and revise the listing as they see appropriate. The original group will then be given the same opportunity. Findings will again be edited in an attempt to develop a complete listing of services in your community. In the final step of the survey, additional communities of interest will be given a statement of the project's purpose and a response form. They will be asked to review the results we have obtained and add to the list those who have been overlooked. After a full and verified listing is completed, we will work with these organizations and individuals to identify specific expectations and requirements for retirement community life.

Why are we doing this?

We all know that the retirement community industry is facing challenges and opportunities that will lead to a redefinition of the products we offer. For our deliberations, we need a reliable list of the full spectrum of professionals who work with the elderly and associated communities of interest. How would you go about establishing the most extensive listing of resources for the elderly? How would you assure the completeness of your listing? We are taking an approach that centers around those most knowledgeable, the people in your community who are familiar with existing services for the elderly.

What would we like you to do?

Each of the sheets making up this workbook refers to a general group. Would you please write down as many people and organizations as you can think of that fall into these preliminary categories? Thank you. We will keep you informed of our progress and findings.

Category No. 1: Community organizations in your area.

This is your first task. Please list here the names of groups in the community that have an active interest in the elderly, such as the AARP, church groups, Home Visit Volunteers, and RSVPs. We would like to contact as many organizations as possible and have them help us in our work.

1. _____
2. _____
3. _____
... _____

Category No. 2: Local medical services, professional care organizations, and related business firms in your area.

Please list here the names of the medical, care, and business organizations in your area that play an important part in the care of the elderly and provide the services they need.

1. _____
2. _____
3. _____
... _____

Category No. 3: Federal, state, and local agencies in your area that play an important role in the life of the elderly.

Please list here the names of the agencies that provide important services to the elderly.

1. _____
2. _____
3. _____
... _____

Category No. 4: Educational programs in your area providing professional development and education opportunities.

Please list here the various people, programs, and organizations that provide professional development and educational opportunities for those who serve the elderly.

   1. _____

   2. _____

   3. _____

   ... _____

Category No. 5: There are private individuals in your community who provide care and services to the elderly. These people work without recognition to keep elderly individuals active and pleased with life in the community and at home.

Please list here all the individuals who come to mind.

   1. _____

   2. _____

   3. _____

   ... _____

After our listing of knowledgeable sources is complete, we approach these people with the following task.

Identifying Market Characteristics

Please help us identify the characteristics of elderly people who might benefit from living in a retirement community. The resulting information will help retirement community executives and marketing and sales associates maintain an awareness of the full spectrum of potential clients.

This is your first task. Think of the elderly you have seen in the community. Where do they live? What kinds of living situations are common or exceptional? Please write down as many different situations as you can think of.

   1. _____

   2. _____

   3. _____

   ... _____

> *Now think about the elderly you know. What are their interests, concerns, and most pressing needs? Please list as many as possible. When you are finished with your listing, pass it on to a friend. You'll probably get another dozen possibilities added to your list.*
>
> 1. _____
> 2. _____
> 3. _____
> ... _____

After these responses are collected, additional groups will be asked to review and add to the work. As we proceed through this application sequence, it is extremely important to maintain a record of those who contributed information. We often need to be able to recheck facts with those who provided them. In strategic research, we always maintain this link.

■ Community Characteristics

Let's consider this question:

> 4.1.6 WORKING WITH THE COMMUNITY. Recognizing that the local community can foster a positive view of the development, what steps should be taken to familiarize people with the retirement community opportunity?

Here we deal with the most frustrating aspect of our business—gaining enterprise approval from the community. Despite the merit of the enterprise, it will always create controversy within the local community. No matter what we say about our responsibility to the community, the approval process poses the greatest potential for enterprise delay and may even lead to abandoning the whole project. Too often, local government and community interests work against us because they project their concerns into the enterprise. We are always dealing with perceptions and interpretations of the facts we present and not with the reality of the situation. This means that we must be thoroughly prepared for public presentations. Effort and hours are justified because failure to prepare adequately for hearings may delay the enterprise and add another year of public relations work. We begin this research with a study session designed to identify the most influential people in the community.

> ## Community Research: Study Session
>
> **Step One:** Prepare a description of your study objectives.
>
> We need to discover all the problems, challenges, and opportunities associated with the proposed development. The executives of this enterprise want to be sure that every individual and family, community organization, interest group, business firm, shop, public service organization, and those not heretofore identified as important for deliberations, are considered during this enterprise. We want to respond to every concern and interest, particularly in terms of the possible impact on neighborhood life, community life, public and private services, property values, visual impact, and ecological and environmental factors.
>
> We need to know what must be done to gain neighborhood and community support. We need people who can help us identify community leaders and neighborhood groups, and those who can help us understand the town's concerns and interests.
>
> **Step Two:** Ask people identified in the progressive survey to review your study objectives. Their task is to recommend participants for study sessions.
>
> **Step Three:** Schedule several meetings with people representative of various sources of information.
>
> **Step Four:** In each meeting, ask the participants to identify and discuss as many members of the neighborhood and community as they can think of, with particular emphasis on the views held by neighborhood leaders, active groups, contentious individuals, and those least likely to be well represented during the community review process.
>
> **Step Five:** Divide the listing into logical groupings and indicate the relationship between groupings.
>
> **Step Six:** Ask all those who participated in study sessions to review the results obtained.
>
> **Step Seven:** Edit the collected information into the clearest possible description that takes into account and gives identity to all community groups, sources of influence, and points of view.

■ Creating a Positive Market Image

Too many people, in preparation for a public hearing, spend their time developing statements and graphics that show enterprise features. This is certainly necessary, and we enjoy talking about our ideas, plans, and progress. However, before we present our concepts and action plan, those at the hearing or meeting must first see that their concerns are addressed. When you demonstrate that you know what is in people's minds and have taken the time to learn and understand, you may be seen as a community advocate as much as the promoter of a development.

Research Design

We need information that allows us to open our public presentations with the following statement: "We have studied the impact of our enterprise on the community. Please listen to what we have learned. We believe it fairly represents your interests and concerns." The guiding standard of performance question item is

> 2.4.4 PREPARATION. For community board presentations and public meetings, what preparation is required to present the features of the enterprise?

As is so often the case, we find other standard of performance question items that can be used to guide research. We find specific information objectives identified in the following set of questions:

> 8.1.4 NEIGHBORHOOD GROUPS. Who lives and works in the neighborhood surrounding the site? How may these people be grouped by activities and concerns?
>
> 8.1.5 NEIGHBORHOOD IMPACT. What is the possible impact of facility activities on neighborhood life?
>
> 8.1.6 COMMUNITY GROUPS. Who lives and works in the local community? How may these people be grouped by activities and concerns?
>
> 8.1.7 COMMUNITY IMPACT. What is the likely impact of retirement community activities on community life and public and private services?
>
> 8.1.8 PROPERTY VALUE IMPACT. What is the possible impact of the retirement community on community property values?
>
> 8.1.9 VISUAL IMPACT. Anticipating the visual impact of the retirement community, what are the possible objectives?
>
> 8.1.10 ECOLOGICAL AND ENVIRONMENTAL IMPACT. What is the anticipated impact of the retirement community development in terms of ecological and environmental factors?
>
> 8.1.11 NEIGHBORHOOD AND COMMUNITY SUPPORT. In terms of community objections and resistance, what is the strategy for gaining neighborhood and community support?

Research Objectives

We can formalize our objectives as a scope of work:

RESEARCH REPORT ELEMENTS	SCOPE OF WORK
Applications system files	Create a file within the applications system, entitled: 2.3.4 preparation.
I. Topic and associated concerns	Develop a strategy for community board presentations and public meetings. Determine the community's views regarding the need for retirement community services.
II. Recommendations	Recommend the details that should be included in every presentation. Address question items 8.1.4 to 8.1.11 in your recommended presentation strategy.
III. Points of view	Discuss the points of view that exist in the community regarding the enterprise. What are the conflicting points of view that exist in the community? What can be said about the dilemma of bringing an economic opportunity to the community that may not be perceived positively by those neighboring the proposed site?
IV. Situational factors	What is the history of the community regarding new developments? Where have real estate developments adversely impacted the community?
V. Financial analysis	What will the enterprise bring to the community in taxes or negotiated payments? What are the anticipated community service costs?
VI. Research design	Summarize the research design. Indicate what steps were taken to reduce misinterpretation of the community's interests and concerns.
VII. Supplemental Information	Identify all the individuals and community entities that participated in study sessions and interviews.

Community Publications

When creating an image for marketing purposes, publications that contribute to quality of life should be identified. For instance, in the highly detailed 71 pages of *Access Expressed! Massachusetts: A Cultural Access Directory,*[11] we find that Very Special Arts Massachusetts, an advocacy group, has worked to make this state a more accessible, culturally vibrant place for people with disabilities and those who work and live with them. This publication lists all accessibility features for museums, theaters, and cultural sites, and, after some experience with what people mean by "culture," now includes sports facilities, movie theaters, public parks, and more. Very Special Arts Massachusetts publishes a calendar of cultural events that offer physical and/or programmatic access. For instance, during Family Fun Days at Old Sturbridge Village, the elderly can enjoy such lively activities as candle making, musical performances, storytelling, and sleigh rides. The calendar item notes when a sign-language interpreter will be available and that more than half the historic buildings are wheelchair-accessible. Are you aware of such sources in your local area? In the Boston area, these include such organizations as Boston Aid to the Blind; D.E.A.F., Inc.; Deaf-Blind Contact Center, Inc.; Disability Law Center; Massachusetts Office for Transportation Access and Architectural Access Board; Talking Information Center; and Theater Access Consortium.

■ Market Dynamics

This question item tells us that we must anticipate new market forces and opportunities:

> 4.2.5 MARKET DYNAMICS. Where are fundamental changes in the market developing?

The challenge here was stated in the call for papers for the 44th Annual Meeting of the American Society on Aging:[12]

> Our theme for the 1998 Annual Meeting was selected because the future is now. The age boom we have been talking about for so many years is upon us. The 20th century added a full generation to our life expectancy. Now our institutions must catch up; they must adopt the long-term view we will need to make the most of our life span. Our decisions—or our indecision—will determine how . . . tomorrow's generations will understand their longevity. . . . What will be our polestar as we calibrate our cultural and ethical compasses? How will we guide ourselves between the extremes of individualism and community, public and private responsibility, saving and spending?

The agenda for this meeting confirms that many people and professionals are prepared to help us look to the future. However, since we are addressing a specific market situation for a CCRC enterprise, we have to conduct our own research.

Progressive Surveys

Analysis of demographics, competing retirement communities, and market characteristics frame our study of the future with descriptions of what exists today. Starting with what has been learned, we share this information with people associated with the market segment of interest and ask them who in their community is best prepared to speak to the future. Similar to the

progressive survey applied to market characteristics, their task is to provide us with the identity of those to whom we should be listening to gain an enriched and verified understanding of the future market for CCRCs.

Study Sessions

Study sessions build on what has been accomplished by means of various progressive survey undertakings. The basic procedure for study sessions is to select seven or eight individuals, with additional groups as necessary to achieve a balance of experience, views, interests, and intensity of feeling about future prospects for the elderly. The most convenient way to orchestrate the study session is to select question items from the standard of performance and ask people to share their insights and experiences. Too often, we overlook the fact that a study session is not primarily a forum in which we hear from individuals. It is an opportunity for individuals to talk to one another. As we listen to these exchanges, we discover valuable information. In order for this to work effectively, we must create an opportunity for interaction between participants that results in new information or evaluation of existing information. This is a highly efficient way of developing an understanding of how people perceive the future. During study sessions, individuals talk to one another and exchange information as they work to complete the tasks assigned to them. In this way, we learn things that would never be discovered in a questionnaire survey or even in an interview.

It is very helpful to conduct study sessions before interviews. In fact, let's state this more strongly: Never interview without the experience gained from a study session. Study sessions reveal the important questions and concerns on which to concentrate further research. There is another reason for doing the study session work first. If you start your research with interviews, your focus is too narrow. Start with study sessions and your base is expanded. When you use this information to guide interviews, individuals and groups of individuals will immediately recognize that you have attempted to understand the situation as they understand it. Without this background, interviews too often seem to be conducted by someone who is completely unfamiliar with the situation.

Interviews

With the results obtained from progressive surveys and study sessions, we are prepared to undertake a program of interviews. We gain so much when we interview the elderly. First of all, it is a rehearsal for the presales endeavor. The elderly can be very analytical when they discuss their future and suggest ways to enhance the settings for their daily affairs. People will want to talk about their situation, requirements, and expectations. When an interview is completed, you know what an individual wants, what he or she thinks others need, what is most important and least important to the individual with regard to possible CCRC features, and, most helpful of all, the feelings behind the various statements made.

Qualitative Interviewing: The Art of Hearing Data [13] is a valuable resource for conducting a good interview. Essentially, before any interviews are undertaken, topics based on your needs must be selected, although people will not confine themselves to your topics. This is particularly true when you interview the elderly about the future. You will hear the stories they want to tell, and this is just what you want. In this way, you will learn what is significant to them. When we conducted the interviews for *The Cypress* and *The Stratford* case studies, we were in a different situation. We were dealing with highly experienced and motivated professionals. They stayed on target. As you can see from the case study materials, they knew exactly what story should be told. The only structure for these interviews was provided by the logos and titles for each of the eight critical success factors. We did find it helpful to use two interviewers. When there are two people present, the person being interviewed works all that much harder to make sure his or her point of view is understood. In both instances, with the elderly and with CCRC professionals, we kept things informal. We let people create the interview dynamics. As expressed so well by Studs Terkel, whose oral history of World War II[14] won a Pulitzer Prize, the goal is to create the type of interview in which, at the end, you might find the individual saying, "I never realized I felt that way."[15]

■ Contracted Research

When contracting for marketing research services, you should certainly require that such services follow the presented standards and safeguards for strategic research. Demand a detailed research design. Require evidence in the final report that the contracted scope of work was correctly executed and incorporates all specified information development safeguards. When evaluating a research firm's offer of service, maintain a healthy skepticism about claims and performance. Douglas Blackmon reports[16] on a nationally recognized human resources and benefits consulting firm that offered to study a company in detail and then "customize" a program to fit the client's needs. In fact, the firm was using a boiler-plate approach. Seven of the 10 final reports examined were identical in most places, duplicating nearly all of the recommended strategies and tactics.

Human Factors Research

The work specified in the preceding section, Market Research, and in the following, Design Research, is more thoroughly undertaken when we combine this work with a study of the expectations and requirements of residents and staff. Accordingly, 5.1 Residents' Expectations and Requirements guides human factors research with the following questions:

5.1.1 DISTINGUISHING CHARACTERISTICS. What characteristics and factors can be used to distinguish residents?

5.1.2 DAILY ACTIVITIES. What are the daily activities of residents? What is known about the extent, time of occurrence, and duration of activities?

5.1.3 INDIVIDUAL PERCEPTIONS. How are residents likely to perceive themselves, other residents, and staff in terms of their individual rights and anticipated perquisites?

5.1.4 LIFE-STYLES. What are the social customs, relationship norms, and cultural traditions of residents?

5.1.5 RESIDENTS' SERVICE PREFERENCES. What are the service preferences of residents?

5.1.6 RECREATION AND LEISURE PREFERENCES. What are the recreation and leisure preferences of residents?

5.1.7 CUISINE AND FOOD SERVICE PREFERENCES. What are the cuisine and food service preferences of residents?

5.1.8 HEALTH CARE PREFERENCES. What are the health care preferences of residents?

5.1.9 RESIDENTIAL DESIGN AND SERVICE CHALLENGES. In summary, what are the facility design and service challenges associated with residents' abilities, activities, preferences, and health?

The study of these question items must lead to the identification and thorough characterization of every possible expectation and requirement that pertains to the achievement of quality of life for residents. This requires attention to the immediate. We need to hear directly from people and learn how to correctly interpret their words and actions. We use study sessions, interviews, and activity analyses to accomplish this. Each result enriches every enterprise deliberation. The budget and man-hours for this work are modest because of the economies associated with the standard of performance, which precisely guides research activities. In addition, expertise with the recommended research methods requires only minimal training. This means that all enterprise participants can play a role, giving us people with expert knowledge, alert to what is important and critical of what is of little concern or insignificant.

Individual Differences

Success in meeting presale requirements is essentially in the hands of prospective residents. An effective sales strategy must be responsive to personal views and situations and all the associated concerns, perceptions, and values. We rely on our experience, recollections, perceptions, and judgment to establish how we can best distinguish one elderly individual from another. Although these insights are valuable and may be trusted, we need to validate them by means of this question item:

> 5.1.1 DISTINGUISHING CHARACTERISTICS. What characteristics and factors can be used to distinguish residents?

The results of the study of market characteristics and dynamics contribute to this effort. Throughout the entire CCRC enterprise, everyone should be alert to distinguishing features of prospective residents.

Personal Experience

We advance our study of individual differences and distinguishing characteristics when we find real stories and personal accounts of the aging experience.[17] We can read narratives written by the elderly, diaries, published accounts of what aging means to an individual, and biographical excerpts. Videocassette productions are also a source of both insight and important information about service and care for the elderly. Michel Jones's video[18] focuses on a 77-year-old woman and her daughters as they debate what is "overprotect" and what is good care. *Harriet's People*,[19] a 28-minute guided walk through the daily world of a nursing home care giver, portrays what we all recognize—care givers create bonds that endure through every difficult moment and crisis. *When She Gets Old*[20] illustrates the value of these resources. Here we see challenged retired homemakers as they struggle to live independently in an urban environment. The details of life we must anticipate in the CCRC enterprise can be found in such work as *Fear of Falling: A Matter of Balance*,[21] which demonstrates the importance of independence.

Conferences

We improve the likelihood that our characterization of distinguishing features is complete when we attend meetings of special-interest organizations responding to the challenge of elderly care. At the 43rd Annual Meeting of the American Society on Aging, for example, the agenda included such topics as redefining retirement—the baby-boomer challenge, aging network, Alzheimer's disease and related disorders, care management, cultural and minority issues, education and training, disability and rehabilitation, housing and aging in place, status assessment program for CCRCs and long-term care, home and community-based care, and institutional care issues.

The publications of interest groups also contain a wealth of accumulated experience and knowledge that can support deliberations and decision making. Consider the interests and activism of the American Association of Retired People (AARP) and American Association of Homes for the Aging. The publications circulated by these organizations help us understand current issues facing the elderly, as well as helping the elderly acquire the skills necessary to become wise consumers.

■ Activity Limitations and Capabilities

A study of the psychology of aging, gerontology, and geriatrics help us address this question:

> 5.1.2 DAILY ACTIVITIES. What are the daily activities of residents? What is known about the extent, time of occurrence, and duration of activities?

There is a domain of knowledge descriptive of the activity limitations and capabilities of the elderly that establishes a basis for facility design and services. When we call attention to this information and knowledge and show its enterprise significance, this research helps identify where our work might be expanded to embrace overlooked or superficially considered design criteria or service possibilities. Further, when we study the characteristics of residents, we help people see what is particularly unique about the current enterprise challenge. Essentially, this research succeeds when enterprise participants "see life in the retirement community before there is a community."

The Gerontological Society of America

Let's review what a professional association finds important enough to call to the attention of its membership. The program schedule for the 49th Annual Scientific Meeting of the Geronto-logical Society of America[22] included such conference work-shops as follows:

- Alzheimer's Disease Special Care Units: Findings from the National Institute on Aging
- Gathering Data from Rural Elders: Techniques that Work
- Interpersonal Psychotherapy in the Treatment of Late Life Depression
- The Use of the Internet in Gerontological Research

Fostering interdisciplinary interaction among attendees, a number of symposia were developed to present research issues:

- Adult Day Care and the Relief of Caregiver
- Quality of Life for the Aging: Cross-Cultural Perspectives
- The Impact of Managed Care

Interest groups were shown as meeting to discuss:

- Abuse, Neglect and Exploitation of Elderly
- AIDS and Aging
- Business and Aging
- Death, Dying, Bereavement and Widowhood
- Elderly Use and Misuse of Alcohol and Drugs
- Geriatric Rehabilitation and Independent Living
- Mental Health Practice and Aging
- Nursing Care of Older Adults
- Physical Environments and Aging
- Emotion and Aging

Activity Analysis

Activity analysis is a means to verify that what we have learned from progressive surveys, study sessions, interviews, and archi-val research accurately reflects the activity limitations and capa-bilities of the elderly. Activity analyses within a CCRC can yield many additional insights concerning individual differences. For example, the meals you share with residents, the moments you spend in the library, the walks you take around a CCRC facility, and the observation of group activities provide a range of insight-ful and perhaps significant impressions. Pick an open space for an interview with broad fields of view. The activities of people around you can simultaneously be noted. In fact, if you see some-thing interesting, stop the interview and ask a question. It is easy to become aware of the varied and rich aspects of the daily activi-ties of the elderly. Visits can be made to places in the community where the elderly are engaged in what is important to them. You will soon recognize that the range of abilities is both broad and select. You will become familiar with what is convenient or challenging to the elderly. At the very least, you have guarded against relying too heavily on your own past experience.

The activities described in the preceding paragraph are valuable only when they are appropriately directed. Do not forget that the results of activity analysis capture only moments in time from which we are asking people to infer that such activities exist elsewhere or at other times. The most convenient way to control a study of distinguishing characteristics is to arrange observations by space and activity. We recommend that the observer be familiar with the spaces and the associated activities. You may need someone familiar with the situation to help you determine not just what is interesting, but what is significant.

In application, activity analysis is used to produce a characterization of the sequence of actions and activities that are expected to comprise the residents' day. If you spend time in a CCRC, in community spaces, assisted-living units, and special care centers, you will readily understand where to apply activity analysis. It is a commonsense approach to identifying important facility design and care and service considerations. We know that the elderly differ from one from another in terms of their tolerance of fatigue or boredom, their reaction to constant or prolonged stress, their tendency to become disoriented or confused, and their behavior in emergency or crisis situations. Other distinguishing features may be the inability to deal with anything other than a perfectly designed environment, cognitive disabilities, low tolerance of frustration, and emotional problems. Some individuals may require special consideration because of physical disabilities that affect vision, speech, or motor movement and coordination.

Activity analysis is quite extensive. We observe every movement of elderly individuals (walking, grasping, reaching, sitting) and give the closest scrutiny to common daily tasks such as bathing, cooking, or mailing a letter, which can assume major importance. Certain activities may also require attention because of the characteristics of the facility being considered, such as long corridors, stairs, common spaces, limited space, and hazardous areas such as parking lots and crosswalks. Detailed attention must be given to activities that are likely to cause stress, fatigue, boredom, or confusion, as well as detailed, demanding, or critical functions. Lack of support for such activities will adversely affect convenience, safety, and security.

After identifying the individual and group activities toward which activity analysis will be directed, we begin to determine the important relationships between people, their activities, and the immediate environment. Interviews, study sessions, and systematic observations are all possible methods for activity analysis. It should not be difficult to determine which will work best in a given situation. The method selected and its application will depend on the kind of results required. The more specific and quantified the results of activity analysis, the more value they will have. Because activity sequences are frequently used as a guide for space planning, the sequences of activities occurring in a physical setting should be described as completely as possible. Mapping and flow diagrams are excellent formats for depicting occupancy and movement patterns.

Sociocultural Dynamics

To grasp the significance of this consideration, think about the fact that sociocultural factors dominate the economy, politics, education, and public services in every state. In this context, we can certainly see the significance of these question items:

5.1.3 INDIVIDUAL PERCEPTIONS. How are residents likely to perceive themselves, other residents, and staff in terms of their individual rights and perquisites?

5.1.4 LIFE-STYLES. What are the social customs, relationship norms, and cultural traditions of residents?

Bias

Bias is a major concern when answering these two question items. We are always influenced by the limitations of our own sociocultural experience, and, as a result, often misinterpret the preferences of the elderly. We need to recognize the existence of different roles for the elderly in our society due to situations, ability, financial factors, and the many distinct life-styles that result. Of further concern is that statistical descriptions of the elderly, such as those seen in market analyses, frequently obscure important sociocultural differences. Guarding against these sources of bias, we must be constantly aware that with their individual customs, traditions, and life-styles, the elderly have their own unique view of the appropriateness or inappropriateness of CCRC design and service features.

As warranted by these considerations, human factors research must determine the possible effects of not responding to the structural and dynamic properties of sociocultural factors. Social interactions are particularly vulnerable in this respect. Where successful activities within a retirement community are dependent on social transactions, such as in common recreation areas, dining rooms, and assisted-living units, sociocultural dynamics must be considered in detail. To our benefit, culture is not an abstraction but is a directly observable composite of customs, life-styles, norms, and practices. Our research should show which features of residential design may be of critical importance to the elderly in various market segments. William Breger,[23] for example, in response to the rejection of standard designs by black and Spanish-speaking elderly, has stressed ethnic identification in two retirement community designs. In New York City, one was designed on the premise that its occupants share a common rural southern background, and is arranged so that all living room windows look out on a greenhouse. This creates an opportunity for all residents to live with flowers and shrubs, and to help plant and tend them. The residence created by the Consumer Action Program of Bedford-Stuyvesant is designed for Puerto Ricans who are made to feel at home on their own roofed courtyard with palm trees and other tropical plants, benches, and other encouragements to a Latin-style street life. How does Breger know his designs work? "I can tell when the design works when everybody comes right out in the morning."

Five Levels of Inquiry

To achieve a somewhat valid understanding of sociocultural dynamics, we should consider five levels of inquiry:

1. Small fact-to-face situations (staff to residents, residents to residents, and residents to families and friends)
2. Structured phenomena (recreational activities, educational classes, and regular and special-event dining)
3. Formal organizations and institutions (churches, community social services, nearby colleges, police, and local hospitals)
4. Dominant cultural streams along which residents may differentiate themselves from other residents (religion, social status, life experience, political interests, and sexual mores)
5. Broad expressions that integrate mass culture (interest in national and world events, concern for the future of a culture or treasured tradition, and confidence in national institutions)

Cultural Relevance

CCRCs, if they are to achieve market significance, must often be responsive to specific cultural expectations and requirements. Failure to do so risks alienation of prospective clients. Consider the differences between a CCRC marketed to retired military officers and one developed in association with a university community, and between a CCRC located in San Antonio and one situated on the coast of Maine. In such contrasting markets, determining what sociocultural elements are important and developing an explanatory framework that justifies design and service concepts are difficult tasks for which few people in the retirement community industry have been trained. However, much can be accomplished by even a minimum effort in these areas. The following research design has potential:

- On the basis of direct observation and casual conversation, establish a list of impressions for each of the five levels of inquiry in terms of stated objectives of the retirement community.
- Select a group of informants who are available for study sessions and interviews and elicit their comments concerning the validity of the initial set of impressions.
- Employ those impressions that withstand evaluation by you and your informants.

Any time strategic research leads to an understanding of the elderly that does not distort the reality of their situation and is aware of where preferences may be overtaken by sociocultural events, this work is moving toward an effective retirement community. When we assume that every previously established design or service feature can be improved by means of intense, critical analysis, successful CCRC design and service features are guaranteed.

■ Preferences

Preferences are identified during the study of individual differences, activity limitations and capabilities, and sociocultural dynamics. These question items guide our work:

5.1.5 RESIDENTS' SERVICE PREFERENCES. What are the service preferences of residents?

5.1.6 RECREATION AND LEISURE PREFERENCES. What are the recreation and leisure preferences of residents?

5.1.7 CUISINE AND FOOD SERVICE PREFERENCES. What are the cuisine and food service preferences of residents?

5.1.8 HEALTH CARE PREFERENCES. What are the health care preferences of residents?

When studying these questions, we do not ask general questions: What do you like? What are your recreational interests? What are you looking for in a retirement community? Rather, our objective is to determine how environments can enable individuals to lead the life they wish to lead, produce constructive attitudes, and develop more positive alternatives for personal activities. As prospective residents consider a move to a CCRC, it is an opportunity for them and for you to discover what is really important. What about the stress of a high-tech life-style that they may have experienced? Many residents in the future will be men and women who are used to long work hours and have virtually ignored their private lives. Are they now becoming more nature-loving and family-oriented? Maybe they realize that time with their families is the most important aspect of their future. How will you respond to this feeling? Talk about hospitality features and services, places to shop with their children and friends, places they might take a visiting grandchild. Stress the potential for them to lead outings rather than being led. Consideration of these possibilities can never be entirely adequate unless it is based on a thorough assessment of preferences.

For the question items having to do with the recognition of preferences, we always begin our work by conducting study sessions, seeking to confirm what we believe is important. A person experienced with retirement community life will recognize that a desire to be active is a very positive characteristic of older people. They wish to schedule their day to suit themselves, and to be able to participate in community, recreational, and social affairs to the extent that they themselves desire. Acute dissatisfaction with any retirement community design that restricts freedom to choose or that does not allow free expression of individual life-styles is always a possibility. Any situation that fails to ensure privacy is likely to be rejected, as will one whose design leads to passivity or isolation. On the other hand, some elderly people may exhibit a reduced capacity to adapt to changing situations and events and may be subject to fears of failure if the building and space features do not clearly indicate what behaviors are possible or appropriate. Many elderly actually prefer a highly structured environment that includes definite boundaries and security precautions, and readily available companions.

Assessing Recommendations

Each question item in section 5.0 Residents results in an array of CCRC design and service possibilities. This question item identifies the need for a summary statement that brings a cluster of information to the attention of the executive organization:

5.1.9 RESIDENTIAL DESIGN AND SERVICE CHALLENGES. In summary, what are the facility design and service challenges associated with residents' abilities, activities, preferences, and health?

We can assess our recommendations by means of a study session that follows these steps:

Design and Service Assessment

Objective: The objective of this study session is to meet with people who are interested in living in a CCRC. We are asking people to work with us to determine the most desirable arrangement of interior spaces. We are also using this as an opportunity to find new ideas for marketing and sales staff.

Step One: Give copies of the floor plans and the standard of performance to the study team thath is representative of prospective occupants. Review both documents carefully so that participants understand what information is needed and what decisions are required.

Step Two: Provide each participant with two-dimensional cutouts of home and common space furnishings. Ask the participants to respond to the following: "If you were being moved into the building tomorrow, which living unit would you choose, and how would you arrange your furnishings? There are no restrictions on location or arrangement. Paste the cutouts you have been given on the floor plan to show your plan for the space you have selected." (You can provide a similar opportunity for community spaces, asking individuals to arrange spaces and furnishings to their liking.)

At the next meeting, we will ask you to share the results of your work. In this way, we can understand each other's preferences and work out a scheme that is satisfactory to everyone.

We then ask participants to review the standard of performance question items with us and explain that these will be discussed during the following meeting. They are encouraged to take the questions home and collect their thoughts.

Step Three: In the second session, the pasted-up floor plans are displayed. Participants are asked to review all suggestions and discuss necessary compromises.

Step Four: Review the answers to the question items in the standard of performance. Summarize this information and share it with participants. Prepare conclusions and proposals based on this information, and provide all participants with an opportunity to critique these conclusions and proposals from the standpoint of their own background and experience.

■ Organization Performance

Consider the number of standard of performance question items that pertain to organization performance. Within every area of responsibility, the most important mission of the CCRC staff is to develop effective staff relationships and a feeling that staff and residents share the same fate. The emphasis we place on people and group dynamics must be genuine. However, no matter what we prescribe, the future is in the hands of the people hired. No management plan will make community life a success; that can only be done by people.

When working within an organization, how you go about doing things is as important as the end result. Let's consider employee benefits. Imagine that you review your options and decide that a "cafeteria plan" will meet the expectations of individual employees in a fair manner and improve the efficiency with which they use their limited funds. How will you evaluate your decision? According to Shinkai,[24] you first achieve an accurate understanding of your employees' needs, determine what types of benefits should be offered, formulate the basic employee-benefits program, and get a grasp of the total cost of the benefit plan. You ask employees to speak to their friends and report back about benefits offered by competitors. Then you can assign a cost to each type of benefit and estimate how many employees will select each option, based on employee surveys. This process makes it clear that you are committed to your employees.

Activity Analyses

Human factors research devoted to organization dynamics often requires that we develop a communication matrix, showing how individuals, groups, and spaces are linked in order to accomplish a particular service. This information is important for every CCRC service. It is important for health care facilities, recreation and activity centers, and administrative and service offices where information must be routinely exchanged. In the area of housekeeping and facility maintenance, information exchange may be the key to convenience, safety, security, and the prevention of facility misuse. The first step in developing a communication matrix is to identify each means of communication. The next step is to develop a suitable communication log. Measurements of frequency of exchanges and the numbers of individuals involved are achieved by asking staff to maintain a log for a specified period of time.

As the informal aspect of communication between individuals is always important, a communication survey may be used to identify the relationships between staff as perceived by the members themselves. The results of such a survey may be surprising—it is common to find that truly important people have been overlooked, or that staff members do not actually function the way the organization charts would indicate. The survey will also help identify those with management potential.

Staff-to-Staff Communications

The purpose of these questions is to identify the people you work with every day, those who are essential to the performance of your job, and those who contribute to the success of your day. With this information, you will help us to meet your needs.

We will put this information to good use to find the best way to organize and to increase your enjoyment of your day at work. The information we collect will be used by only two people who have been selected for their ability to maintain confidentiality.

Please write your name and department below. On the following lines, please write in the names of three co-workers with whom you have direct contact on a daily basis. It may be helpful if you read through the questions before listing these names.

Name _____

Department _____

Co-workers

1. _____
2. _____
3. _____

Please write the number corresponding to one co-worker only in the space provided. This means that for each question you will select the one individual who is most closely related to the question asked.

___1. Which of these individuals is your most important source of job information?

___2. Who supervises or guides your work routine?

___3. When you need an opinion or wish to discuss a work-related matter before making a decision, to which of these individuals do you usually go?

___4. To whom do you most often give information?

___5. Which of these individuals, if any, frequently comes to you for advice or assistance?

___6. Whose work do you supervise directly?

___7. With whom do you spend most of your time during the day?

___8. Which of these individuals is likely to affect your work the most if he or she is absent or otherwise unavailable?

Thank you for your help.

Assessing Relationships Between Staff Members and Residents

For this discussion, we focus on the situation one finds in a newly acquired, distressed CCRC property. Residents will certainly be angered by past events and apprehensive about the future. What have their recent experiences been? What do they feel should be done to reestablish the feeling that they made the right choice when they invested in this retirement community? What do they say about food service, building maintenance, and community and recreational activities? Likewise, the health care and residential services staff will want to be heard. "This is what we have to say about the current situation." "This is why things got out of hand." "In the future, we must pay the closest possible attention to these things if we are to regain the trust of residents." "These are our specific recommendations regarding the needed improvements in services and the facility amenities." The executive and marketing managers will also have many opinions about the current situation and what must be done immediately and in the long term to reestablish the reputation of the retirement community in the market and with prospective residents.

Once we have identified the best sources for our research, we can invest in a study session and interview program. Residents are quite capable of speaking for themselves. They can answer our questions and, even more important, can supplement the questioning process with their own ideas. We use interview techniques to provide individuals with the opportunity to speak for themselves, to answer questions as they would like to see them answered, and, even more important, to tell us what the missing questions are. It is our way to identify with the elderly, to understand their situation, to share their insights, and to encourage them to state their needs. If people are uncertain about the future, we want to share this uncertainty. When goals and objectives come into conflict, we want to collaborate to achieve the best possible compromise.

This survey is appropriate only when you are taking over a distressed property. With it, you can quickly assess residents' perception of staff, which is the best possible assessment of service preferences possible. In healthy situations, residents do not want to answer personal questions; they will say this is none of our business. In such CCRCs as *The Cypress* and *The Stratford*, moreover, every staff member knows how to provide exceptional service and make each day a success for residents. If it is important to learn more about these relationships, observation is sufficient.

An interesting feature of this guide is that people are asked to give their names and the names of the people they are discussing. If you want serious information from people, you must be seen as serious. Nothing detracts from this more than the statement, "Do not use your name if you do not wish to." Tell people that the recovery of the services they expected when they first moved to the CCRC depends on people. What staff worked to solve problems? Who did not respond to what was needed? Note that we are asking people to identify helpful staff. An analysis will immediately identify those about whom no one wanted to say anything good. One additional point: There should be no concern here about staff resentment regarding the questioning of residents about their performance. Staff recognize how important it is to listen to residents and how much they can contribute to the success of the CCRC.

Staff-to-Resident Relations

The purpose of these questions is to identify the people who you rely on for assistance when you need it and those who contribute to the success of your day. With this information, we will have a better basis for organizing services and staff assignments to meet your needs. The information we collect will be used by only two people who have been selected for their ability to maintain confidentiality.

Please write your name in the line below. On the following lines please write in the names of three staff with whom you have direct contact on a daily basis and who have proven most helpful to you when you needed assistance or information. It may be helpful if you read through the questions before listing these names. We have here pictures of the staff and their names.

Name _____

Staff Members Important to You

1. _____
2. _____
3. _____

Please write the number corresponding to one staff member only in the space provided. This means that for each question you will select the one individual who is most closely related to the question asked.

___1. Which of these individuals is most important to you?

___2. Who has been most helpful when you needed assistance?

___3. When you need an opinion or wish to discuss a matter before making a decision, to which of these individuals do you usually go?

___4. When you have something to say about services, to whom do you most often give this information?

___5. Who seems to be most effective in helping others do a good job?

___6. Which of these individuals is likely to affect your day the most if he or she is absent or otherwise unavailable?

■ Self-Assessment

In the group dynamics on which the success of the CCRC depends, there are principles that set the conditions for success. Assume that people can take it; they are tough. Assume that everyone prefers to feel important, needed, useful, and successful. Assume a tendency to want to improve things. Assume the preference for working rather than being idle. Assume that people prefer meaningful work to meaningless work. We must assume the wisdom and efficacy of self-choice. We must assume that everyone likes to be justly and fairly appreciated, preferably in public.[25] As we consider what it takes to do a good job, Chris Argyris[26] suggests that people often avoid asking the necessary questions. People protect themselves by avoiding probes into exactly what it is they do rather than what they say they do. As a result, effort and time committed to improving an organization are wasted. We can only form relationships with tough questions: What am I really like? How well do I know myself? How do others see me?

If you have an interest in the systematic study of staff-to-staff and staff-to-resident relations, the recommended vehicle for assessing these types of relationships is *The Berkeley Personality Profile* developed and validated by Keith Harary and Eileen Donahue.[27] It moves us toward establishing the organization dynamics needed for successful operations and the achievement of exemplary community life for residents.

Design Research

This is one of the most interesting aspects of the executive strategy. Here we share design proposals, present research findings, and subsequently combine research and design into concluding deliberations. As noted elsewhere,[28] we achieve here a continual flow of information between research and design. This open process strategy means that every time a new fact or finding about expectations and requirements is identified, its implications are immediately considered. Every time a design possibility comes to mind, its potential for meeting expectations and requirements is assessed. Though we have crafted a flexible process that relies on immediate application of professional expertise and experience, it is not the least bit chaotic. In the executive strategy, we always have a road map—the standard of performance.

▓ Research and Design—One Process

As we conduct market and human factors research, we are always alert to design possibilities. For example, a proposed design for an assisted-living unit may originate with a director of nursing participating in a study session. That we never wait for formal architectural work before beginning design is evidence of the notable utility of the standard of performance. With this management tool, the architect never wastes time. Preliminary design and schematic design are always on track, guided by and shared with those with hands-on experience and expertise. This is similar to the charrette so common in the professional practice of architecture—learning from people based on the view that everyone is a valuable source of information if we provide the means to share views and recommendations. The architect knows things work both ways. When the architect has an idea, it is sketched and justified and immediately shared for critique. Things move along as they should—realizing the potential of all participants in the enterprise for crafting design possibilities. Wherever a question item asks for a design, those most familiar with the situation put forth their recommendations.

The need to combine research and design into one process is validated by the work habits of architects, developers, marketing executives, and health care and service providers. Unfortunately, the work of many professionals can be too self-centered to allow for critique and too rapid to permit easily the introduction of research findings. For example, architects begin their work by assisting the client to define objectives and resource demands in architectural terms. With the follow-on activity of preliminary design, solutions are conceived within the shortest possible time and at a minimum expense. Then, after some persuasive moments with the client, the architect develops a general description of the project, site plans, drawings of floor plans, and three-dimensional representations of spaces and building image. At this point, the character of the final design is fixed and the production phase begins. As this characterization suggests, architectural work can proceed at a rapid pace. Architects who work in this fashion seldom wait for specifications of user expectations and requirements. Once the architect has set the limits of the program, developed some kind of image of the completed building, he or she is already thinking of tangible products leading to the completion of the project. Likewise, developers have their own pace and milestones that are more a reflection of how they like to work than how they should work. Of course, marketing executives, and health care and service providers also have their preferred ways of working that can lead to a too simplistic understanding of how to make a retirement community enterprise a success. All these professionals need to do more than merely fulfill their contracts. Essentially, we do want developers, architects, marketing executives, and health care and service providers to work as they have always done: work on a project and produce solutions. The modification here is that all project participants have a say in every matter. It is certain that what is crafted here reduces time spent on meetings, trying to find out what other people are thinking and doing, and sharing with others our most recent thoughts. The necessary safeguard provided is the discipline of critique.

■ Industry Archives

As we begin to address design questions, we certainly want to have a compilation of best practices that pertain to the enterprise at hand. A continuing study of all sources pertaining to the retirement community industry is an investment that is required of every CCRC professional. The men and women who lead an organization need to be aware of the issues of the day and the concerns for the future. This knowledge is gained primarily as a matter of good practice. Arthur Gensler, F.A.I.A., founder of America's foremost interior architectural firm, notes that reading is a critical part of his life. He reads three newspapers a day and fifty magazines a month. He reads two weekly business newspapers, as well as *The Wall Street Journal*. He reads many business books and circulates articles throughout the firm. He makes sure anyone who needs a particular piece of information gets a copy. In return, he receives two or three articles a day from his associates.[29] Charles Luckman, F.A.I.A., describes the investment required to have at hand the information that makes a firm competitive. Recognizing that Los Angeles needed a new zoo, Mr. Luckman sent a research team to study and analyze the major zoos in the country. Its charge was to find the basis for a competitive master plan. This advance work helped the firm win this project.[30] This type of effort prepares the executive organization to address the demands of the retirement community enterprise at hand.

To further our knowledge, we start each enterprise with a study of industry archives. The purpose is not simply to collect information. We study events and information sources in terms of specific standard of performance question items and index them accordingly. There are many sources that pertain to each question item in the standard of performance.

Professional Associations

Archival research can begin with material available from associations that are dedicated to the interests of the elderly, such as the

American Association of Homes and Services for the Aging, the American Association of Retired People, the American Seniors Housing Association, the American Society on Aging, the Assisted Living Federation of America, the National Academy on Aging, the National Association for Senior Living Industries, the National Association of Jewish Homes, and the National Council on the Aging.

The value of membership in these associations is evident. For instance, at the National Association for Senior Living Industries EXPO 97,[31] the subject of the keynote address was the more than 380,000 Americans who move across state lines to retire each year, and the billions of dollars a year in sales, from real estate to health care, generated by this migration. One special event, "Assisted Living: A Penetrating Look at What's Right, What's Wrong, What's Next," explored some fundamental issues. Are we focused too much on a single model? How do we or should we accelerate new developments in maturing markets? Is there a cure for increasing turnover rates? How do we live with managed care?

Retirement Community Archives

There is no shortage of good information and expertise within the retirement community industry. Consider Paul A. Gordon's[32] *Developing Retirement Facilities*, the Urban Land Institute's publication *Housing for Seniors: Developing Successful Projects*,[33] and Sylvia Sherwood et al.'s *Continuing Care Retirement Communities*.[34] These are noteworthy accomplishments. Regnier's *Assisted Living Housing for the Elderly: Design Innovations from the United States and Europe*,[35] Regnier, Hamilton, and Yatabe's *Assisted Living for the Aged and Frail*,[36] and Brummett's *The Essence of Home: Design Solutions for Assisted-Living Housing*[37] provide many promising design options and alternatives.

We must also be alert to advances in technology and to new products that suggest possible design features. In the future, as prospective residents are aware of the benefits of "greening" and sustainable architecture, they will be likely to accept facility features that are innovative in this direction. It may even be that when we introduce design and environmental features associated with energy conservation, nature husbandry, and recycled building materials, we will increase the attractiveness of the CCRC enterprise. Such design features as energy-efficient fluorescent fixtures, electronic ballasts, and motion detectors that dim lights in unoccupied spaces are certainly valued design features. We all benefit when we are alert to application possibilities for such features as superinsulating windows, digital sensors that raise and lower the lights according to sunlight level, nontoxic paints, and environmentally sensitive heating and air-conditioning systems.

Government and Research Center Sources

Managers and staff members of government programs are significant sources of information. These are the men and women in local, county, state, and federal offices dedicated to housing for the elderly and associated facilities and services. Information of significance originates from such centers of activity as the State of California, Department of Social Services; National Academy on Aging; Office of Public Policy, Volunteers of America; Department of Veterans Affairs; National Indian Council on Aging; and Agency for Health Care Policy and Research.

Gerontology and Geriatrics Archives

This is a source of information that is underutilized by the retirement community industry, primarily because translating theory and research into applications is demanding. The information you find may be remote from the specific problems you face. It is certainly common that archival research broadens problems and more often than not leaves you with more unanswered questions. Nonetheless, you should consider this source of enrichment, which provides an opportunity to recombine information to create new concepts.

Graduate Studies

Graduate study programs in public health, social welfare, biological, behavioral, medical, and social sciences, as well as humanities departments, are significant sources of information. An example of the publications produced is the study of continuing care retirement communities[38] directed by Sylvia Sherwood, director of Housing and Long-Term Care Research, Research and Training Insitute, Hebrew Rehabilitation Center for the Aged. This is a multifaceted longitudinal study in which data were obtained directly from almost two thousand residents in nineteen CCRCs. Here is a very short list of the academic and research centers studying the knowledge domain of housing and life service to the elderly: Andrus Gerontological Center, University of Southern California; Penn State Gerontological Center; UCLA Center for the Aging; Institute on Aging, University of Pennsylvania Health System; Braceland Center for Mental Health and Aging; American College of Health Care Administrators; Consortium for Learning and Research in Aging; and the Center for Applied Gerontology, University of Chicago.

The Internet

According to J. A. Post, librarian of the Philadelphia Geriatric Research Center, a great deal of information regarding senior services is available on the Internet. In articles written for *The Gerontologist*, she cites valuable Web sites. For instance, in "Internet Resources on Aging: Ten Top Web Sites,"[39] she directs attention to what she calls the most current and comprehensive directory of all Internet sites on aging and related topics, Directory of Web and Gopher Aging Sites (http://www.aoa.dhhs.gov/aoa/webres/craig.htm). GoldenAge Net (http//elo.mediasrv.swt.edu/goldenage/script.htm) is noted as the best place for links related to the long-term care industry. What do we know about the currency and reliability of these sources? It's empirical. It is best to try them out and see what meets your needs. Unfortunately, due to the transitory and poorly maintained state of many sites and home pages, you are as likely to be disappointed as pleased with what you find. In the future, the Internet will become a reliable and comprehensive means of information exchange as our content and search protocols improve.

Travel

In a study of activities in other countries, Joseph Carella,[40] executive director of the Swedish Home for Scandinavians, suggests that the American retirement community industry may wish to reconsider its service package, which he refers to as the "maid/servant syndrome." He notes that people come to expect a great deal of service when they should be encouraged to do as much as possible for themselves. During a visit to a three-story, 110-unit retirement community in Tokyo, the authors noted a very interesting amenity. The facility provides two home-style kitchens and dining rooms for residents, complete with utensils and chinaware service. Residents use these rooms for family gatherings, for the sharing of favorite foods, the pleasure of working together and talking about old times, and letting the young children visit grandparents or great-grandparents. It is one of the most used and appreciated amenities. During the site visits in Japan, we studied the use of space in residences for college students and corporate executives living away from home. The compact furnishings, fixtures, and equipment features were quite distinct from the American standard and most praiseworthy. This inventive use of space is driven by more than the cost of land. It is evidence of vitality in design countering what Ashihara[41] sees as the limits of a Western architecture committed to form and facades.

■ Design of a Reception Area

Design research tends to almost casually produce verified design recommendations. In the study of the reception area for a retirement community, for instance, discussions among the designer, service providers, and the elderly living in a senior residence may have established a number of facts and considerations. For example, observation of exterior parking, entryways, reception areas, and elevators may at first lead to emphasis on the need for areas that are free from hindrances to movement and noise. However, it may later be observed that from time to time, this is a place for conversation and prolonged waiting for arriving guests. These observations would indicate that one should provide for individuals who wish to use the reception area as a lounge as much as a service area. Observations of activities may lead to the conclusion that such areas should not be centralized but dispersed. Conversations with family and guests may indicate critical aspects of the reception area and may suggest that activities correlate more with social gatherings than with reception services. As the listing of activities begins to stabilize, there is sufficient information to develop a flow diagram encompassing a typical day. The flow diagram may either attempt to characterize the entire spectrum of activities or to highlight particular critical considerations. A time profile added to the flow diagram offers some idea of duration, density, and frequency of activities.

During this work, findings and design possibilities are entered into the applications system. A list of possible furniture, fixture, equipment, and storage unit requirements is developed, ranging from benches, desks, and lounge chairs through special security fixtures. A synthesis of findings provides the justification for resulting design schemes, forms, and features. The end result is more than a design proposal; it is a justified design.

Note that this type of study will often show that there is little demand for a proposed space or design feature. In post-occupancy evaluation, nothing is more diagnostic of a poorly conceived design than empty space or a feature that is never used. This comment leads to the next topic—design undertaking.

■ Design Undertaking

Let's consider the development of an assisted-living unit. We want to realize the potential of the participants in the enterprise for crafting design possibilities. Those who know about assisted-living units can, on the basis of past experience, develop a reasoned set of options and alternatives. These options and alternatives are now subject to evaluation, argument, and modification. Essentially, architects do what they have always done, work on a project and produce solutions. The modification here is that all project participants have a say in every design matter. This is not chaotic because deliberations are guided by the standard of performance and the open record of deliberations maintained within the applications system.

Step One: Specify Design Objectives

6.3 Health Care Units Interior Architecture in the standard of performance provides the questions that may become the objectives of the assisted-living unit research endeavor. As noted previously, we can always make a question item more specific by editing the title and text. The following examples show how question items may be changed to reflect the specific topic of assisted-living units, without changing the numerical index.

The original questions ask

Areas to Address

6.3   HEALTH CARE UNITS INTERIOR ARCHITECTURE

6.3.1 HEALTH CARE UNIT DESIGN OBJECTIVES. Which expectations and requirements of health service and care staff and residents should be emphasized in interior architecture design deliberations?

6.3.2 HEALTH CARE UNITS. What health care unit design options best correspond to staff and resident expectations and requirements? How are design features justified in terms of benefits and costs?

6.3.3 HEALTH CARE UNIT FURNISHING, FIXTURES, AND EQUIPMENT. With regard to safety, security, and convenience, what furnishing, fixtures, and equipment options, fixed or mobile, do health care units require?

These items are changed to

Areas to Address

6.3   ASSISTED-LIVING UNIT INTERIOR ARCHITECTURE

6.3.1 ASSISTED-LIVING UNIT DESIGN OBJECTIVES. Which expectations and requirements of health service and care staff and residents should be emphasized in assisted-living unit design deliberations?

6.3.2 ASSISTED-LIVING UNIT DESIGN. What assisted-living unit design options best correspond to staff and resident

---

expectations and requirements? How are design features justified in terms of benefits and costs?

6.3.3 ASSISTED-LIVING UNIT FURNISHING, FIXTURES, AND EQUIPMENT. With regard to safety, security, and convenience, what furnishing, fixtures, and equipment options, fixed or mobile, does the assisted-living unit require?

Step Two: Identify Critical Information Sources

In the context of the selected design questions, we select our research questions from the standard of performance. Here we present the basic standard of performance question items and the revisions that precisely indicate our interest.

The original items ask

6.2   HEALTH CARE PROGRAMS

6.2.4 HEALTH CARE ACTIVITIES. What are the daily and emergency activities of health care staff? What is known about the extent, time of occurrence, and duration of activities?

6.2.5 HEALTH CARE DESIGN CHALLENGES. What are the facility design challenges associated with health care programs?

These are revised to

6.2   ASSISTED-LIVING PROGRAMS

6.2.4 ASSISTED-LIVING UNIT ACTIVITIES. What are the daily and emergency activities of assisted-living unit staff? What is known about the extent, time of occurrence, and duration of activities?

6.2.5 ASSISTED-LIVING UNIT DESIGN CHALLENGES. What are the assisted living unit design challenges associated with health care programs?

Step Three: Scope of Work

In anticipation of the deliberations concerning an assisted-living unit, we frame the problem in terms of the design and research questions and the research method applications.

RESEARCH REPORT ELEMENTS	SCOPE OF WORK
Applications system files	Create files within the applications system, entitled 6.2 Assisted-Living Programs and 6.3 Assisted-Living Unit Design.
I. Topic and associated concerns	Evaluation of best practices in assisted-living unit design. Respond to regulatory standards and specifications. Consider how assisted-living unit design contributes to the performance of health service and care staff. Identify residents' health care expectations and requirements associated with assisted-living services.
II. Recommendations	Establish a design guideline for the assisted-living unit interior architecture.
III. Points of view	Discuss design possibilities with members of the executive organization. For specific design recommendations, what are the conflicting points of view and how can these been addressed?
IV. Situational factors	How did market and financial conditions influence findings? What was the significance of such factors such as regional customs and competitive health care services?
V. Financial analysis	How does the proposed assisted-living unit design compare in cost with designs found in best practices?
VI. Research design	Summarize the 6.2 Assisted-Living Program and 6.3 Assisted-Living Unit Architecture Research Design.
VII. Supplemental information	Identify references, state regulations, applicable building codes, and vendors' descriptions of furnishing, fixture, and equipment items.

■ Supplemental Questions

The standard of performance question items are often supplemented with additional questions that refine the research activity. For instance, when asking professionals experienced with assisted living to review and evaluate the proposed design and offer recommendations, a supplemental line of questioning may go something like this:

- Here is a proposed plan for the assisted-living unit. Let me explain what we are trying to accomplish. Does this make sense?
- Where does it need to be improved?
- What is accomplished if these changes are made?

Each response may lead to a new possibility, with follow-up questions such as

- What would happen if we did this, rather than what you propose? Would it be an improvement?

Turning our attention to furnishing, fixtures, and equipment, we might ask health service and care staff:

- What essential items have been overlooked?
- Is there an especially attractive option that might be included?
- How can this be justified?
- Have you seen this done before? How much did it add to convenience, efficiency, or satisfaction?

■ Research Safeguards

To assure that the data and information derived from research are as error-free and effective as possible, we must craft a research design that has safeguards in place. The data and information on which we rely must be qualified as to source and reliability. Consider a very basic question: Are the obtained data and information valid for the task at hand? Absolute assurance is impossible; reasonable assurance can be established. We can test the proposed research application with this series of questions:[42]

- Have the research objectives been identified?
- What is this research meant to achieve?
- Is the research application logical and appropriate for the stated aims?
- Where was the research undertaken and at what times?

As we evaluate the execution of the research and obtained results, we first ask who participated in the study. Then:

- Were adequate steps taken to control bias?
- Were specific individuals identified as favoring one side of the issue or the other?
- If important individuals and groups were not available for participation, was this noted?
- Were the research participants guided in a manner that resulted in a sense of cooperation, collaboration, and shared responsibility?
- What was said to participants to achieve a sense of shared responsibility?
- Were there opportunities for two-way discussion?

As we review the research application, we ask:

- Did the research team go back and confirm findings and recommendations?
- Were there deviations from the research design?
- Were the results and interpretations reviewed by an independent source?

- Was there agreement as to interpretations of findings?
- Were alternative interpretations of findings given?
- Were unresolved issues identified?

■ Critical Thinking

Design deliberations are characterized by the fact that we tend to quickly and confidently, perhaps overconfidently, accept what our expertise leads us to believe are promising options and alternatives for every challenging situation. Safeguarding our deliberations from shallow thinking is the purpose of this discussion,

First, consider this facility design scenario. A design/build team has previously agreed that one feature of the three-story, residential facility will be single-loaded corridors, with direct access from individual units to a covered arcade and the interior courtyard. Two design concepts are on the table for the design of the entry from the semipublic corridor and arcade to the residential units. One proposal, justified on the basis of a perceived need for visual, sound, and activity privacy, is a private entry with a solid wall and door. The other proposed entry providing residents an opportunity to vary the degree of openness between the unit and the semipublic spaces is to have a porch alcove for each unit with windows and a Dutch door opening to an alcove.[43] Both schemes have been applied in retirement communities. Interviews indicate the pros and cons of each scheme. The questions for discussion by the design team are as follows: What relationship between residential units and the semipublic spaces is most desirable from the residents' perspective? Which design concept has the greater market potential? What are the costs associated with each design concept? Is climate a factor of concern? How does the health care staff perceive the two options? How does the service staff perceive the two options?

Now, let's reframe this information into its fundamental parts:

Goal: Select the better residential entry design concept
Alternatives: Private entry or variable, open entry
Judgment Criteria:
    Design image
    Residents' perspective
    Market potential
    Cost
    Climate
    Health care impact
    Services impact
Deliberation Matrix: Each cell is a place for comparison comments, comparing the two alternatives in terms of the seven criteria.

	PRIVATE ENTRY ALTERNATIVE	VARIABLE, OPEN ENTRY ALTERNATIVE
Design image		
Residents' perspective		
Market potential		
Building cost		
Climate		
Health care impact		
Services impact		

The benefits of specifying options and alternatives and evaluation criteria are notable. Specifying objective and subjective criteria and using these to frame our deliberations represent the very best of critical thinking. First, the engagement of enterprise participants in the process of identifying criteria and distinguishing their relative importance facilitates all subsequent deliberations. A great deal of time can be lost when people argue their positions without agreeing beforehand how proposals will be judged. When mutually agreed upon criteria are established, subsequent deliberations have a reference point. Enterprise participants can debate in the most intense fashion as long as there is a means for concluding discussions. Second, there can be times when a detailed, rigorous assessment of options and alternatives is the best way to protect valuable resources, meet a challenge with merit, or gather commitment for designs and plans of action.

The Analytic Hierarchy Process

■ The Analytic Hierarchy Process

Expanding this discussion, let's consider that when we use a decision-making program, we are looking into the future of every enterprise. Decision making is progressing from simple individual and group deliberations to an application of information technology and associated analytic programs. We have selected Thomas L. Saaty's theoretical construct, the analytic hierarchical process,[44] as the means for conducting such analyses and the application program *Expert Choice* by Decision Support Software, Inc.,[45] as our exhibit software vehicle. Saaty hypothesized that a means could be developed to assess a complex system of interrelated components such as seen in the preceding design scenario. As his methodology matured, Saaty began to understand how people conceptualize and structure a complex problem. He saw that it is essential to maintain the benefits of intuition while realizing the clarity and consistency associated with quantification. Further, he began to see the need to "mix apples and oranges," that is, to deal with both the tangible and intangible in the same deliberative process.

How does Saaty's construct translate into a deliberative process for a retirement community enterprise? A retirement community enterprise has many stakeholders and a range of professional associates. Each will bring their expertise and knowledge. Our concern is how to synthesize these various perspectives within an enterprise deliberation. What weight do you give to tangible considerations versus intangible considerations? Can such directly measurable factors as market demand, land availability, land cost, and interest rates be made to blend with such subjective factors as reluctance to relocate, family traditions, life-style norms, location and climate preferences, and cultural and recreation preferences? How do you account for the perceived differences in the relative importance of facility and services features? Can a synthesis be developed that accounts for all the factors involved in such complex deliberations? Answers to these questions result in the arrangement of deliberation criteria into hierarchies and priorities.

Hierarchies and Priorities

Saaty states that "When we think, we identify objects or ideas and also relations among them. When we identify anything, we decompose the complexity which we encounter. When we discover relations, we synthesize. This is the fundamental process underlying perception: decomposition and synthesis. The elaboration of this concept and its practical implications interest us here."[46] From this evolved the concept of decision-making hierarchies, which is a structuring of functional interactions descending from the goal apex down to the elements contributing to deliberations. Subsequently these elements are assessed in terms of relative importance and the results added to the hierarchy.

Judgment

The assessment of the relative importance of hierarchical elements is a personal judgment. Pick up two books, move your hands up and down, comparing weights. You conclude that one book is heavier than the other. This is a fundamental judgment and certainly the most basic and reliable of human judgments—something is more heavy, more valuable, more beautiful, or more important. Of course, we could have weighed the books.

However, not everything can be measured. Saaty puts this human judgment to work. He takes the elements of the hierarchy, makes a series of comparisons of all possible pairings, and asks one to judge which of the two is more favorable.

Expert Choice *Program*

Saaty's theoretical construct for assessing options and alternatives becomes a convenient methodology when we employ *Expert Choice* by Decision Support Software in a deliberative process. You are encouraged to review this and other decision support systems on the market to find what will work for you.

■ Selection and Evaluation Criteria

Eight question items in the standard of performance call for the specification of decision-making criteria.

> 1.1.2 CONCEPT EVALUATION CRITERIA. What criteria will be used to evaluate candidate concepts?
>
> 2.1.1 EXECUTIVE COUNCIL SELECTION CRITERIA. What are the selection criteria for members of the executive council?
>
> 4.3.2 SALES STAFF SELECTION CRITERIA. What are the skill and licensing criteria for appointing individuals to sales management and staff positions?
>
> 6.1.2 HEALTH CARE MANAGEMENT AND STAFF SELECTION CRITERIA. What are the criteria for appointing individuals to health care management and staff positions?
>
> 7.1.2 MANAGEMENT SELECTION CRITERIA. What are the skill and licensing criteria for appointing individuals to service management positions?
>
> 8.2.2 SITE SELECTION CRITERIA. What are the retirement community site selection criteria?
>
> 8.4.2 MASTER PLAN EVALUATION CRITERIA. What are the criteria for evaluating master plan options and alternatives?
>
> 8.6.4 DESIGN EVALUATION CRITERIA. What are the criteria for evaluating proposed design concepts, schemes, forms, and features?

The task now is to consider the possible judgment criteria for these question items.

Developing Judgment Criteria

In the preceding scenario regarding the evaluation of residential unit entry alternatives, we saw the benefit of stating criteria in simple terms and, so that deliberations do not become overly complex, to limit the number of criteria to six or seven. Let's first consider item 2.1.1 Executive Council Selection Criteria. What are the appropriate criteria?

1. Professional achievements
2. Retirement community experience
3. Architectural/engineering/construction experience
4. Ability to work with others
5. Commitment to the enterprise
6. Ethics
7. Community relations

Now, let's suggest possible judgment criteria for item 1.1.2.

Concept Evaluation Criteria:

1. Design image
2. Market potential
3. Financial feasibility
4. Community acceptance
5. Health care benefits
6. Residential service benefits
7. Quality of life

These factors are common to the real estate development industry and remain basic to a retirement community enterprise. For more possibilities, *The Hierarchon: A Dictionary of Hierarchies*[47] contains more than 400 decision problems and their associated judgment criteria. This is where you should begin your study of the recommended evaluation process. The important aspect of the evaluation process is not whether or not you apply Saaty's construct. The important thing is to make critical thinking an intrinsic part of your applications of the CCRC executive strategy.

Legal Research

When the legal analyst works to identify the regulatory and licensing requirements that must be met and to characterize the mandates for safeguarding the rights of investors and homeowners, the results set a performance standard for every deliberation. Consider that you are already competitive in the senior living industry. You have an extensive knowledge base, expert staff, alliances in place, and a market situation that you fully understand. What you need to know is how to safeguard the proposed investment. This is the primary objective of legal research. The following discussion ranges from the study of regulatory statutes and licensing requirements to the development of homeowner contracts and residents' associations. These question items have a bearing on every other critical success factor.

Areas to Address

3.2   LEGAL AND REGULATORY CONSIDERATIONS

3.2.1 LEGAL RESEARCH. What must be undertaken to diligently address the rights of enterprise participants, health care and service providers, and residents?

3.2.2 LEGAL AGREEMENTS. What contracts must be produced to address transfer of property rights and service agreements?

3.2.3 REGULATORY AGENCIES. What federal, state, and local regulatory and licensing bodies are responsible for enterprise approval?

3.2.4 MEETING REGULATORY REQUIREMENTS. How are regulatory and licensing requirements met? What reporting requirements are mandated by state agencies?.

3.2.5 RESIDENTS' RIGHTS. How must contracts and manuals be formulated to encode the legal rights of residents?

CCRC Regulatory and Legal Considerations[48]

In response to the growth of continuing care retirement communities and to several well publicized CCRC failures, many states have passed statutes and drafted regulations to address the perceived and real risks or potential shortcomings of CCRCs.[49] A CCRC developer must become completely conversant with the regulatory scheme of the state in which the proposed facility is to be located. Failure to do so may result in ownership of a costly unlicensed and empty facility that is unable to contract with potential residents. In addition, to avoid costly and lengthy legal entanglements and expensive potential liabilities, developers should become familiar with the legal liabilities imposed by the common law, such as contract and fraud law, as well as applicable state and federal statutory provisions.

    Individuals considering residence in a continuing care retirement community are usually faced with committing a substantial portion of their liquid retirement assets,[50] and potentially making a lifetime residential decision. Potential residents must understand the limits to the protections offered by state and federal statutes and the common law, and what they can do to maximize the financial security of their investment, as well as enhance the recognized personal rights in their residence.

This section will introduce the unique regulatory and legal issues CCRC providers must address, and the limits to the legal protections on which potential resident must rely. Both providers and residents will also face numerous real estate, estate planning, tax, and other legal issues in their participation in a CCRC, but a detailed discussion of these issues is beyond the scope of this section. Finally, reading this section cannot substitute for experienced legal counsel, especially as the legal issues may differ substantially from state to state. Providers and residents must retain legal counsel early in the development or residential decision-making process.[51]

Developer/Owner Considerations

Continuing care retirement community providers face two legal challenges. First, they must comply with the regulatory and licensing requirements of the state in which the residence will be located. Second, developers must be cognizant of the legal liabilities that can result from the development and operation of any proposed residence, so they can proceed in a manner that minimizes costly and lengthy legal complications. This section will generally outline and describe typical state requirements for CCRC licensing and operation, as well as introduce potential legal liabilities for providers.

■ State Regulatory Compliance and Licensing

CCRCs Subject To Regulation

A prudent developer must first determine whether the state in which a proposed retirement community will be located regulates or licenses CCRCs, and most states do. A provider should not assume that a proposed facility is not a "traditional" nursing home, and therefore does not require state licensing or other compliance. A provider should also not conclude that, because a prior development in another state did not require licensing, a new development will not, or conclude that no licensing is required because none was required for an earlier development.

The risks engendered by these assumptions may be dramatic: Not only may the developer who fails to seek licensing or otherwise comply with state statutes face fines[52] or even criminal liability,[53] a court may also enjoin the provider from marketing the new community.[54]

States commonly define continuing or life care retirement communities subject to state regulation as facilities that provide board or lodging, plus additional personal, medical, or nursing care, pursuant to a contract for life or at least 1 year, requiring an entrance fee.[55] For example, Virginia defines continuing care as follows:

> "Continuing care" means providing or committing to provide board, lodging and nursing services to an individual, other than an individual related by blood or marriage, (i) pursuant to an agreement effective for the life of the individual or for a period in excess of one year, including mutually terminable contracts, and (ii) in consideration of the payment of an entrance fee. A contract shall be deemed to be one offering nursing services, irrespective of whether such services are provided under such contract, if nursing services are offered to the resident entering such contract either at the facility in question or pursuant to arrangements specifically offered to residents of the facility.[56]

However, state definitions of regulated continuing care communities can vary widely. South Carolina much more broadly defines a continuing care contract subject to state licensing and regulation to include merely providing board or lodging, with some additional nursing, medical, or other health services, to a person 65 years of age or older.[57] South Carolina does not require that continuing care contracts be for life or greater than 1 year, or that residents pay an entrance fee. Georgia defines a continuing care contract to be merely an agreement of any duration for food and shelter, with additional nursing care or personal services, to an individual of any age on the payment of an entrance fee.[58] Such contracts actually differ very little from a typical residential lease or a boarder agreement.

Accordingly, providers should assume that the state in which the proposed residence will be located will regulate the proposed residence, and retain legal counsel to provide regulatory compliance guidance. Prudent providers who wish to avoid protracted legal entanglements should do so very early in the process.

State Licensing

Most states require the life care retirement community provider to have a license, permit, or some other certificate of authority issued by the state regulating department, often prior to initiating construction, marketing or soliciting residents and entrance fees, or entering into a life care contract.[59] In California, for example, a provider must apply for a permit prior to executing any continuing care contract or deposit agreement; initiating construction of a new CCRC or expansion of an existing CCRC; converting an existing development into a CCRC; commencing marketing of a CCRC; or closing the sale or transfer of a CCRC.[60] Florida prohibits any person from engaging in the business of providing continuing care or issuing continuing care agreements, or even constructing a facility for the purpose of providing continuing care, without a state certificate of authority to do so.[61]

States requiring life care community licensing may require an initial or provisional license,[62] or may require a periodic review and reauthorization.[63] In some states, certificates of authority are often valid until revoked by the state licensing authority.[64] Grounds for revocation or suspension may include violation of a provision of a continuing care retirement statute; insufficient provider qualifications; failure to file a disclosure statement; misrepresentation of a material fact; misappropriation, conversion, or wrongful withholding of money; unsound financial condition; failure to file annual financial reports; or lack of fitness or trustworthiness.[65] A certificate of authority may be nontransferable; any transferee provider usually must apply for a new certificate of authority.[66]

Disclosure Statements

Either as part of the license application process, or as a distinct requirement, most states regulating CCRCs require that a detailed disclosure statement be provided to the state and prospective residents. States may require that the disclosure statement be given to prospective residents before the CCRC executes any life care contracts or accepts any fees.[67] States that mandate a disclosure statement may require the inclusion of biographical information on the individuals and legal entities involved in the CCRC; a description of the community and services offered; sample documents such as the life care contract or the escrow agreements; a description of fee structures, marketing information and reserve funding; and financial statements and projections.

States may mandate the disclosure of personal information regarding the officers, directors, trustees, partners, equity holders, or other principals, such as names and business addresses, and whether any have been convicted of a felony, been held liable in a civil judgment (especially one involving fraud or embezzlement), been subject to state disciplinary proceedings, or are currently under any state or federal investigation or prosecution.[68] Florida even requires evidence that a provider is reputable and of responsible character, or, if an entity, that the members or shareholders are reputable and of responsible character.[69] The providing organization may have to disclose its experience in managing the day-to-day operations of similar facilities.[79] If the provider is a legal entity, it may have to identify its precise legal nature, each principal, and the interest held thereby.[71] The entity may also have to disclose its affiliation with any religious, charitable, nonprofit, or for-profit entity, as well as the extent to which such an entity will be responsible for the financial obligations of the provider, and the names of all directors, trustees, general partners, or other interested parties of the affiliated party.[72] A legal entity may also have to identify its parent or other affiliated entities, and disclose the contracts or other documents governing the relationship between those parties.[73]

Disclosure statements may also have to identify the location and status of the proposed CCRC, describe the real property of the proposed community, give the estimated number of proposed residents, and summarize the services and care to be offered, including medical care and the basic fee structure.[74] Most states mandate full disclosure of the facility's proposed fee structure, including entrance fees, periodic charges, service fees, or other charges.[75] The provider may also have to disclose the services considered in determining the fees and the manner by which the provider may adjust the fees in the future.[76] A provider may also have to disclose the terms and conditions under which a provider or resident may cancel the life care contract, any health or financial conditions required of a resident, and the conditions under which a provider may refund any portion of the entrance fee.[77]

Copies of any agreements the provider intends to execute with future residents, such as a sample continuing care contract or deposit and escrow agreement, may also be required.[78] A provider may also have to submit for state approval its advertisements, brochures, and other marketing materials.[79]

States also generally require broad financial disclosure. A common requirement is to identify provisions for reserve funding or other financial security measures to ensure the provider's financial performance.[80] A provider will likely have to provide past audited financial statements, and perhaps current and projected financial statements,[81] as well as disclose the source and application of funds to purchase and construct a facility.[82] California and Florida require a detailed professional financial and marketing feasibility study that must include the financing provisions and fund sources, provider experience, all development costs, interest, insurance and taxes, projected cash flows and revenues, and a detailed description of marketing plans.[83]

Continuing Care Contract

State regulatory approaches to life care contracts vary widely. Some states such as Illinois mandate very few contractual provisions,[84] whereas other states such as California, New Hampshire, or Virginia require numerous detailed contractual provisions, dictate contract style, and require state approval of any contract prior to its use.[85] Provisions often required in continuing care contracts include a description of all entrance fees and other consideration transferred to the provider; the specific services provided; any periodic charges and whether these charges are subject to provider modification; the terms under which either party may terminate the contract and the effect on the fees and consideration transferred; any health or financial conditions required of residents; the effect of death or financial difficulties of a resident; and the provisions for resident transfer, recission, or refunds.[86]

A related and very important matter to be considered by a provider when entering into a life care contract is to be certain that the potential resident has the capacity to enter knowingly into the contract. A contract executed by an individual incapable of intelligent assent can render the contract void or voidable,[87] perhaps requiring the refund of all fees paid. Challenges to capacity can include physical infirmities or age.[88] Such a set of facts may also subject the provider to greater judicial scrutiny in any fraud or consumer protection claims brought on behalf of the individual.[89]

Resident Entrance and Periodic Fees

Most states regulate the payment and disposition of entrance fees paid by prospective residents. Regulations commonly define entrance fees as an initial transfer of money or property to a provider in return for acceptance as a resident.[90] The CCRC developer usually must initially deposit the fees into an escrow account, and states often establish the conditions for the accounts and under which the fees may be released.[91] A common prerequisite for release of the escrowed fees of a new facility is having a minimum resident occupancy level,[92] or meeting minimum aggregate financing and construction requirements.[93] In some states, a developer may post a bond, negotiable securities, or a letter of credit in lieu of depositing entrance fees into an escrow account.[94] Florida allows a provider to apply entrance fees to meet outstanding debt if it grants residents a first mortgage on the land, buildings, and equipment of the facility.[95] A CCRC's periodic resident charges may also be subject to state regulation.[96]

Community Financial Security Provisions

States commonly mandate that a CCRC satisfy reserve funding requirements to ensure that it can meet its financial obligations to the community residents. A common requirement is that a provider maintain, often in an escrow account, several months' principal and interest payments,[97] plus several months' operating expenses.[98] The state may even prescribe escrow conditions, require approval of the escrow agent, and determine the conditions under which fees may be returned to a resident.[99] Florida allows a provider to acquire an irrevocable unconditional letter of credit in lieu of the liquid reserve requirement.[100]

Some CCRC statutes may also allow the state to record a lien in favor of residents against the real estate and other assets of the provider, to secure the performance of the life care contract obligations.[101] The lien will be in an amount approximating the value of the property transferred and the services to be performed.[102] The state statute may provide for the release of the lien given certain conditions.[103] Note that the resident lien is not granted priority over preexisting liens, mortgages, or other encumbrances, but only over subsequently recorded interests.[104]

States also generally require providers to complete and submit an annual financial statement to the regulatory department,[105] and even more frequently if warranted.[106] The statement is quite detailed and must often be audited.[107] Finally, states may even mandate a minimum ratio of assets and liabilities to be possessed by providers,[108] and failure to meet this requirement may trigger state examination and remedial action.[109]

Recission or Termination

States also commonly require that continuing care contracts include a recission period to follow an individual's execution of the life care contract.[110] A recission period is a time during which a prospective resident may change his or her mind and terminate the life care contract, usually without penalty or further financial obligation. Recission periods may be as brief as 7 or 10 days,[111] or as long as 30 days.[112] States usually require the refund of all property or other consideration paid should the individual rescind the agreement.[113] A state may also allow for a trial residency period, during which either party may cancel the agreement, with limited financial consequences.[114]

Some continuing care statutes also regulate the circumstances under which a resident may leave the CCRC, or under which a CCRC may terminate a resident's contract,[115] and, if this occurs, whether the resident will receive a refund of the entrance or other fee or consideration paid.[116] States may also mandate that the contract specify the consequences of a resident's death, and the disposition of all consideration paid by the deceased resident to the CCRC.[117]

Provider Transfer or Sale of Interest

States may closely regulate a provider's right to sell or otherwise transfer part or all of its interest in a continuing care retirement community. Some states mandate that a provider notify the state of any intended transfer, including the details thereof.[118] A further disclosure may be required of the new provider, or an entirely new application for a certificate of authority.[119] Ultimately, the state may refuse to grant the new provider a certificate of authority, thereby effectively preventing the proposed transfer.

State Examinations and Rehabilitation

Given the broad state regulation of continuing care retirement communities, providers should not be surprised that state regulatory statutes often invest state authorities with the power to investigate the facilities. Florida even allows an interested party to request an inspection of a provider's finances.[120] Often states have the authority to audit or conduct financial or other examinations of facilities and providers,[121] sometimes assisted by subpoena power.[122] Pennsylvania requires the state to audit each CCRC at least once every 4 years.[123]

States may also have the power to appoint a trustee to rehabilitate or liquidate a CCRC. In the event that a facility becomes insolvent, fails to maintain sufficient liquid reserves, wrongfully releases escrowed funds, fails to meet cash flow requirements, has its certificate of authority revoked, transfers its interest or control to another entity without state approval, or otherwise violates regulatory requirements, the state may take possession of the CCRC and manage and operate it, or appoint another individual or entity to do so at the direction of the state.[124] If successfully rehabilitated, the state may return the facility to the provider.[125] Other states may require the CCRC to obtain new management to address its shortcomings.[126] Moreover, should rehabilitation fail, states may have the power to liquidate the facility and direct the allocation of any resulting proceeds.[127]

Waiver of Statutory Provisions

Finally, many states expressly state that no act, agreement, or statement by a resident shall constitute an enforceable waiver of any provision in the state's continuing care retirement community statute.[128] Accordingly, providers must simply comply with all state CCRC provisions. Furthermore, a provider may have to advise potential residents of the existence of the applicable state continuing care retirement statute.[129]

■ Potential Provider Legal Liabilities

Although developers must comply with state statutes and regulations governing the operation of continuing care retirement communities, and if required, acquire and maintain a valid certificate of authority, doing so does not necessarily insulate a provider from all civil or criminal liability based on the common law or pursuant to other state or federal statutes.[130] Although this section addresses several major potential legal liabilities that may arise from the development and operation of a CCRC, it is by no means comprehensive.[131]

Potential Civil Causes of Action

Breach of Contract. Any life care contract will be the subject of and governed by numerous documents that will enumerate the respective rights and obligations of both residents and the provider. Should a provider fail to comply with its agreed-to obligations, a resident may sue for breach of contract, and, if successful, recover all consequential damages, or seek to enforce the obligations.[132] Agreements subject to suit may include written contracts, as well as other written documents, brochures, or agreements.[133] Contract actions may also generally be maintained on an oral agreement, so any oral representation or promise made by the provider or any of its employees or representatives may be the basis of a future suit by a resident, if the provider fails to perform. Furthermore, courts may find that the parties impliedly agreed to terms and conditions that may not have been expressed or written, and have done so in the context of a life care community.[134] Finally, in every contract, there is an implied covenant of good faith and fair dealing on both parties,[135] which one court recognized as "particularly important in a contract governing a CCRC because of the long-term nature of the contract, the vital importance of its subject matter and the fact that elderly persons—some of whom may, towards the end of their lives, encounter diminished competence—are affected by such contracts."[136]

Common Law Fraud. In addition to breach of contract, continuing care retirement community residents may also sue providers for common law fraud.[137] The elements of common law fraud are a false representation of a present or past fact made by a defendant or the failure to disclose a pertinent fact, the victim's reliance thereon, and damages suffered by the victim.[138] Life care community residents have sued providers for damages for fraudulent conduct including fraudulent promotion and operation of such a community.[139]

State Consumer Protection Acts. Continuing care retirement community providers must also take notice of pervasive state consumer protection acts, drafted to protect consumers from a broad range of unfair, deceptive, or unscrupulous business practices.[140] Deceptive business practices can include, but are certainly not limited to, causing misunderstanding as to the source, sponsorship, approval, or certification of services; causing misunderstanding as to the affiliation, association, or certification of another; or representing that services have qualities, uses, or benefits that they do not have,[141] all of which can arise in the context of a CCRC. Under these acts, the state attorney general may be empowered to initiate enforcement actions, to either temporarily or permanently enjoin the activity, or to seek restitution.[142] The attorney general may also seek the appointment of a receiver with broad powers to take over the business to prevent any further unlawful activity.[143]

A very important feature of these acts is that they generally provide for a private right of action for the consumer, allowing him or her to bring a civil suit for actual damages, or for a minimum statutory sum.[144] The affected consumer may also seek equitable relief such as an injunction against the wrongful activity of the provider.[145] A CCRC resident who prevails in such an the action may be awarded reasonable attorney's fees and costs.[146] Even more important, the court may award double or triple damages where the violation was willful or knowing.[147]

Private Right of Action Pursuant to CCRC Regulatory Statutes. Continuing care retirement community statutes may recognize a private right of civil action for residents based on a provider's statutory violation.[148] In such cases, the resident need prove only a specific violation of the state's life care statute, not a breach of contract, fraud, or other cause of action. The state may allow a successful resident to recover damages, the return of entrance or other advance fees with interest, costs, or attorney's fees.[149] This liability may also extend to other entities or individuals who willfully or recklessly aid or abet a provider in violating a continuing care statute.[150] Some states even provide that negligent misrepresentation or omission will not be a valid defense to any such action.[151] The state may provide, however, a defense where the provider makes a good-faith offer to refund specific fees and costs to the resident.[152] Note that the existence of a private right of action pursuant to a state's CCRC statutes should not limit a provider's liability under other state or federal laws.[153]

Criminal Liability

As a final but important note, most statutes provide criminal penalties for providers who violate life care statutes, fail to obtain a valid certificate of authority, or commit other wrongdoing in connection with the operation of a CCRC. For example, the New Hampshire statute provides that: "Any person, partnership, association or corporation . . . establishing, conducting, managing, or operating any facility within the meaning of this chapter without first obtaining a certificate as provided in this chapter, or who violates any rule adopted under this chapter, shall be guilty of a misdemeanor if a natural person, or guilty of a felony if any other person."[154] The penalty is usually a misdeameanor,[155] but some states make such acts a felony.[156] Furthermore, these statutes may determine that each wrongful act is a separate violation.[157] State consumer protection acts may also provide that a violation of these acts constitutes a misdemeanor or felony.[158] Finally, courts have allowed the criminal prosecution of individual controlling officers, directors, or other principals of CCRCs who engage in criminal conduct.[159]

Resident Issues

No state regulation, or other state or federal law, guarantees the financial security of any continuing care retirement community. Prospective residents are therefore investing a substantial portion or all of their liquid retirement assets in a continuing care retirement community that may fail. Furthermore, state statutes also commonly fail to mandate broad personal rights that would protect the resident's quality of life. This section will discuss the limits to legal protections afforded residents and highlight legal action prospective residents can take to limit their financial risk and expand their personal rights in a facility. However, the most important protection for a prospective resident is the advice of experienced legal counsel prior to agreeing to or signing any life care contract or related document.

■ Personal Financial Security and Property Rights

Financial Security

State-mandated resident financial protections discussed previously, such as regulated escrow of entrance fees, financial reserves requirements, and broad financial reporting and disclosure obligations, certainly enhance a resident's financial security. Prospective residents who are considering communities in states that do not provide these protections should demand that the provisions be included in any resident contract, or consider communities in states that do require these provisions.

However, potential residents must recognize and accept that states and their regulatory departments do not guarantee the financial security of any CCRC. In fact, several states expressly disclaim any representation regarding a community's financial security. Arizona, for example, states: "Nothing in this article is deemed to require the director to determine the actual financial condition of any life care contract provider. The approval of a permit indicates only that the entity appears to be financially viable based upon the information provided to the director."[160] Arizona, Illinois, New Hampshire, and Pennsylvania require the provider to advise residents that the issuance of a permit does not constitute approval, recommendation, or endorsement by the regulatory department or director, nor does such a permit evidence the accuracy or completeness of the information set out in the application or the annual report of the provider.[161] Moreover, residents must recognize that any state financial review can be rather limited; often the licensing process must be completed in less than 60 days.[162]

Regulatory statutes may provide for state intervention when a CCRC encounters financial difficulty. For example, in Illinois, if the state regulatory official believes that a facility is insolvent or in danger of becoming so, the state attorney general may "file an appropriate action on behalf of the State of Illinois and any or all residents in any court of competent jurisdiction, including the federal bankruptcy court or any other federal court."[163] New Hampshire's statute provides that the state, if necessary to protect the interests of the residents, shall file a lien against a facility's property or take any other action necessary to protect the residents.[164] Nevertheless, these provisions do not guarantee the financial security of any CCRC facility or that a resident will recover all consideration should the facility fail.

These provisions should serve to emphasize to potential residents that a CCRC is a commercial venture that may fail, leaving residents as creditors in a bankruptcy case or a state liquidation, perhaps with very little opportunity to recover their substantial initial entrance fee and forfeiting their right to housing and services. Although a detailed discussion of federal bankruptcy law is beyond the scope of this section, residents should be aware of some basic bankruptcy principles. The Federal Bankruptcy Code favors discharge of a debtor's obligations and the rehabilitation of the debtor. This means that the code provides debtors with broad powers to discharge debts, to restructure financial obligations, and to amend contracts, all of which can have a severely adverse impact on a resident's rights in a continuing care retirement facility.[165]

The most effective method for prospective residents to protect their financial investment is to purchase their residence.[166] Residents should take a full fee-simple interest in the unit, unencumbered by any lien or mortgage except that required by any entity financing the resident's purchase. In this case, units are individually owned in fee simple, and common property and facilities are jointly owned by all residents.[167] Residents also contract separately for all fee services, such as meals, health care, and housekeeping.[168] Given the unique character of any continuing CCRC, there will be restrictions regarding transferability of the unit. The provider may retain an option to repurchase the unit at an agreed-to price, or formula therefor, whenever the life care contract concludes.[169]

Residents who execute the more traditional life care residence lease and pay a substantial entrance fee face greater financial risks. Although the fee is placed in escrow and its release regulated by the state,[170] most fees can be rightfully released to the provider within the first few years of residence.[171] If the community subsequently fails, the resident could lose his home, his benefits or services, and the entrance fee.[172] Furthermore, if the resident leaves the facility or the provider terminates the life care contract, such a resident may not receive a refund of his or her entrance fee.

In some states, the provider must record voluntarily a lien in favor of residents against the CCRC property to help secure the provider's performance of all contract obligations.[173] The same statutes may also provide for foreclosure of the lien or other liquidation proceeding, with any net proceeds distributed to residents,[174] sometimes as a priority claim.[175] This purported resident protection may be of rather dubious value, however, as the lien will not have priority over any preexisting and recorded construction or other mortgage usually required to finance the facility.[176] If the amount of the mortgages exceeds the value of the facility's property, any subsequent resident lien is without value. Some states even allow the resident lien to be subrogated to that of any later recorded mortgage, which would further diminish the resident's security position.[177]

Termination of the Life Care Contract

Whereas state statutes often require that a life care contract specify the grounds under which either the resident or the provider may terminate the contract,[178] only a few states mandate particular language to protect residents.[179] Virginia has a detailed provision governing termination of resident contracts that requires that the provider must have good cause to terminate a resident contract.[180] Good cause is limited to proof that a resident is a danger to himself or others; nonpayment of periodic fees; conduct by a resident that interferes with another resident's quiet enjoyment of the facility; failure to comply with reasonable facility written rules and regulations; material misrepresentations in a resident's application; or material breach by a resident of the terms of the life care contract.[181] If a provider seeks to terminate a contract, the Virginia statute requires written notice to the resident and an opportunity for the resident to remedy the situation.[182] Residents should demand from any provider similar specific provisions regarding termination of any life care contract.

States also often require that life care contracts specify the health and financial conditions for admission to the community, as well as the effect of any change in a resident's health or financial condition.[183] However, states generally do not require specific provisions or standards governing these issues. Accordingly, prospective residents and their legal counsel must carefully negotiate with the provider for inclusion of acceptable contract language governing the effect of any adverse change in health or finances, and the effect, if any, on the entrance or other fees and consideration paid.

Finally, most state statutes require that a CCRC resident contract address the implications of a resident's death, either prior to or after occupying the residence.[184] These statutes commonly provide that if a prospective resident dies or is incapacitated, and is thus unable to become a resident, the life care agreement is automatically terminated, and the provider must refund all consideration paid.[185] Regarding the death of a current resident, some states allow contractual language that specifies that all consideration paid for continuing care becomes earned income of the provider upon a resident's death.[186] However, prospective residents can demand that some portion of the entrance fee be refunded to the deceased resident's estate.

■ Personal Rights

After scrutinizing the financial security of their chosen continuing care retirement community and their property rights, residents must actively seek to clarify their basic personal rights as a

CCRC resident. Despite sales brochures offering a broad view of happy residents engaged in many pleasant activities, it may not be so clear what personal rights residents will have in any particular community. Residents' basic rights can derive from both the contractual language of the continuing care contract and related documents, and from state statutes that may mandate a variety of resident rights.

Contractual resident rights are those expressly or impliedly acknowledged in the continuing care contract. Residents should not rely, however, on oral representations. They should rely only upon those rights clearly expressed in writing in the continuing care contract. If the contract does not specify any right a prospective resident may desire, he or she should demand that this be included in the contract, or perhaps choose to live in another facility that expressly recognizes those rights.

Fortunately for CCRC residents in some states, continuing care statutes may mandate personal rights of residents. Florida, for example, has an exemplary continuing care statute that clearly enumerates these rights:

> No resident of any facility shall be deprived of any civil or legal rights, benefits, or privileges guaranteed by law, by the State Constitution, or by the United States Constitution solely by reason of status as a resident of a facility. Each resident has the right to:
> (a) Live in a safe and decent living environment, free from abuse and neglect.
> (b) Be treated with consideration and respect and with due recognition of personal dignity, individuality, and the need for privacy.
> (c) Unrestricted private communications, including receiving and sending unopened correspondence.
> (d) Freedom to participate in and benefit from community services and activities and to achieve the highest possible level of independence, autonomy, and interaction within the community.
> (e) Exercise civil and religious liberties. No religious beliefs or practices, and no requirement of attendance at religious services, may be imposed on any resident.
> (f) Present grievances and recommend changes in policies, procedures, and services to the staff of the facility, governing officials, or any other person without restraint, interference, coercion, discrimination, or reprisal. This right includes access to ombudsman volunteers and advocates and the right to be a member of, and active in, and associate with, advocacy or special interest groups.
> (g) Freedom from governmental intrusion into the private life of the resident.[187]

Residents of states without similar statutes should demand that these rights be stated clearly in the resident contract.

Some states also provide for resident community groups through which residents can organize to negotiate more effectively with the provider.[188] Florida and New Hampshire expressly recognize that all residents have the right to self-organize, the right to be represented by an individual of their own choice, and the right to engage in concerted activities for their own purposes.[189] Florida even requires communities to hold quarterly meetings with residents of the community to freely discuss financial issues and proposed policy changes.[190] Of course, residents do not need a legislative mandate to organize, and any resident contract limiting resident organization would be subject to court review.

Notes

1. P. Schoemaker. (1995). Scenario planning: A tool for strategic thinking. *Sloan Management Review.* (Winter): 41–51.
2. January 1997 address by Dr. Gene Cohen, president of the Gerontological Society of America, to the National Institute on Aging, National Advisory Council on Aging.
3. W. Achenbaum. (1996). Handbooks as gerontological maps. *The Gerontologist* (December): 825.
4. H. Wolcott. (1975). Criteria for an ethnographic approach to research in schools. *Human Organization* 34: 111–127.
5. J. Harrigan (1997). Architecture and interior design. In *Handbook of Human Factors and Ergonomics,* ed. G. Salvendy. New York: John Wiley & Sons, p. 2019.
6. J. P. Kotter. (1995). Leading change: Why transformation efforts fail. *Harvard Business Review* (March–April): 59–67.
7. Crown Research Corporation, Troutdale, Oregon, provided the financial and market analyses for *The Stratford.* Mark Miles gave permission for the authors to share the work of his corporation with our readers. Crown Research Corporation. (1990a). *Market Analysis: The Stratford.* Troutdale, OR: CRC. Crown Research Corporation. (1990b). *Financial Feasibility Report: The Stratford.* Troutdale, OR: CRC.
8. F. Hertz. (1997). Comment. *The Boston Globe,* April 10, p. D4.
9. W. Scanlon (1997). *How Continuing Care Retirement Communities Manage Services for the Elderly,* HEHS-97-36. Washington, D.C.: General Accounting Office.
10. H. Itami. (1987). *Mobilizing Invisible Assets.* Cambridge: Harvard University Press.
11. M. Abrams. (1995). *Access Expressed! Massachusetts: A Cultural Access Directory.* Boston: Very Special Arts Massachusetts.
12. American Society on Aging. (1997). *Critical Choices.* Call for papers for the 44th Annual Meeting of the American Society on Aging, San Francisco.
13. H. Rubin, and I. Rubin. (1995). *Qualitative Interviewing: The Art of Hearing Data.* Thousand Oaks, CA: Sage.
14. S. Terkel. (1984). *"The Good War": An Oral History of World War Two.* New York: Ballantine.
15. S. Terkel. (1972) *Working.* New York: Pantheon, pp. xx–xxi.
16. D. Blackmon. (1997). Consultant's advice on diversity was anything but diverse. *The Wall Street Journal,* March 11, pp. A1, A16.

17. R. Kastenbaum, (1997). A dash of bitters for seasoning. *The Gerontologist* (February): 131–134.

18. M. Jones, (1995). *Curtain Call: Managed Care vs. Independent Living.* Videocassette, 52 min. Sherborn, MA: Aquarius Productions, Inc.

19. Video Press. (1995). *Harriet's People.* Videocassette, 28 min. Baltimore: University of Maryland, School of Medicine.

20. WTTW/Chicago. (1993). *When She Gets Old.* Videocassette, 28 min. Chicago: Terra Nova Films.

21. New England Research Institutes Media Development Center. (1994). *Fear of Falling: A Matter of Balance.* Videocassette, 40 min. Princeton: Films for the Humanities and Sciences.

22. The Gerontological Society of America. (1996). *Economic & Health Security for the Aging, Agenda.* Paper presented at the 49th Annual Scientific Meeting, November 17–21, Washington, D.C.

23. W, Von Eckhardt. (1975). Making the patient feel better. *San Francisco Chronicle.* June 17, p. 8.

24. Y. Shinkai. (1996). Thinking about a cafeteria plan. *The Nikkei Weekly*, September 30, p. 7.

25. A. Maslow. (1965). *Eupsychian Management.* Homewood, IL: Dorsey Press.

26. C. Argyris. (1994). Good communications that blocks learning. *Harvard Business Review* (July–August): 77–85.

27. K. Harary and E. Donahue. (1994a). *Who Do You Think You Are?* San Francisco: HarperCollins. Idem. (1994b). *Who Do You Think You Are?* (CD-ROM). San Francisco: HarperCollins Interactive.

28. J. Harrigan and P. Neel. (196). *The Executive Architect: Transforming Designers into Leaders.* New York, John Wiley & Sons, pp. 145–146.

29. Ibid., pp. 37–38

30. Ibid., p. 18

31. National Association for Senior Living Industries. (1997). *EXPO 97*, New Orleans, June.

32. P. Gordon. (1993). *Developing Retirement Communities*, 2nd ed. New York: John Wiley & Sons.

33. D. Porter. (1995). *Housing for Seniors: Developing Successful Projects.* Washington, D.C.: Urban Land Institute.

34. S. Sherwood, H. Ruchline, C. Sherwood, and S. Morris. (1997). *Continuing Care Retirement Communities.* Baltimore: John Hopkins University Press.

35. V. Regnier. (1994). *Assisted Living Housing for the Elderly: Design Innovations from the United States and Europe.* New York: Van Nostrand Reinhold.

36. V. Regnier, J. Hamilton, and S. Yatabe. (1995). *Assisted Living for the Aged and Frail.* New York: Columbia University Press.

37. W. Brummett. (1997). *The Essence of Home: Design Solutions for Assisted-Living Housing.* New York: Van Nostrand Reinhold.

38. S. Sherwood, H. Ruchline, C. Sherwood, and S. Morris (1997). *Continuing Care Retirement Communities.* Baltimore: John Hopkins University Press.

39. J. Post.(1996). Internet resources on aging: Ten top Web sites. *The Gerontologist* (December): 728–734.

40. J. Carella. (1996). Scandinavians champion resident independence. *Contemporary Long Term Care* (September): 139–140.

41. Y. Ashihara. (1989). *The Hidden Order: Tokyo Through the Twentieth Century.* Tokyo: Kodansha International.

42. J. Harrigan. (1987). *Human Factors Research: Methods and Applications for Architects and Interior Designers.* Amsterdam: Elsevier Science, pp. 128–130.

43. V. Regnier. (1994). *Assisted Living Housing for the Elderly: Design Innovations from the United States and Europe*. New York: Van Nostrand Reinhold, p. 56.

44. T. Saaty. (1980). *The Analytic Hierarchy Process*. New York: McGraw-Hill.

45. Decision Support Software, Inc. , Pittsburgh, PA.

46. T. Saaty. (1980). *The Analytic Hierarchy Process*. New York: McGraw-Hill, p. 3.

47. T. Saaty and E. Forman. (1992). *The Hierarchon: A Dictionary of Hierarchies*. Pittsburgh: RWS Publications.

48. The discussion and materials presented herein were prepared by Patrick F. Harrigan, J.D. of Chubrich & Harrigan, P.A., Portsmouth, N.H. Statutory case law cited was current as of July 1, 1997.

49. See *Certification and Financial Management of Life Care Facilities: Hearing on HB571 Before the Senate Insurance Committee*, 1987–88 Sess. (N.H. 1987) (statements of Representatives Townsend and Park); 40 PA. Cons. Stat. Ann. §3202 (West 1992). See also *Barr v. United Methodist Church*, 153 Cal. Rptr. 322 (Ca. Ct. App. 1979) (Pacific Homes life care retirement community failure).

50. Entrance fees for the traditional lifetime residential leases can range between $50,000 and $250,000. See N.H. Rev. Stat. Ann. §420-D (1991) (legislative findings and declaration of purpose).

51. This is intended as general introductory information to be used by providers and residents only in conjunction with experienced independent legal counsel of their own choosing. Original and fully current legal authorities should be professionally researched and consulted.

52. See, for example, Fla. Stat. Ann. §651.108 (West 1996); Va. Code Ann. §38.2-4916 (Michie 1994).

53. See, for example, Fla. Stat. Ann. §651.125(1) (West 1996); Va. Code Ann. §38.2-4915, 4916 (Michie 1994).

54. See, for example, Colo. Rev. Stat. Ann. §12-13-117 (West 1996); Fla. Stat. Ann. §651.125(3) (West 1996); 40 Pa. Cons. Stat. Ann. §3221 (West 1992); Va. Code Ann. §38.2-4915 (Michie 1994).

55. See, for example, Ariz. Rev. Stat. Ann. §20-1801, 6 (1990); Cal. Health & Safety Code §1771(a)(8) (Deering Supp. 1997); 210 ILL. Comp. Stat. Ann. §40/2(c) (West 1993); N.H. Rev. Stat. Ann. §420-D:1, III (1991); 40 Pa. Cons. Stat. Ann. §3203 (West 1992); Va. Code Ann. §38.2-4900 (Michie 1994). See also Fla. Stat. Ann. §651.011 (2) (West 1996)(contract may be for any duration).

56. Va. Code Ann. §38.2-4900 (Michie 1994). Interestingly, Virginia also exempts from application of its statute providers that do not charge an entrance fee and which only accept assignments of government payments, charitable organization contributions, and third-party health care coverages as regular periodic charges. Va. Code Ann. §38.2-4917 (Michie 1994).

57. S.C. Code Ann. §37-11-20 (Supp. 1996).

58. Ga. Code Ann. §33-45-1 (1) (1994).

59. See, for example, Ariz. Rev. Stat. Ann. §20-1802 (1990); Fla. Stat. Ann. §651.021 (1) (West 1996); Ga. Code Ann. §33-45-5 (1994); 210 Ill. Comp. Stat. Ann. §40/3 (West 1993); N.H. Rev. Stat. Ann. §420-D:2, I (1991); 40 Pa. Cons. Stat. Ann. §3204(a) (West 1992); S.C. Code Ann. §37-11-30 (Supp. 1996).

60. Cal. Health and Safety Code §1779(a) (Supp. 1997).

61. Fla. Stat. Ann. §651.021 (1) (West 1996).

62. See, for example, Fla Stat. Ann. §651.022 (1) (West 1996).

63. See, for example, Fla. Stat. Ann. §651.0235 (West 1996); 40 Pa. Cons. Stat. Ann. §3205(a) (West 1992); S.C. Code Ann. §37-11-30 (Supp. 1996).

64. See, for example, 210 Ill. Comp. Stat. Ann. §40/11 (West 1993); N.H. Rev. Stat. Ann. §420-D:2,3 (1991).

65. See, for example, Fla. Stat. Ann. §651.106 (West 1996); N.H. Rev. Stat. Ann. §420-D:5, I (1991); 40 Pa. Cons. Stat. Ann. §3205(a) (West 1992).

66. See, for example, Ariz. Rev. Stat. Ann. §20-1803, D (1990); 210 Ill. Comp. Stat. Ann. §40/6 (West 1993); N.H. Rev. Stat. Ann. §420-D:3 (1991); 40 Pa. Cons. Stat. Ann. §3206 (West 1992); S.C. Code Ann. §37-11-30 (Supp. 1996).

67. See, for example, N.H. Rev. Stat. Ann. §420-D:4 (1991); 40 Pa. Cons. Stat. Ann. §3207(a) (West 1992); Va. Code Ann. §38.2-4903 (Michie 1994).

68. See, for example, Ariz. Rev. Stat. Ann. §20-1802 (1990); Cal. Health and Safety Code §1779.4(h), (i) (Supp. 1997); Fla. Stat. Ann. §651.022(2)(b), (c) (West 1996); 40 Pa. Cons. Stat. Ann. §3207(a)(3) (West 1992); S.C. Code Ann. §37-11-30(B)(2) (Supp. 1996); Va. Code Ann. §38.2-4902, A (Michie 1994).

69. Fla. Stat. Ann. §651.022(2)(c) (West 1996).

70. See, for example, Ariz. Rev. Stat. Ann. §20-1802 (1990); 40 Pa. Cons. Stat. Ann. §3207(a)(3) (West 1992); S.C. Code Ann. §37-11-30(B)(2)(a) (Supp. 1996); Va. Code Ann. §38.2-4902, A (Michie 1994).

71. See, for example, Ariz. Rev. Stat. Ann. §20-1802 (1990); Va. Code Ann. §38.2-4902, A (Michie 1994).

72. See, for example, Ariz. Rev. Stat. Ann. §20-1802 (1990); Cal. Health and Safety Code §1779.4(j) (Supp. 1997); 40 Pa. Cons. Stat. Ann. §3207(a)(4) (West 1992); S.C. Code Ann. §37-11-30(B)(2) (Supp. 1996); Va. Code Ann. §38.2-4902, A (Michie 1994).

73. See, for example, Ariz. Rev. Stat. Ann. §20-1802 (1990); Cal. Health and Safety Code §1779.4(j) (Supp. 1997).

74. See, for example, Ariz. Rev. Stat. Ann. §20-1802 (1990); Cal. Health and Safety Code §1779.4(c),(d),(e) (Supp. 1997); 40 Pa. Cons. Stat. Ann. §3207(a)(5), (6) (West 1992); S.C. Code Ann. §37-11-30(B)(4),(5) (Supp. 1996); Va. Code Ann. §38.2-4902, A (Michie 1994).

75. See, for example, Ariz. Rev. Stat. Ann. §20-1802 (1990); Cal. Health and Safety Code §1779.4(r) (Supp. 1997); 40 Pa. Cons. Stat. Ann. §3207(a)(7) (West 1992); S.C. Code Ann. §37-11-30(B)(6), (7) (Supp. 1996); Va. Code Ann. §38.2-4902, A (Michie 1994).

76. See, for example, Cal. Health and Safety Code §1779.4(r) (Supp. 1997); 40 Pa. Cons. Stat. Ann. §3207(a)(7) (West 1992); S.C. Code Ann. §37-11-30(B)(6) (Supp. 1996); Va. Code Ann. §38.2-4902, A (Michie 1994).

77. See, for example, Ariz. Rev. Stat. Ann. §20-1802 (1990); S.C. Code Ann. §37-11-30(B)(6) (Supp. 1996); Va. Code Ann. §38.2-4902, A (Michie 1994).

78. See, for example, Ariz. Rev. Stat. Ann. §20-1802 (1990); Cal. Health and Safety Code §1779.4(l),(n),(o),(p),(q) (Supp. 1997); Fla. Stat. Ann. §651.022 (2)(d) (West 1996); 210 Ill. Comp. Stat. Ann. §40/4 (West 1993); 40 Pa. Cons. Stat. Ann. §3207(a)(13) (West 1992); S.C. Code Ann. §37-11-30(B)(13) (Supp. 1996); Va. Code Ann. §38.2-4902, C (Michie 1994).

79. Fla. Stat. Ann. §§651.022 (2)(e), 651.095 (West 1996).

80. See, for example, Cal. Health and Safety Code §1779.4(r) (Supp. 1997); 40 Pa. Cons. Stat. Ann. §3207(a)(8) (West 1992); S.C. Code Ann. §37-11-30(B)(8) (Supp. 1996); Va. Code Ann. §38.2-4902, A (Michie 1994).

81. See, for example, Cal. Health and Safety Code §1779.4(r),(w) (Supp. 1997); Fla. Stat. Ann. §651.022 (2)(f) (West 1996); 40 Pa. Cons. Stat. Ann. §3207(a)(9) (West 1992); S.C. Code Ann. §37-11-30(B)(9) (Supp. 1996); Va. Code Ann. §38.2-4902, A (Michie 1994).

82. See, for example, Ariz. Rev. Stat. Ann. §20-1802 (1990); 40 Pa. Cons. Stat. Ann. §3207(a)(10) (West 1992); Va. Code Ann. §38.2-4902, A (Michie 1994).

83. Cal. Health and Safety Code §1779.4(v) (Supp. 1997); Fla. Stat. Ann. §651.022(3) (West 1996). See also Ariz. Rev. Stat. Ann. §20-1802 (1990).

84. 210 Ill. Comp. Stat. Ann. 40 (1993).

85. Cal. Health and Safety Code §1787 (Supp. 1997); N.H. Rev. Stat. Ann. §420-D:12 (1991); Va. Code Ann. §38.2-4905, A and D (Michie 1994).

86. See, for example, Colo. Rev. Stat. Ann. §12-13-114 (West 1996); Fla. Stat. Ann. §651.055(1) (West 1996); Ga. Code Ann. §33-45-7(b) (1994); N.H. Rev. Stat. Ann. §420-D:12 (1991); 40 Pa. Cons. Stat. Ann. §3214(a) (West 1992); Va. Code Ann. §38.2-4905 (Michie 1994).

87. See 17A AM.JUR.2D Contracts §23 (1991).

88. See 17A AM.JUR.2D Contracts §24 (1991).

89. See infra notes 92–95, and accompanying text.

90. See, for example, Ariz. Rev. Stat. Ann. §20-1801, 4. (1990); Colo. Rev. Stat. Ann. §12-13-101(3) (West 1996); Fla. Stat. Ann. §651.011(4) (West 1996); 210 Ill. Comp. Stat. Ann. 40/2(h) (West 1993); N.H. Rev. Stat. Ann. §420-D:1, V (1991); 40 Pa. Cons. Stat. Ann. §3203 (West 1992); S.C. Code Ann. §37-11-20(3) (Supp. 1996); Va. Code Ann. §38.2-4900 (Michie 1994).

91. See, for example, AZ. Rev. Stat. Ann. §20-1804 (1990); Colo. Rev. Stat. Ann. §12-13-104 (West 1996); Fla. Stat. Ann. §§651.022(7), 651.023(4), 651.033 (West 1996); 210 Ill. Comp. Stat. Ann. 40/7(a) (West 1993); N.H. Rev. Stat. Ann. §420-D:10 (1991); 40 Pa. Cons. Stat. Ann. §3212 (West 1992).S.C. Code Ann. §37-11-90(B) (Supp. 1996); Va. Code Ann. §38.2-4904.1 (Michie 1994).

92. See, for example, Fla. Stat. Ann. §651.023(4)(b) (West 1996); 210 Ill. Comp. Stat. Ann. 40/7 (a)(2) (West 1993); N.H. Rev. Stat. Ann. §420-D:10, III (1991); 40 Pa. Cons. Stat. Ann. §3212 (West 1992).

93. See, for example, Colo. Rev. Stat. Ann. §12-13-104 (West 1996); 40 Pa. Cons. Stat. Ann. §3212 (West 1992).S.C. Code Ann. §37-11-90(B) (Supp. 1996).

94. See, for example, N.H. Rev. Stat. Ann. §420-D:10 (1991); 40 Pa. Cons. Stat. Ann. §3212(5) (West 1992).

95. Fla. Stat. Ann. §651.023(5) (West 1996).

96. See, for example, Fla. Stat. Ann. §651.055 (1)(i) (West 1996) and 40 Pa. Cons. Stat. Ann. §3214(a)(10) (West 1992)(sixty day notice of periodic fee changes).

97. See, for example, Ariz. Rev. Stat. Ann. §20-1806 (1990); Colo. Rev. Stat. Ann. § 12-13-107 (1) (West 1996); Fla. Stat Ann. §651.035 (1)(a) (West 1996); 210 Ill. Comp. Stat. Ann. 40/7 (b) (West 1993); 40 Pa. Cons. Stat. Ann. §§3209, 3210 (West 1992);.

98. See, for example, Colo. Rev. Stat. Ann. § 12-13-107 (1) (West 1996); Fla. Stat Ann. §651.035 (2) (West 1996); N.H. Rev. Stat. Ann. §420-D:8 (1991).

99. See, for example, 210 Ill. Comp. Stat. Ann. 40/7 (b) (West 1993).

100. Fla. Stat. Ann. §651.035 (7) (West 1996).

101. See, for example, Ariz. Rev. Stat. Ann. §20-1805, A (1990); Colo. Rev. Stat. Ann. § 12-13-106 (1) (West 1996); N.H. Rev. Stat. Ann. §420-D:5, II (1991); 40 Pa. Cons. Stat. Ann. §3211 (West 1992).

102. See, for example, Ariz. Rev. Stat. Ann. §20-1805, B (1990); Colo. Rev. Stat. Ann. § 12-13-106 (2) (West 1996).

103. See, for example, Ariz. Rev. Stat. Ann. §20-1805, D or H (1990); Colo. Rev. Stat. Ann. § 12-13-106 (8) (West 1996).

104. See, for example, Ariz. Rev. Stat. Ann. §20-1805, G (1990); Colo. Rev. Stat. Ann. § 12-13-106 (7) (West 1996); 40 Pa. Cons. Stat. Ann. §3211 (West 1992).

105. See, for example, Ariz. Rev. Stat. Ann. §20-1807, A (1990); Colo. Rev. Stat. Ann. § 12-13-108 (West 1996); Fla. Stat. Ann. §651.026 (West 1996); Ga.

Code Ann. §33-45-6 (1994); N.H. Rev. Stat. Ann. §420-D:7 (1991); 40 Pa. Cons. Stat. Ann. §3207(b) (West 1992).

106. See, for example, Fla. Stat. Ann. §651.0261 (West 1996).

107. See, for example, Fla. Stat. Ann. §651.026 (West 1996); Ga. Code Ann. §33-45-6 (1994); N.H. Rev. Stat. Ann. §420-D:7 (1991).

108. See, for example, Ariz. Rev. Stat. Ann. §20-1808, A (1990).

109. See, for example, Ariz. Rev. Stat. Ann. §20-1808, B (1990).

110. See, for example, Ariz. Rev. Stat. Ann. §20-1802, D (1990); Fla. Stat. Ann. §651.055 (2) (West 1996); Ga. Code Ann. §33-45-7 (b) (1994); 210 Ill. Comp. Stat. Ann. 40/5 (b) (West 1993); 40 Pa. Cons. Stat. Ann. §3214(b) (West 1992).Va. Code Ann. §38.2-4905, B (Michie 1994).

111. See, for example, Ariz. Rev. Stat. Ann. §20-1802, D (1990); Fla. Stat. Ann. §651.055 (2) (West 1996); Ga. Code Ann. §33-45-7 (b) (1994); 40 Pa. Cons. Stat. Ann. §3214(b) (West 1992); Va. Code Ann. §38.2-4905, B (Michie 1994).

112. See, for example, S.C. Code Ann. §37-11-35 (Supp. 1996).

113. See, for example, Ariz. Rev. Stat. Ann. §20-1802, D (West 1990); Fla. Stat. Ann. §651.055 (2) (West 1996); Ga. Code Ann. §33-45-7 (b) (1994); 210 Ill. Comp. Stat. Ann. 40/5 (b) (West 1993); 40 Pa. Cons. Stat. Ann. §3214(b) (West 1992); S.C. Code Ann. §37-11-35 (Supp. 1996); Va. Code Ann. §38.2-4905, B (Michie 1994).

114. See, for example, Ga. Code Ann. §33-45-7(a)(7)(A) (1994).

115. See, for example, Fla. Stat. Ann. §§651.055(1)(g), 651.061 (West 1996); 40 Pa. Cons. Stat. Ann. §3214(a)(7), (d) (West 1992); Va. Code Ann. §38.2-4905, A, 8. (Michie 1994).

116. See, for example, Colo. Rev. Stat. Ann. §12-13-105 (West 1996); Fla. Stat. Ann. §§651.055(1)(g), 651.061 (West 1996); 40 Pa. Cons. Stat. Ann. §3214(d) (West 1992).

117. See, for example, Fla. Stat. Ann. §651.055(1)(h) (West 1996); 40 Pa. Cons. Stat. Ann. §3214(a)(9) (West 1992).Va. Code Ann. §38.2-4905, A, 10. (Michie 1994).

118. See, for example, N.H. Rev. Stat. Ann. §420-D:13 (1991); Va. Code Ann. §38.2-4906 (Michie 1994).

119. See, for example, N.H. Rev. Stat. Ann. §420-D:13 (1991).

120. Fla. Stat. Ann 651.111 (West 1996).

121. See, for example, Ariz. Rev. Stat. Ann. §20-1809 (West 1990); Colo. Rev. Stat. Ann. §12-13-110 (West 1996); Fla. Stat. Ann. §651.105 (West 1996); 210 Ill. Comp. Stat. Ann. 40/10 (West 1993); N.H. R.S.A. §420-D:23 (1991); 40 Pa. Cons. Stat. Ann. §3218(a) (West 1992); S.C. Code Ann. §37-11-80 (Supp. 1996); Va. Code Ann. §38.2-4914 (Michie 1994).

122. See, for example, N.H. Rev. Stat. Ann. §420-D:21 (1991); 40 Pa. Cons. Stat. Ann. §3218(b) (West 1992); Va. Code Ann. §38.2-4914 (Michie 1994).

123. 40 Pa. Cons. Stat. Ann. §3219 (West 1992).

124. See, for example, Ariz. Rev. Stat. Ann. §20-1808, C, D, E (1990); N.H. Rev. Stat. Ann. §420-D:16, I and II (1991); 40 Pa. Cons. Stat. Ann. §3216(a), (b) (West 1992).

125. See, for example, Ariz. Rev. Stat. Ann. §20-1808, G (1990); 40 Pa. Cons. Stat. Ann. §3216(c) (West 1992).

126. See, for example, S.C. Code Ann. §37-11-105 (Supp. 1996).

127. See, for example, Ariz. Rev. Stat. Ann. §20-1808, H (1990); N.H. Rev. Stat. Ann. §420-D:16, III and IV (1991); 40 Pa. Cons. Stat. Ann. §3216(d), (e), (f), (g) (West 1992).

128. See, for example, Fla. Stat. Ann. §651.065 (West 1996); 40 Pa. Cons. Stat. Ann. §3214(e) (West 1992).Va. Code Ann. §38.2-4908 (Michie 1994).

129. See, for example, Fla. Stat. Ann. §651.055(3) (West 1996).

130. Providers must also closely consider a variety of legal entities in which to do business, including not-for-profit, for-profit and limited-liability corporations, trusts, partnerships, and asociations. Use of such an entity may limit the personal liability of the individuals with a legal or equitable interest in the entities. A discussion of this issue is beyond the scope of this section.

131. The claims introduced herein are not intended to be exhaustive, and residents may bring other claims, depending on applicable state and federal law and specific facts, including causes of action for personal injury.

132. See, for example, *Estate of Riedel v. Life Care Retirement Communities, Inc.*, 505 N.W.2d 78 (Minn.Ct.App. 1993)(breach of contract claim for miscalculating deceased CCRC resident refund).

133. See, for example, *Van Brunt v. Peninsula United Methodist Homes, Inc.*, No. 8043, 1987 WL 7953, at 4, (Del.Ch. 1987)(resident breach of contract claim based in part on language in provider brochures and annual report).

134. See, for example, *Onderdonk v. Presbyterian Homes of N.J.*, 425 A.2d 1057 (N.J. 1981) (provider impliedly obligated to furnish annual financial statements to residents).

135. See, for example, *Onderdonk v. Presbyterian Homes of N.J.*, 425 A.2d 1062 (N.J. 1981) (provider impliedly obligated to furnish annual financial statements to residents).

136. *Van Brunt v. Peninsula United Methodist Homes, Inc.*, No. 8043, 1987 WL 7953, at 3, (Del.Ch. 1987).

137. In addition to suits for common law fraud, disgruntled residents may also bring a civil action based on the federal Racketeer Influenced and Corrupt Organizations Act, or R.I.C.O. 18 U.S.C.A. §§1961–1968 (1984 & Supp. 1997). Although a very complicated statute, to prevail in a civil R.I.C.O. suit, a plaintiff must generally prove that he was injured from criminal activity by an enterprise engaging in a pattern of racketeering conduct that threatens to continue. See generally Albert D. Spaulding, *How to Start a Civil RICO Lawsuit*, 38 PRAC.LAW 15 (1992). Originally designed to combat racketeer influences in the economy, more specifically organized crime, courts have broadly applied the act to an enterprise of common law fraud and many other examples of fraud in a commercial context, including the financial mismanagement of a life care facility and self-dealing by the facility principals. See, for example, *Bennett v. Berg*, 685 F.2d 1053 (8th Cir. 1982) (overruling dismissal of RICO claim by life care community residents alleging fraud in the inducement of residents to live in the community and in the operation of the community). R.I.C.O. provides for both treble civil damages and criminal sanctions for conduct found to violate the statute. See generally Albert D. Spaulding, *How to Start a Civil RICO Lawsuit*, 38 PRAC.LAW 15, (1992).

138. *Black's Law Dictionary* 594 (1979).

139. *Bennett v. Berg*, 685 F.2d 1053, 1057 (8th Cir. 1982).

140. See, for example, Mass. Gen. Laws Ann. §93A (West 1984 & Supp. 1997); N.H. Rev. Stat. Ann. §358-A (1995 & Supp. 1996). See also *Estate of Riedel* v. *Life Care Retirement Communities, Inc.*, 505 N.W.2d 78 (Minn. Ct. App. 1993) (state Consumer Fraud Law claim by estate of deceased life care community resident for miscalculating refund).

141. See, for example, N.H. Rev. Stat. Ann. §358-A:2 (1995 & Supp. 1996).

142. See, for example, Mass. Gen. Laws Ann. §93A, §4 (West Supp. 1997); N.H. Rev. Stat. Ann. §358-A:4, III (Supp. 1996).

143. See, for example, N.H. Rev. Stat. Ann. §358-A:4, III-a (Supp. 1996).

144. See, for example, Mass. Gen. Laws Ann. §93A, §9(3) (West Supp. 1997); N.H. Rev. Stat. Ann. §358-A:10, I (1995).

145. See, for example, Mass. Gen. Laws Ann. §93A, §9(2) (West 1984); N.H. Rev. Stat. Ann. §358-A:10, I (1995).

146. See, for example, Mass. Gen. Laws Ann. §93A, §9(4) (West 1984); N.H. Rev. Stat. Ann. §358-A:10, I (1995).

147. See, for example, Mass. Gen. Laws Ann. §93A, §9(3) (West Supp. 1997); N.H. Rev. Stat. Ann. §358-A:10, I (1995).

148. See, for example, Fla. Stat. Ann. §651.13 (West 1996); Ga. Code Ann. §33-45-11 (1994); N.H. Rev. Stat. Ann. §420-D:20 (1991); 40 Pa. Cons. Stat. Ann. §3217 (West 1992); Va. Code Ann. §38.2-4911 (Michie 1994). See also *American Nat'l Bank and Trust of New Jersey v. Presbyterian Homes of New Jersey*, 372 A.2d 1147 (N.J. Super .Ct. App. Div. 1977) (dismissing claim by deceased resident's estate based on the New Jersey Retirement Community Full Disclosure Act).

149. See, for example, Ga. Code Ann. §33-45-11 (1994); N.H. Rev. Stat. Ann. §420-D:20, I (1991); 40 Pa. Cons. Stat. Ann. §3217(a) (West 1992); Va. Code Ann. §38.2-4911 (Michie 1994).

150. See, for example, Va. Code Ann. §38.2-4911 (Michie 1994).

151. See, for example, N.H. Rev. Stat. Ann. §420-D:20, II (1991).

152. See, for example, N.H. Rev. Stat. Ann. §420-D:20, III (1991); 40 Pa. Cons. Stat. Ann. §3217(c) (West 1992).

153. See, for example, 40 Pa. Cons. Stat. Ann. §3217(e) (West 1992); Va. Code Ann. §38.2-4911 (Michie 1994).

154. N.H. Rev. Stat. Ann. §420-D: 26 (1991).

155. See, for example, Ariz. Rev. Stat. Ann. §20-1811 (1990); Colo. Rev. Stat. Ann. §12-13-112 (West 1996); Ga. Code Ann. §33-45-10(a) (1994); 210 Ill. Comp. Stat. Ann. 40/12 (West 1993); S.C. Code Ann. §37-11-120 (Supp. 1996).

156. See, for example, Fla. Stat. Ann §651.125 (West 1996). See also 40 Pa. Cons. Stat. Ann. §3222(a) (West 1992)(willful and knowing violation subjects person to fines up to $10,000 and imprisonment up to 2 years).

157. See, for example, Fla. Stat. Ann §651.125 (West 1996); Ga. Code Ann. §33-45-10(a) (1994).

158. See, for example, N.H. Rev. Stat. Ann. §358-A:6 (1995).

159. See 18B AM.JUR.2D *Corporations* §1893-96 (1985).

160. Ariz. Rev. Stat. Ann. §20-1802, G. (1990).

161. Ariz. Rev. Stat. Ann. §20-1803, C. (1990); 210 Ill. Comp. Stat. Ann. 40/6 (West 1993); N.H. Rev. Stat. Ann. §420-D:4, IV (1991); 40 Pa. Cons. Stat. Ann. §3207(a)(12) (West 1992). See also Va. Code Ann. §38.2-4903, B (Michie 1994).

162. See, for example, 40 Pa. Cons. Stat. Ann. §3204(c) (West 1992); S.C. Code Ann. §37-11-40 (Supp. 1996). National organizations such as AASHA accredit continuing care community providers, which can assist a potential resdient in choosing a facility. Florida may recognize independent accreditation in lieu of its statutory requirments. Fla. Stat. Ann. §651.028 (West 1996). However, AASHA accreditation does *not* guarantee the financial success of any facility.

163. 210 Ill. Comp. Stat. Ann. 40/9 (West 1993). *See also* Va. Code Ann. §38.2-4903, B (Michie 1994) (state may issue cease and disist orders or seek injunctions to enforce compliance with statute).

164. N.H. Rev. Stat. Ann. §420-D:5, II (1991).

165. However, the Bankruptcy Code does not allow for the modification of a creditor's *secured* interest in the assets of the debtor. Where the residents pay an entrance fee and lease their units, a lien granted to the residents by the provider may afford some financial protection. If the provider grants a

resident a valid mortgage, lien, or other encumbrance against the property of the provider, and the value of that property exceeds all of the valid prior recorded interests of other creditors or residents as well as the interest of the resident, then the resident has a secured interest that may protect him or her in the event of a financial failure of a facility. If not, then the resident lien may be of little value.

166. Although certainly beyond the scope of this section, purchasing their unit may also afford residents tax advantages. See, for example, *Maddock* v. *Greenville Retirement Community*, No. 12564, 1997 W.L. 89094, at 2, n. 4, 7 (Del. Chan., Feb. 26, 1997).

167. See, for example, *Maddock v. Greenville Retirement Community*, No. 12564, 1997 W.L. 89094, at 2 (Del. Chan., Feb. 26, 1997).

168. See, for example, *Maddock v. Greenville Retirement Community*, No. 12564, 1997 W.L. 89094, at 3 (Del. Chan., Feb. 26, 1997).

169. See, for example, *Maddock v. Greenville Retirement Community*, No. 12564, 1997 W.L. 89094, at 2 (Del. Chan., Feb. 26, 1997).

170. See supra notes 90–96 and accompanying text.

171. See supra notes 90–96 and accompanying text.

172. *Moravian Manors, Inc. v. Commonwealth Ins. Dept.*, 521 A.2d 524, 527 (Pa. Commw. Ct. 1987).

173. See, for example, Ariz. Rev. Stat. Ann. §20-1805 (1990).

174. See, for example, Ariz. Rev. Stat. Ann. §20-1805 (1990); Fla. Stat. Ann. §651.071 (West 1996); N.H. Rev. Stat. Ann. §420-D:16, III (1991).

175. See, for example, N.H. Rev. Stat. Ann. §420-D:16, III (1991).

176. For example, New Hampshire provides: "Nothing in this chapter shall be construed to impair the priority, with respect to the lien property, of mortgages, security agreements, lease agreements, or installment sales agreements on property not otherwise encumbered which have been entered into by a provider with an issuer of bonds or notes and bonds which are secured by a resolution, ordinance, or indenture of trust if such mortgages or agreements were duly recorded at least four months prior to the institution of liquidation proceedings." N.H. Rev. Stat. Ann. §420-D:16, V (1991). See also Fla. Stat. Ann. §651.071 (West 1996).

177. See, for example, Ariz. Rev. Stat. Ann. §20-1805, I. (1990); Colo. Rev. Stat. Ann. §12-13-106 (9) (West 1996).

178. See, for example, 40 Pa. Cons. Stat. Ann. §3214(a)(7), (d) (West 1992); Va. Code Ann. §38.2-4905 (Michie 1994).

179. See, for example, 40 Pa. Cons. Stat. Ann. §3214(d) (West 1992); Va. Code Ann. §38.2-4905 (Michie 1994).

180. Va. Code Ann. §38.2-4905, A, 8. (Michie 1994). See also Fla. Stat. Ann. §651.061 (West 1996); 40 Pa. Cons. Stat. Ann. §3214(d) (West 1992).

181. Va. Code Ann. §38.2-4905, A, 8. (Michie 1994).

182. Va. Code Ann. §38.2-4905, A, 8. (Michie 1994).

183. See, for example, Fla. Stat. Ann. §651.055(1)(c), (d), and (e) (West 1996); 40 Pa. Cons. Stat. Ann. §3214(a)(3), (4), (5) (West 1992).

184. See, for example, 40 Pa. Cons. Stat. Ann. §3214(a)(9), (c) (West 1992); Va. Code Ann. §38.2-4905, A, 10 (Michie 1994).

185. See, for example, Fla. Stat. Ann. §651.055(5) (West 1996); 40 Pa. Cons. Stat. Ann. §3214(c) (West 1992); Va. Code Ann. §38.2-4905, C (Michie 1994).

186. See, for example, Fla. Stat. Ann. §651.055(1)(h) (West 1996); 40 Pa. Cons. Stat. Ann. §3214(a)(9) (West 1992); Va. Code Ann. §38.2-4905, A, 10 (Michie 1994).

187. Fla. Stat. Ann. §651.083(1) (West 1996).

188. See, for example, Fla. Stat. Ann. §651.081 (West 1996); N.H. Rev. Stat. Ann. §420-D:15 (1991); 40 Pa. Cons. Stat. Ann. §3215 (West 1992); Va. Code Ann. §38.2-4910 (Michie 1994).

189. Fla. Stat. Ann. §651.081 (West 1996); N.H. Rev. Stat. Ann. §420-D:15, I (1991).

190. Fla. Stat. Ann. §651.085(1) (West 1996).

CCRC STANDARD OF PERFORMANCE

1.0 Enterprise Concept

■ 1.1 Enterprise Concept Development

1.1.1 CANDIDATE CONCEPTS. Taking into account the existing situation, anticipated events, desired enterprise outcomes, and image of the future, what are the candidate retirement community concepts?

1.1.2 CONCEPT EVALUATION CRITERIA. What criteria should be used to evaluate candidate concepts?

1.1.3 EVALUATION RESULTS. What are the evaluation results and concluding recommendations for candidate concepts?

1.1.4 ENTERPRISE CONCEPT. What is the mutually agreed-upon enterprise concept?

■ 1.2 Enterprise Action Plan

1.2.1 ACTION PLAN. What is the proposed enterprise action plan?

1.2.2 ENTERPRISE SCHEDULE. What are the enterprise milestone events and schedule?

1.2.3 REQUIRED RESOURCES AND ASSETS. What resources and assets are needed to fulfill the promise of the enterprise concept and action plan?

1.2.4 REQUIRED RESEARCH. What research is required to augment the enterprise strategy?

2.0 Executive Organization

■ 2.1 The Executive Council

2.1.1 EXECUTIVE COUNCIL APPOINTMENT CRITERIA. What are the criteria for appointment to the executive council?

2.1.2 EXECUTIVE COUNCIL CANDIDATES. Who are the candidates for placement on the executive council?

2.1.3 EXECUTIVE COUNCIL APPOINTMENTS. Applying the selection criteria to candidates, which individuals are recommended for appointment to the executive council?

2.1.4 EXECUTIVE COUNCIL MANDATE. What are the primary responsibilities of the executive council?

2.1.5 INDIVIDUAL RESPONSIBILITIES. What are the responsibilities of individual executive council members?

■ 2.2 Enterprise Associates

2.2.1 OWNERS, INVESTORS, AND LENDERS. Who represents the owners, investors, and lenders during executive organization deliberations?

2.2.2 MARKETING AND SALES MANAGER. Who represents the marketing and sales perspectives during executive organization deliberations?

2.2.3 DEVELOPER'S REPRESENTATIVE. Who represents the developer's interests and concerns during executive organization deliberations?

2.2.4 ARCHITECTS. Who represents the architectural design interests and concerns during executive organization deliberations?

2.2.5 DESIGN/BUILD MANAGEMENT. Who represents the design/build management team during executive organization deliberations?

2.2.6 SERVICE PROVIDERS. Who represents the service providers' interests and concerns during executive organization deliberations?

2.2.7 HEALTH CARE REPRESENTATIVE. Who represents the interests and concerns of those managing and maintaining the health care program during executive organization deliberations?

2.2.8 FOOD SERVICE REPRESENTATIVE. Who speaks for the interests and concerns of those who provide food services?

2.2.9 LEGAL COUNSEL. Who provides legal counsel to the executive organization?

2.2.10 FINANCIAL ADVISORS. Who provides financial advice to the executive organization?

2.2.11 INSURANCE PROVIDERS. Who represents the interests and concerns of the insurance providers?

2.2.12 RESIDENTS' SPOKESPERSONS. Who represents the interests and concerns of residents during executive organization deliberations?

2.3 Performance Assessment

2.3.1 OVERSIGHT. As the cornerstone of the enterprise, how is the work of the executive organization evaluated?

2.3.2 PEER REVIEW. What experts are responsible for assessing proposed and in-progress work?.

2.3.3 BOARD OF DIRECTORS. Recognizing that liaison and oversight are the primary responsibilities of the enterprise board of directors, what qualifications for appointment are proposed? Who are the most outstanding candidates?

2.3.4 RESIDENTS' ENTERPRISE REVIEW BOARD. As executive performance is most challenged when confronting the customer directly, who should serve on the residents' enterprise review board?

2.4 Liaison

2.4.1 LOCAL GOVERNMENT LIAISON. What are the points of liaison between the executive organization and local government planning, design review, and code enforcement staff and associated community boards?

2.4.2 REGULATORY AGENCIES LIAISON. What are the points of liaison between the executive organization and regulatory and licensing agencies?

2.4.3 SPOKESPERSONS. What individuals should speak for the executive organization within the community?

2.4.4 PREPARATION. For community board presentations and public meetings, what preparation is required to present the features of the enterprise?

2.5 Applications System

2.5.1 APPLICATIONS SYSTEM REQUIREMENTS. Responding to enterprise objectives and executive and associates responsibilities, what are the applications system requirements?

2.5.2 APPLICATIONS SYSTEM DESIGN. Responding to specified applications system requirements, what are the best software suites and network features for the enterprise?

2.5.3 APPLICATIONS SYSTEM COMPLIANCE. Considering that the applications system is mandated for enterprise deliberations, what is the means for familiarizing all enterprise participants with its structure and utility features?

3.0 Finance and Law

3.1 Financial Considerations

3.1.1 ENTERPRISE BUSINESS PLAN. What enterprise business plan is proposed to achieve sustainable profits and respond to financial opportunities, anticipated pitfalls, and ethical considerations?

3.1.2 PROFIT/NONPROFIT CONSIDERATIONS. What information is needed to identify and evaluate profit/nonprofit options?

3.1.3 FINANCIAL STRUCTURE. What are the financial requirements for the various development phases of the retirement community enterprise?

3.1.4 OPERATING COSTS. What are the anticipated operating costs for the enterprise, prior to occupancy, at occupancy, and over time?

3.1.5 MANAGING ENTERPRISE COSTS. What is the oversight process for milestone approvals and scheduled allocation of funds for each phase of the enterprise?

3.1.6 POTENTIAL INVESTORS AND LENDERS. Who are the potential investors and lenders?

3.1.7 SOLICITATION OF SUPPORT. What steps must be taken to attract investors and lenders?

3.1.8 EQUITY REQUIREMENTS. What are the equity requirements for each phase of the enterprise?

3.1.9 REPORT TO UNDERWRITERS. What question items in the standard of performance must be addressed when preparing the report to underwriters?

3.1.10 PRESALE REQUIREMENTS. What are the presale and nonrefundable deposit requirements for the various enterprise phases?

3.1.11 ON-SITE SOURCES OF INCOME. What are the revenue categories and anticipated on-site revenues for the enterprise?

3.1.12 OFF-SITE SOURCES OF INCOME. What are the revenue categories and anticipated revenues associated with off-site activities?

3.1.13 LOCAL ECONOMIC BENEFITS. As the enterprise means tax or negotiated revenues, jobs, and increased economic activity in the local community, what is the best way to present the associated financial benefits?

3.1.14 FINANCIAL FEASIBILITY PRESENTATION. As each of the preceding question items are candidates for inclusion in the enterprise feasibility study, what is the best possible financial feasibility presentation? What detailed information is required in this presentation?

▪ 3.2 Legal and Regulatory Considerations

3.2.1 LEGAL RESEARCH. What must be undertaken to diligently address the rights of investors, lenders, enterprise participants, health care and service providers, and residents?

3.2.2 LEGAL AGREEMENTS. What contracts must be produced to address transfer of property rights and service agreements?

3.2.3 REGULATORY AGENCIES. What federal, state, and local regulatory and licensing bodies are responsible for enterprise approval?

3.2.4 MEETING REGULATORY REQUIREMENTS. How are regulatory and licensing requirements met? What reporting requirements are mandated by state agencies?

3.2.5 RESIDENTS' RIGHTS. How should contracts and manuals be formulated so as to clearly present the legal rights of residents?

4.0 Marketing and Sales

▪ 4.1 Market Strategy

4.1.1 MARKET POTENTIAL. The assessment of market potential is the initial step in the development of a market strategy; thus, what do the results of market research (question items 4.2.1 through 4.2.5) identify as opportunities and challenges?

4.1.2 MARKETING STRATEGY DEVELOPMENT. Which identified market strategies have promise for the enterprise? What are the pros and cons of each? What are the costs associated with each? What program of activities best meets the needs of the enterprise?

4.1.3 MARKETING PROGRAM SCHEDULE. What are the first steps in the marketing program? What is the timeline for all subsequent activities? What are the costs associated with each activity?

4.1.4 MARKETING AUDIT PLAN. What is the audit plan for assessing the effectiveness of the market strategy and associated activities?

4.1.5 PROMOTIONS. Which media have been selected to promote the retirement community enterprise? Which hold the greatest potential and why is this so? What are the projected costs for promotional activities?

4.1.6 WORKING WITH THE COMMUNITY. Recognizing that the local community can foster a positive view of the development, what steps should be taken to familiarize people with the retirement community opportunity?

4.1.7 LIMITED MARKET RESPONSE. When interest in the retirement community is below expectations, what additional efforts should be undertaken?

4.1.8 CONTRIBUTING TO THE FEASIBILITY STUDY. As each of the preceding question items is a candidate for inclusion in the enterprise feasibility study, what is the best possible description of our marketing and sales strategy? What detailed information is required?

■ 4.2 Market Research

4.2.1 DEMOGRAPHICS. What are the demographics of the market region for the general and elderly populations? What is the current and anticipated future demand for retirement communities?

4.2.2 COMPETITORS. What are the existing competing developments? Where are others proposed?

4.2.3 COMPETING CONCEPTS. What do competing developments offer in terms of admission standards, services, quality of life, and financial arrangements?

4.2.4 MARKET CHARACTERISTICS. What descriptive categories best identify and distinguish potential residents?

4.2.5 MARKET DYNAMICS. Where are fundamental changes in the market developing?

■ 4.3 Sales Strategy

4.3.1 INITIAL PRESENTATION. How should the retirement community opportunity be presented to prospective residents?

4.3.2 SELLING TO FAMILY MEMBERS AND FRIENDS. How should the retirement community opportunity be presented to the families and friends of prospective residents?

4.3.3 CLIENT RELATIONS. What steps should be taken to establish in prospective residents a sense of trust in the sales staff?

4.3.4 FOLLOW-UP STEPS. After the initial presentation to prospective residents, what is the strategy for maintaining contact and encouraging reconsideration of the retirement community opportunity?

4.3.5 COMPETING SALES STRATEGIES. Within the market area, what are the sales strategies of competing retirement communities?

4.3.6 INFORMATION BROCHURE. What should be included in the retirement community marketing brochure regarding distinguishing facility features, the master plan, qualification standards, resident services, financial arrangements, quality of life, and health care services?

4.3.7 CLIENT COMPLAINTS. What complaints are common regarding the sales experience? What is the process for dealing with complaints and ensuring that problems are remedied?

4.3.8 LOST CLIENTS. What do we know about prospective clients who did not respond to the retirement community opportunity?

4.4 Sales Staff Selection and Training

4.4.1 SALES STAFF MANDATE. What are the primary responsibilities of the sales staff?

4.4.2 SALES STAFF SELECTION CRITERIA. What are the skill and licensing criteria for appointing individuals to sales management and staff positions?

4.4.3 SALES STAFF CANDIDATES. Who are the candidates for sales management and staff positions?

4.4.4 SELECTION OF SALES STAFF. Applying the selection criteria to candidates, which individuals should be appointed to sales staff and management positions?

4.4.5 SALES STAFF ORGANIZATION. How should the sales staff be organized to fulfill its mandate?

4.4.6 WORKING WITH THE ELDERLY. What knowledge and skills are required to promote an interest in the enterprise among prospective residents?

4.4.7 WORKING WITH FAMILIES AND FRIENDS. What knowledge and skills are required to promote an interest in the enterprise among family and friends of prospective residents?

4.4.8 ROLE OF RETIREMENT COMMUNITY STAFF. Recognizing that every person with whom a prospective client comes in contact influences sales, what values and attitudes should be developed in the retirement community staff?

5.0 Residents

■ 5.1 Residents' Expectations and Requirements

5.1.1 DISTINGUISHING CHARACTERISTICS. What characteristics and factors can be used to distinguish residents?

5.1.2 DAILY ACTIVITIES. What are the daily activities of residents? What is known about the extent, time of occurrence, and duration of activities?

5.1.3 INDIVIDUAL PERCEPTIONS. How are residents likely to perceive themselves, other residents, and staff in terms of their individual rights and anticipated perquisites?

5.1.4 LIFE-STYLES. What are the social customs, relationship norms, and cultural traditions of residents?

5.1.5 RESIDENTS' SERVICE PREFERENCES. What are the service preferences of residents?

5.1.6 RECREATION AND LEISURE PREFERENCES. What are the recreation and leisure preferences of residents?

5.1.7 CUISINE AND FOOD SERVICE PREFERENCES. What are the cuisine and food service preferences of residents?

5.1.8 HEALTH CARE PREFERENCES. What are the health care preferences of residents?

5.1.9 RESIDENTIAL DESIGN AND SERVICE CHALLENGES. In summary, what are the facility design and service challenges associated with residents' abilities, activities, preferences, and health?

■ 5.2 Interior Architecture of Residences

5.2.1 RESIDENTIAL DESIGN OBJECTIVES. Which expectations and requirements of residents should be emphasized in interior design deliberations for private residences?

5.2.2 RESIDENTIAL UNIT AND SPACE PLAN OPTIONS. What residential unit and space plan options best correspond to residents' expectations and requirements? How are these justified in terms of benefits and costs?

5.2.3 RESIDENCE FURNISHING, FIXTURES, AND EQUIPMENT. With regard to safety, security, and convenience, what furnishing, fixtures, and equipment options, fixed or mobile, do residential units require?

5.2.4 RESIDENCE COMMUNICATION, SURVEILLANCE, AND COMPUTER EQUIPMENT. What are the communication, surveillance, and computer equipment requirements of residences?

5.2.5 RESIDENCE ENVIRONMENTAL CRITERIA. What provisions should be made for the effect on residents of temperature, humidity, air quality, air movement, illumination, noise, distractions, annoyances, hazards, and climatic conditions?

5.2.6 SURFACE TREATMENTS. Where do surfaces require special attention in terms of durability, maintainability, and safety?

5.2.7 INFORMATION REQUIREMENTS. What general and emergency information is required in residences?

5.2.8 INFORMATION PRESENTATIONS. Considering the possible sensory limitations of the residents, how should general and emergency information be presented?

5.2.9 RESIDENTIAL DESIGN CHALLENGES. In summary, what are the residential design challenges associated with residents' abilities, activities, preferences, and health?

■ 5.3 Community Life

5.3.1 COMMUNITY SPACE REQUIREMENTS. What community spaces are required?

5.3.2 COMMUNITY SPACE ACTIVITIES. What is known about the extent, time of occurrence, and duration of community activities?

5.3.3 COMMUNITY SPACE PERCEPTIONS. How are residents likely to perceive community space in terms of their individual rights and perquisites?

5.3.4 COMMUNITY LIFE-STYLES. What are the social customs, relationship norms, and cultural traditions common to community space?

5.3.5 COMMUNITY RECREATION AND LEISURE PREFERENCES. What are the community recreation and leisure preferences of residents?

5.3.6 HOSPITALITY. What are the preferences of residents regarding hospitality services, food service, and spaces for guests and family members?

5.3.7 COMMUNITY FACILITY DESIGN CHALLENGES. In summary, what are the community facility design challenges associated with residents' abilities, activities, preferences, and health?

■ 5.4 Community Space Interior Architecture

5.4.1 COMMUNITY SPACE DESIGN OBJECTIVES. Which expectations and requirements of residents and staff should be emphasized in design deliberations for community space?

5.4.2 COMMUNITY SPACE DESIGN OPTIONS. What community space design options best correspond to residents' and staff expectations and requirements? How are these justified in terms of benefits and costs?

5.4.3 COMMUNITY SPACE FURNISHING, FIXTURES, AND EQUIPMENT. With regard to safety, security, and convenience, what furnishing, fixtures, and equipment options, fixed or mobile, do community spaces require?

5.4.4 COMMUNITY SPACE COMMUNICATION, SURVEILLANCE, AND COMPUTER EQUIPMENT. What are the communication, surveillance, and computer equipment requirements of community spaces?

5.4.5 COMMUNITY SPACE ENVIRONMENTAL CRITERIA. What provisions should be made for the effect of temperature, humidity, air quality, air movement, illumination, noise, distractions, annoyances, hazards, and climatic conditions in community spaces?

5.4.6 COMMUNITY SPACE SURFACE TREATMENTS. Where do surfaces require special attention in terms of durability, maintainability, and safety?

5.4.7 COMMUNITY SPACE INFORMATION REQUIREMENTS. What general and emergency information is required in community spaces?

5.4.8 COMMUNITY SPACE INFORMATION PRESENTATIONS. Considering the sensory limitations of the residents, how should general and emergency information be presented?

6.0 Health Care

■ 6.1 Health Care Management and Staff

6.1.1 MANAGEMENT AND STAFF MANDATE. What are the primary responsibilities of health care managers and staff?

6.1.2 HEALTH CARE MANAGEMENT AND STAFF SELECTION CRITERIA. What are the criteria for appointing individuals to health care management and staff positions?

6.1.3 STAFF MANAGEMENT CANDIDATES. Who are the candidates for health care management and staff?

6.1.4 SELECTION OF HEALTH CARE MANAGEMENT AND STAFF. Applying the selection criteria to candidates, which individuals should be appointed to health care management and staff positions?

6.1.5 HEALTH CARE STAFF ORGANIZATION. How should health care management and staff be organized to fulfill their mandate?

6.1.6 MEDICAL COUNCIL. What is the medical council charter and how should it be organized to fulfill its mandate?

6.1.7 HEALTH CARE STAFF PERCEPTIONS. How are health care staff members likely to perceive themselves, other staff members, and residents in terms of their individual rights and perquisites?

6.1.8 HEALTH CARE STAFF LIFE-STYLES. What are the social customs, relationship norms, and cultural traditions of health care staff?

6.1.9 HEALTH CARE MANAGEMENT AND STAFF RESPONSIBILITIES. What are the responsibilities of individual health care managers and staff?

6.1.10 MANAGEMENT AND STAFF TRAINING. What continuing education programs should be offered to health care managers and staff?

6.1.11 LICENSED SERVICES. Who should be assigned the responsibility of managing licensed services? What are the job responsibilities and position requirements?

6.1.12 MANAGEMENT OF OFF-SITE SERVICES. Who should be assigned the responsibility of managing off-site services? What are the job responsibilities and position requirements?

6.1.13 PERFORMANCE MONITORING. What process should be followed when monitoring and evaluating management and staff performance in terms of residential life contributions and costs of operations?

■ 6.2 Health Care Programs

6.2.1 HEALTH CARE PROGRAMS. What is the scope and content of mandated and support health care programs?

6.2.2 HEALTH CARE STAFF DISTINCTIONS. How may health care staff be distinguished in terms of program responsibilities? How many individuals are expected in each category?

6.2.3 HEALTH CARE ACTIVITIES. What are the daily and emergency activities of health care staff? What is known about the extent, time of occurrence, and duration of activities?

6.2.4 HEALTH CARE DESIGN CHALLENGES. In summary, what are the facility design challenges associated with health care programs?

■ 6.3 Health Care Units Interior Architecture

6.3.1 HEALTH CARE UNIT DESIGN OBJECTIVES. Which expectations and requirements of health service and care staff and residents should be emphasized in interior architecture design deliberations?

6.3.2 HEALTH CARE UNIT DESIGN. What health care unit design options best correspond to staff and resident expectations and requirements? How are design features justified in terms of benefits and costs?

6.3.3 HEALTH CARE UNIT FURNISHING, FIXTURES, AND EQUIPMENT. With regard to safety, security, and convenience, what furnishing, fixtures, and equipment options, fixed or mobile, do health care units require?

6.3.4 HEALTH CARE UNIT COMMUNICATION, SURVEILLANCE, AND COMPUTER EQUIPMENT. What are the communication, surveillance, and computer equipment requirements of health care units?

6.3.5 HEALTH CARE UNIT ENVIRONMENTAL CRITERIA. What provisions should be made for the effect on staff and residents of temperature, humidity, air quality, air movement, illumination, noise, distractions, annoyances, hazards, and climatic conditions?

6.3.6 HEALTH CARE UNIT SURFACE TREATMENTS. Where do surfaces require special attention in terms of durability, maintainability, and safety?

6.3.7 HEALTH CARE UNIT INFORMATION REQUIREMENTS. What general and emergency information are required? How can these be made responsive to sensory limitations?

6.3.8 HEALTH CARE UNIT INFORMATION PRESENTATIONS. How can health care unit general and emergency information presentations be made responsive to sensory limitations?

7.0 Residents' Services

■ 7.1 Service Management

7.1.1 EXECUTIVE MANAGER. What are the responsibilities of the executive manager?

7.1.2 SERVICE MANDATE. What are the primary responsibilities of service managers?

7.1.3 MANAGEMENT SELECTION CRITERIA. What are the skill and licensing criteria for appointing individuals to service management positions?

7.1.4 SERVICE MANAGEMENT Candidates. Who are the candidates for service management positions?

7.1.5 SELECTION OF SERVICE MANAGEMENT. Applying the selection criteria to candidates, which individuals should be appointed to service management positions?

7.1.6 SERVICE MANAGEMENT ORGANIZATION. How should the service management be organized to fulfill its mandate?

7.1.7 MANAGEMENT RESPONSIBILITIES. What are the responsibilities of individual managers?

7.1.8 MANAGEMENT TRAINING. What continuing education opportunities should be offered to managers?

7.1.9 MANAGEMENT OF LICENSED SERVICES. Who should be assigned the responsibility of managing licensed services? What are the job responsibilities and position requirements?

7.1.10 MANAGEMENT OF OFF-SITE SERVICES. Who should be assigned the responsibility of managing off-site services? What are the job responsibilities?

7.1.11 PERFORMANCE MONITORING. What process should be followed when monitoring and evaluating management performance in terms of residential life contributions and costs of operations?

7.1.12 RESIDENTS' COUNCIL. What is the charter of the residents' council and how should the council be organized to fulfill its responsibilities and work with the executive manager?

■ 7.2 Resident Services and Staff

7.2.1 SERVICES. What resident services are expected and required and what is the justification for each? What must each service offer on a scheduled or as-needed basis?

7.2.2 TRANSPORTATION SERVICES. What are the daily and special transportation service requirements of residents?

7.2.3 SERVICE STAFF. Who provides direct service to residents? How may these individuals be grouped by service categories and responsibilities? How many individuals does each category include?

7.2.4 SERVICE STAFF ACTIVITIES. What are the anticipated activities of the service staff? What is known about the extent, time of occurrence, and duration of anticipated activities?

7.2.5 SERVICE STAFF CUSTOMS. What are the significant work customs, life-styles, norms, and traditions of the service staff?

7.2.6 SERVICE STAFF SELECTION. What are the selection criteria for each staff category? How should prospective staff be screened with regard to undesirable traits and criminal activity history?

7.2.7 SERVICE STAFF TRAINING. For each staff category, what initial and continuing training is required?

7.2.8 SERVICE DESIGN CHALLENGES. In summary, what are the facility design challenges associated with service staff activities?

◾ 7.3 Facility Operations

7.3.1 FACILITY OPERATIONS. What facility operations are required?

7.3.2 OPERATIONS STAFF. Who is responsible for facility operations? How may these individuals be grouped by responsibilities? How many individuals does each category include?

7.3.3 OPERATIONS STAFF ACTIVITY DESCRIPTIONS. What are the anticipated activities of the operations staff? What is known about the extent, time of occurrence, and duration of anticipated activities?

7.3.4 OPERATIONS STAFF CUSTOMS. What are the significant work customs, life-styles, norms, and traditions of the operations staff?

7.3.5 OPERATIONS STAFF SELECTION. What are the selection criteria that should be employed in each staff category?

7.3.6. OPERATIONS STAFF TRAINING. For each operations staff member category, what initial and continuing training is required?

7.3.7 FACILITY OPERATIONS DESIGN OBJECTIVES. In summary, responding to identified requirements of facility operations and staff, which should be emphasized in design deliberations?

7.3.8 FACILITY MANAGEMENT SCHEME. What are the required guidelines and manuals that describe to staff and residents the use of facility features?

8.0 Design and Build

■ 8.1 Site Selection

8.1.1 CANDIDATE SITES. What are the candidate sites for the retirement community?

8.1.2 SITE SELECTION CRITERIA. What are the retirement community site selection criteria?

8.1.3 CANDIDATE SITE EVALUATION. What are the results of the application of site selection criteria to candidate sites?

8.1.4 NEIGHBORHOOD GROUPS. Who lives and works in the neighborhood surrounding the site? How may these people be grouped by activities and concerns?

8.1.5 NEIGHBORHOOD IMPACT. What is the possible impact of facility activities on neighborhood life?

8.1.6 COMMUNITY GROUPS. Who lives and works in the local community? How may these people be grouped by activities and concerns?

8.1.7 COMMUNITY IMPACT. What is the likely impact of retirement community activities on community life and public and private services?

8.1.8 PROPERTY VALUE IMPACT. What is the possible impact of the retirement community on community property values?

8.1.9 VISUAL IMPACT. Anticipating the visual impact of the retirement community, what are the possible objectives?

8.1.10 ECOLOGICAL AND ENVIRONMENTAL IMPACT. What is the anticipated impact of the retirement community development in terms of ecological and environmental factors?

8.1.11 NEIGHBORHOOD AND COMMUNITY SUPPORT. In terms of community objections and resistance, what is the strategy for gaining neighborhood and community support?

8.1.12 NEGOTIATIONS. What is the position of the local city manager, city planner, and associated boards regarding restrictions relief and contract zoning? What is the history of these entities on past projects? What is the necessary preparation for each anticipated presentation?

■ 8.2 Critical Circulation Patterns

8.2.1 MOVEMENT OF INDIVIDUALS. What is the anticipated number of people entering, leaving, and moving about within the retirement community, for what purposes, how frequently, and at what times?

8.2.2 EQUIPMENT AND MATERIAL TRANSPORT. What are the characteristics of the equipment and material that must be transported to and within the retirement community? How are these items transported, and what is the frequency and time of occurrence?

8.2.3 VEHICULAR TRAFFIC. From the perspective of neighborhood impact and safety and security, what aspects of vehicular traffic must be considered during facility design, site planning, and master plan development? What are the characteristics of the areas of concern?

8.2.4 RECOMMENDED CIRCULATION DESIGN FEATURES. In summary, what are the recommended facility and master plan circulation design features supportive of residential activities and equipment and material flow? In what way is this proposal a response to concerns for efficiency, convenience, safety, and security?

■ 8.3 Master Plan

8.3.1 RECOMMENDED MASTER PLANS. What are the candidate master plans that achieve quality-of-life objectives, meet requirements for outdoor space, and respond to neighborhood and community concerns?

8.3.2 MASTER PLAN EVALUATION CRITERIA. What criteria should be used to evaluate candidate master plan options and alternatives?

8.3.3 MASTER PLAN EVALUATION OUTCOME. What candidate master plans were evaluated? What were the results and concluding recommendations?

8.3.4 OUTDOOR SPACE. What are the requirements for outdoor space in terms of amenities, landscape development, and enhancement of existing natural features?

■ 8.4 Facility Design

8.4.1 DESIGN CONCEPTS. Which expectations and requirements of residents, health care personnel, and service providers should be emphasized in design deliberations?

8.4.2 FACILITY DESIGN BENEFITS. In terms of residents' and staff expectations and requirements, what is the benefit and problem resolution potential of each suggested facility design concept?

8.4.3 PROPOSED FLOOR PLAN SCHEMES. Responding specifically to research regarding the expectations and requirements of residents and health care and service staff, what are the proposed facility floor plan schemes? What is the estimated square feet for each facility space?

8.4.4 ALTERATION EXPECTANCIES. How soon might it be necessary to modify or expand facilities? What events would most probably lead to this requirement? How do the proposed facility schemes account for this possibility? How do these schemes help reduce the distractions and annoyances associated with remodeling and expansion?

■ 8.5 Design Image

8.5.1 FORM AND STRUCTURE. What are the proposed facility form and structure design concepts?

8.5.2 EXTERIOR DESIGN IMAGES. What are the proposals for exterior facility design images, details, and accents?

8.5.3 INTERIOR DESIGN IMAGES. What are the proposals for interior spatial forms, design images, and surface colors, textures and patterns?

8.5.4 DESIGN IMAGE JUSTIFICATION. What are the quality-of-life and community impact possibilities of each design image recommendation?

■ 8.6 Design/Build Process

8.6.1 DESIGN/BUILD MANAGEMENT TEAM. Which executive council members and enterprise associates are members of the design/build management team?

8.6.2 DESIGN/BUILD MILESTONES. What are the design/build milestones? What is produced at each?

8.6.3 PROGRESS REPORTS. What is the means selected to inform all enterprise participants concerning the activities of the design/build management team and enterprise progress?

8.6.4 DESIGN EVALUATION CRITERIA. What are the criteria for evaluating proposed design concepts, schemes, forms, and features?

8.6.5 PROBLEM RESOLUTION. What is the procedure for resolving existing or anticipated design/build problems?

8.6.6 DOCUMENT CONTROL. What is the information system content and structure for enterprise document control following completion of the application of the standard of performance?

REFERENCES

Abrams, M. (1995). *Access Expressed! Massachusetts: A Cultural Access Directory*. Boston: Very Special Arts Massachusetts.

Achenbaum, W. (1996). Handbooks as gerontological maps. *The Gerontologist* (December): 825.

American Society on Aging. (1997). *Critical Choices*. Call for papers for the 44th Annual Meeting of the American Society on Aging. San Francisco.

Anders, G. (1997). Elderly enjoy better health than expected. *The Wall Street Journal*, March 18, pp. B1, B4.

Anders, G. and L. McGinley (1997). Medical morass. *The Wall Street Journal*, March 6, pp. A1, A8.

Argyris, C. (1994). Good communications that blocks learning. *Harvard Business Review* (July–August): 77–85.

Ashihara, Y. (1989). *The Hidden Order: Tokyo Through the Twentieth Century*. Tokyo: Kodansha International.

Austin, D. (1996). "Value, Performance, and Image." In J. Harrigan and P. Neel, *The Executive Architect: Transforming Designers into Leaders*. New York: John Wiley & Sons, pp. 320–321.

Axelrod, N. (1994). Who's in Charge? *The Nonprofit Times* (December): 32.

Bartlett, C. A., and S. Ghoshal. (1994). Changing the role of top management: Beyond strategy to purpose. *Harvard Business Review* (November–December): 79–88.

———. (1995). Changing the role of top management: Beyond systems to people. *Harvard Business Review* (May– June): 132–142.

Berman, H. (1994). *Interpreting the Aging Self: Personal Journals of Later Life*. New York: Springer.

Bettelheim, B. (1974). *A Home for the Heart*. New York: Alfred A. Knopf.

Binstock, R., and L. George. (1996). *Handbook of Aging and the Social Sciences*. San Diego: Academic Press.

Birren, J., and K. Schaie. (1996). *Handbook of the Psychology of Aging*. San Diego: Academic Press.

Blackmon , D. (1997). Consultant's advice on diversity was anything but diverse. *The Wall Street Journal*, March 11, pp. A1, A16.

Bower, J. and C. Christensen (1995). Disruptive technologies: Catching the wave. *Harvard Business Review* (January–February): 43–53.

Brecht, S. (1996). Trends in the retirement housing industry. *Urban Land* (November): 32–39.

Brummett, W. (1997). *The Essence of Home: Design Solutions for Assisted-Living Housing.* New York: Van Nostrand Reinhold.

Carella, J. (1996). Scandinavians champion resident independence. *Contemporary Long Term Care* (September): 139–140.

Cherof, E. (1996). What to do before the union knocks on your door. *Contemporary Long Term Care* (December): 58.

Chesbrough, H., and D. Teece. (1996). When is virtual virtuous? Organizing for innovation. *Harvard Business Review* (January–February): 65–73.

Cohen, G. (1997). President Cohen Speaks to N.I.A. Advisory Board on Aging. *Gerontology News* (March): 1–3.

Craig, E. (1993). The U.S.A.'s 20 best. *New Choices.* November, 66 - 67.

Crown Research Corporation (1990a). *Market Analysis: The Stratford.* Troutdale, OR: CRC.

———. (1990b). *Financial Feasibility Report: The Stratford.* Troutdale, OR: CRC.

Davidson, R. (1996). Seniors' housing finance: Tight money, big growth. *Urban Land* (November): 33.

Davis, S., and J. Botkin, (1994). The coming of knowledge-based business. *Harvard Business Review* (September–October): 165–170.

Davis, W. (1996). The new retirees. *The Boston Globe,* October 1, pp. D1, D5.

Dewhirst, J. (1997) Letter to American Association of Homes and Services for the Aging Members. Washington, D.C.: AAHSA.

Dorn, S. (1993). The Cypress of Hilton Head Island. *Hospitality Design* (November): 44–49.

Drucker, P. F. (1995). The information executives truly need. *Harvard Business Review* (January–February): 54–62.

Feinberg, P. (1992). Retirement planning: Investing for the good life. *Barron's,* August 31, pp. 5–6.

Foreman, J. (1996). Caregiving from afar isn't easy. *The Boston Globe,* October 7, pp. C1, C2.

The Gerontological Society of America. (1996). *Economic & Health Security for the Aging, Agenda.* Papers presented at the 49th Annual Scientific Meeting, Washington, D.C., November 17–21.

Ghoshal, S., and C. A. Bartlett. (1994). Changing the role of top management: Beyond structure to processes. *Harvard Business Review* (January–February): 87–96.

Gomes-Casseres, B. (1994). Group versus group: How alliance networks compete. *Harvard Business Review* (July–August): 62–74.

Goodman, R. (1995). *Client Assessment Knowledge System for Building Industry Application.* Department of Architecture. San Luis Obispo: California Polytechnic State University.

Gordon, P. (1993). *Developing Retirement Communities,* 2nd ed. New York: John Wiley & Sons.

Grant, W. H., and L. Schlesinger. (1995). Realize your customers' full profit potential. *Harvard Business Review* (September–October): 59–72.

Harary, K., and E. Donahue. (1994a). *Who Do You Think You Are?* San Francisco: HarperCollins.

———. (1994b). *Who Do You Think You Are?* CD-ROM. San Francisco: HarperCollins Interactive.

Harrigan, J., and W. Ward. (1972). Human factors information taxonomy: A guide to user-oriented architectural service. (Grant A72-0-643.) Washington, D.C.: National Endowment for the Arts.

Harrigan, J. (1987). *Human Factors Research: Methods and Applications for Architects and Interior Designers.* Amsterdam: Elsevier Science.

———. (1997). Architecture and interior design. In *Handbook of Human Factors and Ergonomics*, ed. G. Salvendy. New York: John Wiley & Sons, pp. 964–986

Harrigan, J., and P. Neel. (1996). *The Executive Architect: Transforming Designers into Leaders.* New York: John Wiley & Sons.

Hatfield, J. (1996). Family affair. *The Boston Globe*, September 11, pp. F1, F5.

Heifetz, R. (1994). *Leadership Without Easy Answers.* Boston: Belknap Press/Harvard University Press.

———. (1997). The work of a modern leader. *A Newsletter from Harvard Business School Publishing* (April): 4–7.

Heifetz, R., and D. Laurie. (1997). The work of leadership. *Harvard Business Review* (January–February): 124–134.

Hertz, F. (1997). Comment. *The Boston Globe*, April 10, p. D4.

Hout, T., and J. Carter, (1995). Getting it done: New roles for senior executives. *Harvard Business Review* (November–December): 133–145.

Husi, D. (1996). Serving the "silent generation." *Urban Land* (November): 34–35.

Hyatt, L. (1997). Getting physicians on-board. *Nursing Homes* (January): 11

Infante, M. (1996) Preemployment screening: what the record won't show. *Contemporary Long Term Care* (November): 71.

Ishizawa, M. (1996). Spending to improve access for disabled. *The Nikkei Weekly*, March 3, p. 3.

Jones, M. (1995). *Curtain Call: Managed Care vs. Independent Living.* Videocassette, 52 min. Sherborn, MA: Aquarius Productions.

Kanter, R. M. (1994). Collaborative advantage: The art of alliances. *Harvard Business Review* (July–August): 96–108.

Kaplan, R., and D. Norton, (1996). *The Balanced Scorecard: Translating Strategy into Action. Boston.* Boston: Harvard Business School Press.

Kastenbaum, R. (1997). A dash of bitters for seasoning. *The Gerontologist* (February): 131–134.

Katzenbach, J., and D. K. Smith. (1993). *The Wisdom of Teams.* New York: HarperCollins.

Katzenback, J. (1997). *Teams at the Top*. Boston: Harvard Business School Press.

Keeney, R. (1992). *Value-Focused Thinking: A Path to Creative Decision-making*. Cambridge: Harvard University Press.

Kotter, J. P. (1995). Leading change: Why transformation efforts fail. *Harvard Business Review*. March-April, 59-67.

Large-Scale residential award for excellence. (1993). *Urban Land Magazine* (December): 15–16.

Luckman, C. (1996). "The Executive Architect." In J. Harrigan and P. Neel, *The Executive Architect: Transforming Designers into Leaders*. New York: John Wiley & Sons, pp. 19–20.

Maslow, A. (1965). *Eupsychian Management*. Homewood, IL: Dorsey Press.

McCarthy, E. (1997). Avoiding the pitfalls of assisted living development. *Urban Land* (February): 45–49, 55.

McGinley, L. (1997). Rules are proposed by the government for care at home. *The Wall Street Journal*, March 6, p. B6.

Meyer, C. (1994). How the right measures help teams excel. *Harvard Business Review* (May–June): 45–54.

Micklewait, J., and A. Wooldridge. (1996). *The Witch Doctors*. New York: Times Books.

Milojkovic, J. (1995). *Reinventing Organization Learning*. Videocassette, 58 min. Stanford: Stanford Video Media Group.

Moore, J. (1996). How to prepare for a market "correction." *Contemporary Long Term Care* (September): 34.

National Association for Senior Living Industries (1997). *EXPO 97*, New Orleans, June.

National Institute of Standards. (1995). *Malcolm Baldrige National Quality Award: Health Care Pilot Criteria*. Washington, D.C.: NIS.

Ness, J. A., and T. Cucuzza. (1995). Tapping the full potential of ABC. *Harvard Business Review* (July–August): 130–138.

New England Research Institutes Media Development Center (1994). *Fear of Falling: A Matter of Balance*. Videocassette, 40 min. Princeton: Films for the Humanities and Sciences.

Nichols, D. (1996). Florida class-action suit may be first of many. *Contemporary Long Term Care* (October): 11

Nordheimer, J. (1996). A mature housing market: Growing business of not-quite-nursing home care. *The New York Times*, April 10, pp. C1, C4.

NYNEX (1997). *Gerontechnology: New Tools for Independent Living*. Paper presented at the 43rd Meeting of the American Society on Aging, March 23–26. Nashville.

Peck, R. (1997). Do you have the information? *Nursing Homes* (January): 4.

———. (1997). Information systems: Gearing up for the new generation. *Nursing Homes* (January): 13–15.

Pfeffer, J. (1992). *Managing with Power: Politics and Influence in Organizations*. Boston: Harvard Business School Press.

————. (1995). *Managing with Power: Politics and Influence in Organizations.* Videocassette, 60 min. Stanford: Stanford Video Media Group.

Porter, D. (1995). *Housing for Seniors: Developing Successful Projects.* Washington, D.C.: Urban Land Institute.

Porter, M. (1995). The competitive advantage of the inner city. *Harvard Business Review* (May–June): 55–70.

Post, J. (1996). Internet resources on aging: Ten top Web sites. *The Gerontologist* (December): 728–734.

Quinn, J. (1985). Managing innovation: Controlled Chaos. In *Managerial Excellence*, ed. Nan Stone. Boston: Harvard Business Review, p. 114.

Regnier, V. (1994). *Assisted Living Housing for the Elderly: Design Innovations from the United States and Europe.* New York: Van Nostrand Reinhold.

Regnier, V., J. Hamilton, and S. Yatabe. (1995). *Assisted Living for the Aged and Frail.* New York: Columbia University Press.

Romano, M. (1997). Retired Americans should be on guard against abuse from financial advisers. *The Wall Street Journal*, March 28, pp. C1, C15.

Rubin, H., and I. Rubin. (1995). *Qualitative Interviewing: The Art of Hearing Data.* Thousand Oaks, CA: Sage.

Saaty, T. (1980). *The Analytic Hierarchy Process.* New York: McGraw-Hill.

Saaty, T., and E. Forman. (1992). *The Hierarchon: A Dictionary of Hierarchies.* Pittsburgh: RWS Publications.

Sahlman, W. (1997). How to write a great business plan. *Harvard Business Review* (July–August): 98–108.

Scanlon, W. (1997). *How Continuing Care Retirement Communities Manage Services for the Elderly,* HEHS-97-36. Washington, D.C.: General Accounting Office.

Schoemaker, P. J. H. (1995). Scenario planning: A tool for strategic thinking. *Sloan Management Review* (Winter): 41–51.

Senior Highs. (1993). *Builder* (October): 64–66.

Sherwood, S., H. Ruchline, C. Sherwood, and S. Morris. (1997), *Continuing Care Retirement Communities.* Baltimore: John Hopkins University Press.

Shinkai, Y. (1996). Thinking about a cafeteria plan. *The Nikkei Weekly,* September 30, p. 7.

Simons, R. (1995). Control in an age of empowerment. *Harvard Business Review* (March–April): 80–89.

Stephenson, K. (1995). *Strategic Misalignment: Making Networks Work in Your Organization.* Videocassette, 55 min. Stanford: Stanford Video Media Group.

Stevenson, H. and M. Moldoveanu (1995). The power of predictability. *Harvard Business Review* (July–August): 140–143.

Sullivan, J. (1996). Ducking the hazards. *Contemporary Long Term Care* (September): 38–45.

Van Amberg, N. (1993). Cypress wins "Oscar." *Real Estate/Homes* (November): 7.

Video Press. (1995). *Harriet's People.* Videocassette, 28 min.. Baltimore: University of Maryland, School of Medicine.

Von Eckhardt, W, (1975). Making the patient feel better. *San Francisco Chronicle,* June 17, p. 8.

Wetlaufer, S. (1994). Case Study: The team that wasn't. *Harvard Business Review* (November–December): 22–38.

Wilson, R. E. (1994). Communication and learning. *Harvard Business Review* (September–October): 181.

Wolcott, H. (1975). Criteria for an ethnographic approach to research in schools. *Human Organization* 34: 111–127.

WTTW/Chicago (1993). *When She Gets Old.* Videocassette, 28 min. Chicago: Terra Nova Films.

INDEX